Publishing
in the Third World

Publishing in the Third World

Knowledge and Development

Edited by
Philip G. Altbach
Amadio A. Arboleda
S. Gopinathan

Heinemann
Portsmouth, New Hampshire

Mansell
London

Heinemann Educational Books, Inc.
70 Court Street, Portsmouth, New Hampshire 03801, U.S.A.

Mansell Publishing Ltd.
6 All Saints Street, London N1 9RL, England

First Published 1985

Library of Congress Cataloging in Publication Data

Main entry under title:

Publishing in the Third World.

  Bibliography: p.
  Includes index.
  1. Publishers and publishing—Developing countries.
  2. Book industries and trade—Developing countries.
I. Altbach, Philip G.   II. Arboleda, Amadio Antonio.
III. Gopinathan, Saravanan.
Z289.P82 1985   070.5'091724   84–27920
        ISBN 0–435–08006–7 (Heinemann)
        ISBN 0–7201–1760–7 (Mansell)

Printed in the United States of America

Contents

v

Countries and Regions

Tables

Preface

This volume stems from common concerns about Third World publishing and a conviction that a more thorough understanding of the topic will lead to analysis and perhaps improvement. Without question, providing books and journals for the more than half the world's population living in the Third World is a task of paramount importance. Yet book publishing has been ignored by analysts and often by planners. As a result, the publishing industry in the Third World does not provide an adequate output of books—in both quantitative or qualitative terms. The reasons for this lag are complex, and we hope that this volume will shed light on them.

Our aim in this book is to provide the best possible analyses of important issues relating to publishing in key Third World nations. We began searching for contributors in 1981. It was more difficult than we expected to obtain quality manuscripts, due in part to the lack of good statistical information, to the lack of a community of researchers, and to the lack of concern by those in the industry for research and analysis.

The three editors of this volume approached the tasks with a variety of experiences and interests. Philip G. Altbach has been involved in research on Third World publishing for some time, has done fieldwork in India, and has put together the most comprehensive bibliography currently available on Third World publishing.[1] Amadio Arboleda, currently on the staff of the United Nations University in Tokyo, has been associated with the University of Tokyo Press and with scholarly publishers in the United States. S. Gopinathan, on the faculty of the Institute of Education in

Singapore, is also a director of the Singapore Book Development Council. He has written widely on publishing and textbooks in Asia. The challenges of editing a book across international boundaries and with contributors on four continents were considerable. We have overcome problems of distance, sometimes problematical postal services, and occasional difficulties in communication, and we are convinced that this experiment in international editing is a success. We are indebted to our authors for their contributions and for their willingness to work with an editorial committee separated by thousands of miles. We also acknowledge the assistance of Jennifer Newton, who helped copy edit the manuscripts.

This book presents a good "state of the art" on Third World publishing and takes its place with a few other volumes that have looked in some depth at the problems of Third World publishing.[2] But the literature is very limited, and this volume is a beginning rather than the definitive discussion of the topic. Indeed, we hope that our efforts will stimulate further research and analysis.

This book is intended to provide information and increase awareness of one of the most important parts of the knowledge distribution system. Publishing is crucial to education, to scholarship, to intellectual life, and to research. Books are used by everyone, from new literates who require a continuing supply of reading material to scholars and scientists who communicate through sophisticated research monographs. The challenges of book publishing in the Third World are considerable, yet much progress has been made. We can learn from each other, and this book will contribute to this learning process.

Philip G. Altbach
Buffalo, New York, USA

Amadio Arboleda
Tokyo, Japan

S. Gopinthan
Singapore

March 1984

Notes

1. Philip G. Altbach and Eva Maria Rathgeber, *Publishing in the Third World: Trend Report and Bibliography* (New York: Praeger, 1980).
2. See, for example, E. Oluwasanmi, E. M. McLean, and H. Zell, eds., *Publishing in Africa in the Seventies* (Ile-Ife, Nigeria: University of Ife Press, 1974), S. Minowa and A. A. Arboleda, eds., *Scholarly Publishing in Asia* (Tokyo: University of Tokyo Press, 1973), Thomas Nickerson, ed., *Trans-Pacific Scholarly Publishing* (Honolulu: East-West Center Press, 1963), A. Ben Cheikh, *Book Production and Reading in the Arab World* (Paris: UNESCO, 1982), and Alberto Augsburger, *The Latin American Book Market: Problems and Prospects* (Paris: UNESCO, 1981).

Publishing
in the Third World

1. Publishing in the Third World: Some Reflections

Philip G. Altbach
Amadio A. Arboleda
S. Gopinathan

This book is the first study of Third World publishing on an international scale, with chapters on countries in Asia, Africa, Latin America, and the Middle East, many written by nationals of these countries. It provides an opportunity for broader reflection on some of the major issues relating to publishing and for wider discussions on prospects and possibilities in a rapidly changing technological world, particularly as they relate to the Third World. Much progress has been made since UNESCO's International Book Year in 1972 focused attention on the problems of publishing and book distribution in the Third World, but many of these efforts are still hampered by considerable inequalities and continuing difficulties in institutionalizing book industries in many countries. Recent changes in international copyright now make it possible for Third World countries to have greater access to knowledge from the industrialized world. Nevertheless, questions that have international implications, such as the role of the multinationals in Third World publishing, distribution, and the prices and availability of paper continue to plague publishing efforts in the Third World. This chapter will look at some of the key issues facing Third World publishing in the 1980s and beyond in light of the analyses and presentations in this book and based on the considerable recent literature concerning publishing in the Third World.[1]

The literature is quite explicit in stressing that publishing has an important role in the Third World. Although it does not count for much in terms of gross national product, its importance to society outweighs its economic cost and benefit. The provision of books is crucial to education, to the development and maintenance of literacy, to the growth of a national culture, to the production and distribution of knowledge relevant to the nation, and to a sense of intellectual community. For a long time publishing was ignored by policy makers concerned mainly with the more immediate problems of socioeconomic development. Recently the importance of books has been increasingly recognized, and consequently the importance of publishing to educational and cultural policies. Book development councils have been established in most Third World nations. Some of these countries have integrated books into plans for education and development. In spite of such efforts, however, the financial resources devoted to book development remain extraordinarily small, and, as a result, in many countries publishing has lagged behind other developments in education. Of course, the reasons for this, led by the difficulties involved in the process of development generally, are complicated and as varied as the number of countries concerned.

It has long been recognized that publishing is a complex enterprise, being both a business venture and a cultural institution. It has international implications and relationships that have a tremendous cultural impact. Translations, copyright questions, and the role of multinational publishers are, for example, international issues. The fact that more than 80 percent of the world's book titles are published in the industrialized nations also affects Third World publishing and book distribution. A common plight of many nations is the limited supplies of paper, which must, in most cases, be imported. Third World nations must also consider introducing and using advanced printing technology, which is almost exclusively produced in the industrialized nations, in their publishing industries. The possibilities for regional cooperation in publishing and book distribution also involve international considerations.

Furthermore, publishing is complex because it involves a wide range of enterprises and issues. In the Third World, particularly, it is linked closely to the educational system, which is the major purchaser and user of books. Publishing depends on the institutional infrastructures of education and libraries to provide the basic market for books. Libraries are major purchasers of general and scholarly books. The individual market in most Third World countries is largely undeveloped; often there are few bookstores, and almost never book clubs.

Government policies affect the book industry in the Third World to a significant extent. Since public funds provide much of the basic economic support for publishing, the industry is directly influenced by government policies concerning libraries, the price of paper, the purchase of school books, and emphases on literacy programs and nonformal education. The growth of national book development councils in many countries has been important in establishing a forum for discussion among government officials and the book community. To an extent unknown in Western industrialized nations, the Third World publishing industry is dependent on public funds and, therefore, public policy for its success and even its viability.

Many issues affect publishing in all parts of the world regardless of economic realities or literacy rate. Publishers everywhere are affected by new printing technologies, the price of paper, trends in imports and exports of books, international copyright arrangements, and other factors. Third World publishers have special issues as well, and these are of primary concern in this book. The vagaries of international markets—in paper, technology, and even tastes—affect them substantially, and the above mentioned interrelationship between the book industry and educational systems is of special relevance. Publishing in the Third World is more often than not a fragile enterprise. The reasons for this vary, but generally it can be traced to benign neglect by government, the private sector, and the intellectual community.

The Myth of the Third World

Although this volume is about publishing in the Third World, we are not trying to lump Third World nations together without some recognition of the distinctiveness of the different societies and cultures involved. The very concept of the "Third World" needs elaboration, particularly in the context of publishing. The countries considered in this book vary in geographical location, social and cultural orientation, and political attitude. India, for example, is a major publishing nation in its own right but has a low level of literacy, whereas Argentina is one of the major publishing nations of Latin America and has a high literacy rate and well-developed publishing infrastructures. Several African nations suffer from virtually all of the problems of Third World publishing: a multiplicity of local languages, few of which are well developed for publishing purposes; a lack of both the infrastructures and personnel for publishing; much illiteracy; a very limited market for books; and domination of small local book markets by externally controlled multinational publishers. For these countries, problems of developing an independent book industry are numerous and not easily solved. Some proposed solutions argue that regional publishing arrangements could best serve small individual markets, and efforts have been made in this direction, most notably in East Africa. The results, however, have not been impressive, and the problem of serving small markets remains.

The Third World is characterized in the development literature as having low per capita income, low levels of literacy, emphasis in the economy on the production of primary products or the extraction of natural resources, and little industrial capacity. Third World nations are also considered to be dependent on the industrialized countries for the products of high technology, including books and other printed material. Many Third World nations do have these characteristics, but a number of them do not, or, at least, no longer have them. There have been considerable changes in recent years, making the situation somewhat varied.

A few Third World nations that still manifest many of the attributes of a developing country have nonetheless managed to become major forces in publishing. Perhaps the most notable among them are India and Egypt, which are both centers of knowledge distribution in their respective regions. Both of these countries have developed large and sophisticated publishing industries and both export large numbers of books, particularly to neighboring countries. They are centers for translations, and both have significant international markets of their own. India and Egypt have been successful in part because they have significant internal markets for books and they have large populations of educated individuals and well-established educational systems, notably at the university level, which helps to create a demand for high-level published material. There is also both the human and industrial base in these nations for the development of an indigenous publishing industry. One factor that has contributed significantly to their ability to compete internationally and to produce books that local and regional audiences can afford has been low labor costs.

Both publishing industries have been flexible in the kinds of books they publish and have tried hard to fill both the local and regional markets. From these considerations we can see that it is generally possible for certain low-per-capita-income nations to develop sophisticated and effective publishing industries if they have a large internal market and a fairly substantial population of educated individuals.

Several other Third World nations have also become major publishing forces in the international market on a different scale. Singapore and Hong Kong (though Hong Kong is not, strictly speaking, a nation), which are both small as markets and in population, have become centers of printing and, to some extent, for publishing based on an international market position. A combination of low labor costs, high technology, and a commitment to the international marketplace have contributed to the success of these two countries in a number of economic endeavors, including publishing. In Latin America, the two countries that dominate Spanish-language publishing, and are major forces in international publishing are Mexico and Argentina. They both have highly developed publishing infrastructures and major export markets in Latin America. Indeed, the power of these two countries in the region has made the emergence of viable publishing industries in some of the smaller Latin American nations very difficult. A number of Third World nations, with relatively high income levels and a large number of well-educated readers, have fairly substantial publishing industries mainly to serve their local markets. Thailand, the Philippines, and Brazil are examples of this pattern of publishing development. Indeed, Brazil, now the major publisher of books in Portuguese, produces enough to export to Portugal as well as to Angola and Mozambique.

Despite these advances, however, a great many Third World nations remain dependent on external suppliers for virtually all their book needs. Many of the smaller nations of Latin America and Africa have virtually no publishing industry, although basic book needs, such as texts for elementary schools, are often supplied locally. In some instances, competition from either multinational publishers or large regional publishers, such as those in Mexico or Argentina, inhibit local publishing. In others, the lack of appropriate infrastructures, language bifurcation, and fiscal problems have limited the development of a local book industry. Political and economic problems have often limited government attention to publishing, and private enterprise in publishing, where it is permitted, is often limited in scope. In many cases, although it is unlikely that a publishing industry capable of serving basic local needs will develop, it is possible, with careful attention, to develop publishing capability with relatively small capital investment.

Most Third World nations fall somewhere between the world-class publishing nations and those without significant capability. Nations such as Nigeria, Ghana, and Kenya, although they have fairly well-established publishers and are able to meet some of their needs locally, are nonetheless dependent on external forces for many of their books. It would be possible for countries like these to develop significant publishing industries if appropriate financing could be found and sufficient attention given to this problem.

The publishing situation differs widely among Third World nations. Some countries have achieved impressive levels of literacy and have high standards of living—both of these elements are very significant in the development of a book industry, and, in terms of publishing, are equal to levels in most of the industrialized nations. Other countries are so burdened with other problems that publishing has not had a chance to develop. Variations in publishing are also determined by differences in economic systems. In countries such as China, Vietnam, Angola, and Cuba, which have centrally planned economies, publishing is carried on by the state. In other Third World nations, there is often a division of responsibility between the state and private enterprise, with government taking a more active role than is typical in most of the Western industrialized nations. Experiments with parastatal publishing—in which publishers receive state funding but still have a certain degree of independence—have been attempted in several African nations with mixed success. The term "Third World" must be understood with all these variations in mind since the variations are so significant. For the purposes of this book, we include virtually all of the nations of Africa, Asia, and Latin America in our Third World purview, although we recognize the major variations in level of socioeconomic development, political system, and, of course, publishing and book development.

Japan, although it is not a Third World nation, is included in the volume because it is the one major industrial power that does not trace its roots, and inevitably its publishing origins, back to Europe. This, in a sense, makes the Japanese publishing situation similar to that in a number of developing countries. Lacking an international language and having a market that was limited to Japan, the Japanese had to develop their own approaches to publishing on a local scale, including creating an infrastructure that eventually facilitated translations from other languages. Unlike Third World nations, Japan has always had an adequate educational system that produced a large literate population and fueled economic development which enabled Japan to surpass many European nations. The advantage of including Japan in this volume is that it illustrates how a non-European-American nation could develop an adequate publishing system on its own. Of course Japan is one of the world's economic giants and consequently has the advantages that allowed it to develop the necessary infrastructures for a viable and successful publishing industry. Any comparison to Third World countries must keep this in mind.

Themes and Variations

The essays in this volume are diverse in orientation, approach, and, of course, subject matter. Some consider countries that cover a broad spectrum geographically, politically, and in terms of economic development. Others take up issues that affect virtually all Third World nations. Some of these themes recur in almost all the chapters, and they are among the most important issues of Third World publishing.

International Dependency and Neocolonialism

Publishing, more than most other segments of an economy, is very much tied to an international network of knowledge based on books. Knowledge, in all senses of the term, is international. It comprises information that is communicated across international boundaries, and, as a result, gives rise to an important international trade in books and periodicals. In almost every respect, Third World publishers are at a disadvantage in the international marketplace of ideas. Most major periodicals originate in the industrialized nations, with countries such as the United States, France, and Britain at the center of the international knowledge network. Further, the major Western publishers often have branches in the Third World. These branches, in some instances, do original publishing and in this sense contribute to indigenous publishing development, but they also import books from the metropolitan centers. The orientations, policies, and ideas of the home office generally predominate in the branch offices of these multinational publishers. The major world languages (English, French, and, to a lesser extent, Spanish) play a dominant role in international publishing, thus giving Western publishers a key role in the cultural, and ultimately economic, life of many Third World nations. The trends in book translations illustrate this; a large number of books are translated from English into a variety of languages while relatively few Third World books are translated into the major European tongues. A look at UNESCO's giant annual listing of translations throughout the world, *Index Translation,* shows how the problem is further exacerbated: "Of the 50,428 entries in the 1977 edition more than half were produced in eight industrialized countries, including the USSR, the Federal Republic of Germany, Spain, the Netherlands, Japan, the US, Denmark and the UK, in descending order of number of translations, leaving the remaining 21,806 entries to be divided among 62 of the 70 countries in the *Index*."[2]

In addition to the marketplace reflected by the multinational publishers, the deliberate foreign aid policies of the industrialized nations influences the Third World. Many of these countries utilize their foreign assistance funds to export books to the Third World. Furthermore, the nexus of relationships between the Third World publisher and the industrialized nations is complex and deep. Third World publishers depend on the industrialized nations for new equipment and often look to overseas markets for their book sales, sometimes to compensate for the small domestic market. For the most part, however, the power is overwhelming on the side of the industrialized nations with the intellectual balance of payments tilted toward the north. In any discussion of Third World publishing, it is necessary to consider the impact of this complex set of relationships.

Copyright

A subsidiary factor in the relationship between the industrialized nations and the Third World can be found in the issue of copyright. The issues relating to copyright, both domestic and international, are complicated. Without question, the international copyright arrangements were drafted to protect the interests of the major publishing nations and many industrialized countries accepted copyright only when it was in their interest; copyright did not originate in a desire for the free flow of knowledge and ideas. Although recent liberalization has taken place in the regulations governing the transfer of knowledge to the Third World, the balance of power in knowledge production and dissemination still resides with the major publishing nations. The issue of international copyright is, of course, quite controversial in the Third World, and a number of countries persist in flouting or ignoring international regulations. Most Third World nations are members of one of the international copyright treaties and, with some exceptions, generally follow their rules. However, many in the Third World feel that international copyright does not serve their best interests. This is not difficult to understand when one recognizes that many industrialized countries began to observe international copyright only when they felt it fit their particular needs. Many industrialized countries still find ways of getting around the issues of copyright when they feel this is necessary.

A Publishing Balance

A well-balanced publishing industry includes a number of elements that function in a symbiotic relationship. Typically, in the industrialized nations, the book industry is a mix of the production and sale of school textbooks, general books, scholarly books, encyclopedias, mass-market fiction, and the like. These elements coexist in a delicate balance, with the profits from texts often subsidizing the production of uneconomic scholarly books or with mass-market fiction permitting the publication of poetry. In contrast, in the Third World these elements are seldom in balance. Further, peripheral support systems that are crucial to the publishing industry's functioning well are often lacking or underdeveloped in Third World countries. Among these are a well-developed library system, which is a major purchaser of books and an economic pillar of the book industry, and a distribution network system that includes book stores as a major component. Despite the fact that Third World publishing is often overly dependent on the school textbook market, there is little understanding that profits made on textbooks can subsidize the publication of less profitable but, nevertheless, badly needed materials; in many countries the textbook market is in the hands of government textbook boards. Third World nations must also face stiff competition from imported books, which are sometimes "dumped" at concessional prices in Third World markets. In short, the lack of all the usual markets for books and the often unnatural development of the publishing industry means that the economics of the industry are skewed and the publishers do not serve the entire potential market for books.

Emerging Technologies

For the most part, Third World publishing is based on outmoded technologies. As publishing in the advanced industrial countries moves very rapidly into the era of computer-assisted typesetting, photo-offset printing, perfect binding, and other innovative technologies, Third World publishers are being left far behind. The new technologies not only permit very large printings but also enable publishers to print small quantities of a book for scholarly purposes or small audiences. They are capital intensive and labor saving. Such technologies depend, however, on high capital expenditures for the purchase of expensive equipment and on highly trained personnel and sophisticated repair and back-up capability. For these reasons, Third World countries, with a few exceptions, will not be able to leap into the postindustrial modes of production in the fields of printing and publishing. Not only is capital scarce, but the capital to purchase imported equipment must be expended in scarce foreign exchange. Service and spare parts are lacking and consequently sophisticated machines are often nonoperational for long periods. In particular, trained personnel to operate the equipment are in short supply.

The economics of Third World publishing is often based on low-paid, low-skilled labor. For example, the semimechanical binding that is common in India and elsewhere can compete favorably with machine binding. To a small degree in India and, more prominently, in Singapore and Hong Kong, sophisticated state-of-the-art typesetting and, in rare cases, printing equipment has been imported so that local publishing and printing industries can compete internationally. In these cases, the local printers and publishers often focus on doing work commissioned by foreign firms, and so their output contributes little to the local publishing scene, however lucrative these jobs may be in terms of export earnings. The outmoded technologies of most Third World publishers may be better suited to the economics of local publishing in the short and medium term. It is also unlikely that the new technologies can be absorbed (or afforded) effectively under present conditions.

The long-term implications of this technological backwardness are, however, more serious. Using new technologies, publishers in the industrialized nations eventually will reduce their costs even further, giving them an even greater competitive advantage.[3] Further, the new technologies mean that Third World publishing for the foreseeable future will remain dependent on the industrialized nations for equipment and techniques.

The implications of the new technologies, however, go far beyond the mechanical processes of book publishing. They touch upon the very basis of the economies of the future: the extensive use of knowledge as a resource. The development of new technologies in publishing will accelerate the use of knowledge. This in turn will allow the users of such knowledge to advance into other new technologies that will provide the foundations for future major world industries, such as electronics and computers, space technology, deep-sea and ocean technology, and genetic engineering. Without a foothold in these knowledge-based industries, the gap between the Third World and the industrialized world will continue to grow wider. Alvin Toffler writes in *The Third Wave:* "Today, [the] four clusters of related industries are . . . likely to become backbone industries of the [future], bringing with them, once more, major shifts in economic power and in social and political alignments."[4] The dilemmas are considerable and the solutions unclear.

Policy and Practice

Third World publishing is a fragile industry that often needs government help to survive. Because Third World economies, even in the market economies, are more government influenced than in the West, government policies concerning publishing are very important. In many instances, these policies have been vacillating and contradictory and have actually hindered the growth of the industry. The scope of the policies is varied: regulations concerning the import of paper and ink, copyright rules, changes in the curriculum of the schools, and political and ideological constraints on what can be published are all part of the equation. Regulations concerning the import of books and the nature and scope of customs duties on books, paper, and related materials are also important for the publishing industry. In some countries, government took control of textbook publication without understanding the broader implications for the publishing industry of this action. Recently established book development councils in many nations have created forums where the publishing industry can work directly with government officials.

Distribution

In many economic endeavors that involve the production of materials, goods, or information for sale, distribution determines success or failure. While this has been recognized in the Third World for consumer or industrial goods, it is often ignored, neglected, or poorly appreciated, particularly in relation to book publishing. More often than not the prevailing economic infrastructure in many of these countries dictates the approaches that are taken—or, in most cases, not taken—to distributing the products of publishing. The lack of a well-functioning postal system, a well-established countrywide transportation system, and a well-set-up system of bookstores or selling points throughout a country are the main reasons for poor distribution. It is not unusual to find warehouses filled with badly needed textbooks in the capital cities of many Third World countries. Urban distribution systems that are frequently dominated by multinational interests provide adequately for the needs of the cities while neglecting the remote rural areas.

The Economics of Publishing

A detailed consideration of the economics of Third World publishing is beyond the scope of this book. Nevertheless, it is important to point out that economic considerations for Third World publishers differ significantly from those of publishers in the industrialized nations. The cost of books is determined by labor costs, paper availability and costs, and other factors. Paper, which is seldom a problem in the industrialized nations, is often unavailable and costly in the Third World. In many nations, paper must be imported with hard currency and at high prices. Where paper is locally produced, the quality is often deficient and supplies unreliable. Small markets for books mean that large press runs are not possible and the cost of books is high. Most Third World nations are not able to sell books abroad, even in the surrounding region, and this is an economic problem. Certain kinds of books, such as scholarly monographs, cannot be published in most Third World nations without a considerable subsidy. Yet it is important to publish original scholarship if a nation is to establish an independent research base. Government is inevitably involved in the economics of publishing, particularly since commercial credit is seldom available for the book industry due to the unprofitability of publishing in the Third World. It is simply impossible to obtain a rapid return on investment in most instances.

Conclusion

These issues point to some of the problems of Third World publishing and indicate why it is important to consider publishing in these countries on its own terms. Although there are many differences among Third World nations, there are some common themes and problems. The difficulties of developing a successful publishing enterprise in the Third World are real, and yet much has been done in the short space of thirty years. Many Third World nations have developed an indigenous book publishing capability and serve the needs of the educational system and of new literates fairly effectively. These are probably the two most crucial needs in terms of books in much of the Third World. It is our hope that this essay and the chapters that follow will enhance our understanding of the realities and issues of publishing in the Third World, for it is only through such understanding that we can move ahead.

Notes

1. Two substantive resources on Third World publishing are available. *Publishing in the Third World: Trend Report and Bibliography* by Philip G. Altbach and Eva Rathgeber (New York: Praeger, 1980) is the most comprehensive bibliographical source available. The *Studies on Book and Reading Series* and other papers prepared for UNESCO's World Congress on Books,

held in London in 1982, are an excellent source of data and analysis. The Series has continued and most of the papers remain in print. Both are available from UNESCO, 7 Place de Fontenoy, Paris, France. Finally, *African Book Publishing Record* and *Asian Book Development* are the only international journals devoted to the Third World publishing. The former is a valuable source of analysis as well as bibliographical data on material published in Africa while the latter covers Asia, from Iran to South Korea.

2. Amadio A. Arboleda, "Writing about Books: Cultural Inundationum," *Asian Book Development* 14, no. 2 (1982).
3. Datus Smith, Jr., *The Economics of Book Publishing in Developing Countries* (Paris: UNESCO, 1977).
4. Alvin Toffler, *The Third Wave* (New York: Morrow, 1980).

Themes

2. Textbooks in the Third World: Challenge and Response*

Philip G. Altbach
S. Gopinathan

The printed word is a key element in the educational process; textbooks are central to schooling at all levels. Yet the production and availability of textbooks are seldom taken into account by those who plan educational reforms or expansion of school systems. Textbooks are particularly important in the Third World, because governments have seen educational expansion as a primary tool of development. The textbook is a tool of instruction, and its potentials, limitations, and actual use are conditioned by features of the total system.

Where there are shortages of teachers and limited teacher training, as in many Third World countries, textbooks can be crucial in maintaining standards of quality and giving direction to the curriculum. A recent study noted: "From the evidence we have so far, the availability of books appears to be the single most consistently positive school factor in predicting academic achievement. In 15 of the 18 statistics, it is positive; this is, for example, more favourable than the 13 out of 24 recently reported for teacher training."[1] However, this evidence is balanced by the realization that the very expansion that made the text central to education has strained resources and made the supply of textbooks a major problem. Beeby has noted that in Indonesia, "in the towns and small cities of the less developed provinces, in over 50

*This is a revised and integrated essay based on two previous papers: Philip Altbach, "Key Issues of Textbook Provision," and S. Gopinathan, "The Role of Textbooks in Asia," both of which appeared in *Prospects* 13, no. 3 (1983).

13

percent of the schools no child who was questioned had a textbook at all. Even in Grade 6, where textbooks would seem to be completely essential, only 40 percent of the students in the poorer provinces had a book of any kind."[2]

The creation, production, and distribution of textbooks is a complex process involving the publishing industry, the educational establishment, writers, and, inevitably, government departments. In the Third World context, international agencies are often involved as well as international organizations, multinational publishing corporations, and the like. Good textbooks require planning, development, funding, testing, and distribution; textbooks utilize substantial quantities of paper, often imported, and require printing facilities. Providing adequate textbooks is quite clearly the product of coordinated educational, governmental, publishing, and printing resources.

This chapter analyzes the broader context of textbook creation and distribution in the Third World.[3] While publishing and the textbook business are not major financial expenditures in the wider arena of educational and economic development, they involve many elements of a modern society. It is important to understand these interrelationships if the need for textbooks is to be effectively met.[4] It is necessary to examine the history of textbook development, contemporary international implications, the relationship between the text market and general and scholarly publishing, the role of the public and private sectors in the textbook enterprise, and, of course, the articulation between textbooks and the educational system.

The Multiple Roles of Textbooks

In mass-based education systems, the ability to deliver information in an efficient and cost-effective manner is crucial. Good texts raise standards and require only a relatively small investment of resources. The very growth of the school system has enabled the publishing and printing industries to modernize, since a steady market is assured. In turn the cost of books is reduced, provided the basic structure of the textbook is retained. Further, advances in textbook production technologies and in larger printings make textbooks a cheaper proposition than mixed-media curriculum materials. Again, books are portable, easily handled, and reusable, and can be individually purchased and used flexibly in classroom and independent study. It has been argued that textbooks enhance teacher productivity as they free the teacher to do a variety of education-related and noneducation-related tasks. Where teacher skills are deficient, as is unfortunately the case in much of the Third World, well-designed textbooks can improve the quality of instruction.

An often unremarked aspect of textbooks is the role of the state in education, and a study of state-school relationships may reveal a lot about textbooks' dominant place in schooling. The recent Japanese textbook controversy is a case in point; other less dramatic examples could be cited, such as the insistence on a form of civics education and, in many newly independent countries, the reworking of history syllabi and curricula. Textbooks at one level, then, carry the intrinsic values and the historical mirror in which the nation wishes to see itself reflected. The selection and legitimation of content are seen as vital to national needs. Control over textbooks is vital to the state. Textbooks become a major instrument of the schooling process as the state becomes progressively more involved in education. The increasing numbers to be educated point out the need for bureaucratic control, common standards, and uniformity. Textbook content is one way of introducing students throughout a nation to common socializing experiences, thus giving textbooks a vital integrative function. In an equally significant way, because textbooks are the curriculum made explicit, they allow for the very important function of education evaluation—pupils can be assessed publicly at a national level and selection for higher levels made on the basis of achievement. We may also speculate how such communalization could facilitate teacher and pupil mobility; it is certainly an area that requires more study and evidence.

The Historical Context

Historical factors are important in understanding contemporary educational realities in the Third World. The heritage of colonialism has determined the structure of educational systems, the language of schooling, and many aspects of the curriculum. In many instances the most durable contribution of colonialism has been the examination system which many Third World countries still retain, albeit in amended form. The educational and commercial links to metropolitan centers imposed during the colonial period have in many cases remained to the present. Multinational publishers, for example, often headquartered in the former colonial metropole, retain considerable influence in the Third World.[5] Third World nations have attempted to break with colonial traditions, but strong influences remain in many countries.

Textbooks during the colonial period reflected the curricular orientations of the colonizers and were often written by colonial officials, especially those involved in education, and often published in the metropole. Educational policies and curricula reflected the needs of the colonial authorities.[6] Key decisions in education were made by people who had priorities far different from nation building and economic development.

Almost all Third World nations entered the post-World War II period without the basic infrastructure of publishing, though branches of metropolitan publishers existed in some countries. In other cases textbooks were imported from the metropole. Indigenous publishers were rare, and national educational authorities had little expertise in textbook production and distribution. All of the requirements of a modern publishing system—printing facilities, a distribution apparatus, competent editors, and the like—had to be developed almost from scratch. The heritage of colonialism was one of dependency on a foreign country.

The curriculum was also patterned on colonial practices and was outmoded if not irrelevant.[7] Examples from the metropole abounded in the curriculum, and crucial concepts like traditional cultures and colonial rule were treated from a colonial perspective. New conceptions of history, national development, and priorities had to be devised, and then curricula and textbooks developed to suit these needs.

A common problem was that education was limited to a small urban elite and literacy was limited to a small segment of the population. The language of education was often exclusively the metropolitan language, which further limited access. Every newly independent nation had to expand educational opportunities and foster literacy, often in new languages. The problems of creating textbooks for a new curriculum and for rapidly expanding educational systems were substantial.[8]

Colonialism structured an international system that emphasized the power of the metropolitan centers and a dominant-dependent relationship between these centers and their peripheries. The publishing enterprise reflected this unequal distribution of material and intellectual resources. Basic decisions concerning publishing and usually the publishing apparatus itself remained in the metropole. Trade relationships emphasized this arrangement.

Even in those countries not under direct colonial rule, such as Thailand, China, most of Latin America, and Japan, the influence of European educational patterns, ideologies, and emphases was very strong. European experts played a prominent role in educational and curricula planning, and the organizational patterns reflected European models. Noncolonized Third World nations, although they had a greater capability to produce their own textbooks and were less dependent on foreign models for the curriculum, were very much linked to an international system of inequality in education.

Historical factors continue to weigh heavily. The educational policies, language priorities, and curricular orientations of the colonial period still influence many Third World nations. Of the 18,584 books published in India in 1978, 7,089 were in English and only 2,966 in Hindi. The remainder were in India's other languages.[9] The cost of recreating an educational system has been great and has placed special burdens on textbooks, since they are often the first representation of the new educational reality. The historical organization of the text business, with an emphasis on foreign experts, foreign printing capacity, and foreign technology has been difficult to break. The multinational publishers also retain considerable influence in many Third World nations since they continue to function actively, particularly where a European language remains important in education. Historical traditions and policies must be kept in mind in any consideration of contemporary textbook development. It is easy to demand a break with the past; it is much more difficult to implement truly independent policies and practices.

The International Context

Neither educational systems nor textbooks in the Third World exist in a vacuum. Textbook production and distribution are part of an international system of publishing and knowledge distribution, which is dominated by the industrial nations and often used by them to maintain their position. As late as 1978, 34 developed countries representing 30 percent of the world's population produced 81 percent of the world's titles. Thirty-seven percent of all British books are sold overseas, and 20 percent of these are educational books. British publishing, and in particular educational publishing, cannot survive without overseas markets.[10] The elements of the international system include copyright arrangements, the existence and bias of multinational publishing companies, the control of new printing technologies, and the world price of paper. The policies of the industrialized nations and major aid-giving agencies in education also affect the nature of textbooks in the Third World.

Textbook production in the Third World has long been in the hands of a few multinational publishing firms based in the industrialized nations. Macmillan, Longman, McGraw-Hill, Prentice-Hall, and others are household names in many countries. Even such prestigious scholarly publishers as Oxford University Press are deeply involved in the production and distribution of school-level textbooks worldwide. Though the trend is away from the dominance of multinational firms, their influence remains strong.[11] In Zimbabwe, for example, most textbooks have been produced by Longman or Macmillan, which have a well-developed presence in the country.

The multinational firms have a number of distinct advantages over indigenous publishers.[12] With some adaptation they are often able to produce books for more than one country, and through branch offices they can market them regionally. This is the case in both Anglophone and Francophone Africa, where the national markets are small and regional distribution is not too difficult. They can purchase paper on international markets at low cost and can allocate material resources among their regional offices. The multinational firms have access to the most modern technologies and can introduce them, as needed, in the Third World affiliates. Perhaps most important, the multinationals have ready access to cash, a constant problem among Third World publishers, and can invest the sums needed for textbook development. They can thus utilize modern printing techniques and can print in large numbers, thereby reducing unit costs. The multinationals have all the expertise necessary to engage in sophisticated and effective publishing. They are able to do research and development for textbooks to ensure that the final result is of high quality.

The multinationals do not always work to the benefit of the Third World. They are concerned basically with the profitability of the corporation and not of the host country, and their publishing decisions are made with their own interests in mind. Textbooks produced by the multinationals may not be directly relevant for particular Third World nations. Such books are often designed with a regional market in mind and typically retain the perspective of the metropolitan publishers. They are frequently edited and printed in Europe or North America, and consequently local publishers do not benefit; the publishing infrastructure of the consuming nation is not strengthened. The technical quality of the textbooks is generally quite high. Printed on good quality paper and often including pictures, these books may be expensive and unnecessarily elaborate for the local market. Their marketing advantages, quality, and large printings, often make the emergence of indigenous textbooks very difficult. Without question, the multinational publishers retain a good deal of influence in the international textbook configuration: they set the standard for texts and they are able, in some markets, to dominate the production and sales of textbooks. In recent years, they have begun to publish in Third World languages and have thereby spread their influence. Branches of multinational publishers in such countries as Zimbabwe, Nigeria, India, and Malaysia are actively producing books in local languages for specific markets.

The contemporary concept of the textbook is a Western idea, and most Third World nations depend on notions of textbook design, production, and appearance initiated in the industrialized nations. The idea that books should have full-color illustrations, be printed on long-lasting paper, be accompanied by workbooks printed on poorer quality paper, and should generally be hardcover rather than paperback are all Western concepts. Many Third World nations attempt to follow these ideas about text design. In some countries, paperback books printed on cheaper paper are used in order to reduce costs or due to problems of supply. In a few instances, books are specifically designed to meet local needs rather than to conform to international standards.

The international copyright system has implications for textbooks and is symbolic of the international knowledge system. International copyright arrangements are dominated by the industrialized nations, although Third World nations have attempted with some success, through UNESCO and other agencies, to gain more control over the system.[13] It is sometimes difficult for Third World publishers to obtain permission to reprint or translate materials; the bureaucratic procedures involved are complex and time consuming. The copyright issue is more important with university-level textbooks, where there is often a need to translate or reprint materials from the industrialized nations. Metropolitan publishers sometimes prefer to sell their own books (at high prices) rather than to grant licenses for local printings. At the school level, copyright issues are not generally a key concern, but the entire question is symbolic of the nature of the international knowledge system.

New ideas and technologies that emanate from the industrialized nations are important for the advancement of Third World countries, which must try to obtain access to them through the international system. Computer-assisted typesetting, new techniques in graphic design, and printing technologies that utilize fast and efficient presses have all been pioneered in the industrialized nations. This expensive equipment must often be purchased abroad, and personnel trained in the efficient use of the new technologies are not generally available. In the long run these methods are important to the success of indigenous publishers, enabling them to simultaneously reduce unit costs (on large quantities) and improve quality, but a balance between a headlong rush to computerization and the maintenance of outdated yet efficient manufacturing practices must be carefully drawn.

A final element of the international equation is the foreign assistance policies of industrialized nations, which some feel are detrimental to Third World interests.[14] The British government has provided English language college-level textbooks to many Third World countries. Although these books are useful to students, they do not develop local publishing industries or help build capabilities for indigenous textbook development. Similar efforts have been sponsored by the United States, the Soviet Union, and West Germany. Franklin Book Programs, a private American foundation funded by the United States government and other sources, assisted the development of textbook capabilities in a number of Third World nations. UNESCO has also been concerned with textbook production and distribution. Some of these programs have helped develop local textbook capabilities, while others have provided imported books.

The international factor plays an important role in the textbook equation. Third World nations can learn a great deal from the technologies and experiences of the industrialized nations, and in some areas international agencies and individual industrialized nations can constructively assist the Third World. But the negative implications of the international system must also be kept in mind: the restrictions of international copyright, the complex roles of the multinational publishers, and the mixed results of foreign aid programs must be carefully considered.

Language

The issue of language of instruction has implications far beyond textbooks; it has broad educational and political importance. Conflict over language policy is evident in many Third World nations. In numerous countries, educational systems are shifting from the colonial language to one or more indigenous languages. Often indigenous languages have not been used for modern schooling, and agreement on appropriate vocabularies and spelling has to be reached before textbooks can be written. Even where languages have a long educational tradition, new subjects necessitate the "modernization" of the language. Such language shifts, along with the expansion of education and an increasing diversity of curricular offerings, has placed great pressure on textbook development. Thus, language has both policy implications and related technical problems for textbook development.

Additional language-related issues with implications for the development of textbooks include typefaces, printing capability, and translation. It is often necessary to devise new typefaces to meet the needs of languages not previously used for educational purposes.

Printing capability is a broader problem, but facilities for printing in indigenous languages may be scarcer than those for printing in the metropolitan languages. In addition, it is often necessary, at least at the initial stages, to translate textbooks from metropolitan languages into indigenous languages. Problems of copyright, quality of translations, relevance, and vocabularies further complicate this task.

Since Third World nations have increasingly adopted more than one indigenous language for educational purposes, the problems of textbook development become even more complicated. In India, for example, at least fifteen languages are in widespread use for education. The National Book Trust in India as well as several private sector publishers have attempted to utilize common design and graphic and pictorial material in producing textbooks in a number of languages. These texts are simultaneously translated into different languages, resulting in a number of economies.

Textbooks and Publishing

The relationship between textbooks and the publishing industry in the Third World is complex. Increasingly government agencies have taken a direct role in textbook production and distribution, in the interest of producing books more cheaply and ensuring that they meet requirements of the educational system. This has had both positive and negative effects. The private publishing industry has been deprived of its largest and most lucrative market, and this has constrained its development. Governments have found that textbook production is expensive and complicated, and delays have occurred as costs have risen. The development of a full-fledged publishing infrastructure solely for textbooks has been a formidable and costly process.

However, there are certain advantages to government involvement. In Malaysia the sheer volume of new school books needed as a consequence of the adoption of Bahasa Malaysia as the major educational language could not have been provided by commercial publishers alone. Malaysia's language and literature agency supported by government funds had to turn printer to meet the challenge. In India some 514 million copies of textbooks are required annually, far beyond the scope of commercial publishers. In other instances, as with the Curriculum Development Institute of Singapore, government support enabled the utilization of curriculum expertise from abroad—for practically every subject—and resulted in a new generation of textbooks and teaching aids within a comparatively short time span. However, government publishing is not inevitable: in Singapore a tender system enables commercial publishers to share in the enterprise.

Despite persistent structural inequalities, noteworthy advances have been made in textbook provision and a measure of national self-reliance has been achieved in some countries. It is clear, for example, that great strides have been made in providing Asia's schoolchildren with relevant curriculum materials. As table 2.1 indicates, most Asian countries have either maintained or improved on the number of new editions produced annually.

Qualitative improvements have also been made to textbooks, and with the syllabus revision that has been undertaken within many Third World education systems, many of these books now relate more closely to national conditions. More illustrations, the use of color, more pedagogically based structuring of content, the production of workbooks and teachers' guides, the incorporation of study aids within texts have all undeniably made for better texts. Though textbooks in regional languages are not as plentiful as needed, many countries have begun to provide them to ensure that their language policies are effectively implemented; a small state like Singapore produces some instructional materials in four languages.

Finally, infrastructural facilities have been built up in many countries to decrease dependence on imported textbooks. Almost all elementary-level texts are indigenously produced in Asia, and a large number of secondary-level texts are extensive local adaptations, locally produced. An important factor in this has been the state's involvement in the production of curriculum materials. The Indian Education Commission Report called for both statewide and nationwide textbook boards to produce and sell textbooks.[15] Although commercial publishers have generally resisted such moves, it seems clear that a completely free-enterprise textbook publishing system can not always provide sufficient quantities of inexpensive books in situations of

Table 2.1. Production of School Textbooks in Asia

Country	Number of Titles		
	1970	1974	1979
Afghanistan			50*
Bhutan	17	10	
Brunei			34
China			3602‡
Hong Kong		131	107*
India	316	529	467
Indonesia		476	458
Japan			352
Korea, Republic	1263		941
Malaysia	324	240	299
Nepal			2†
Pakistan			50*
Philippines			120
Singapore	99	81	173
Sri Lanka	148	57	22
Thailand	65	336	150*
Vietnam			802†

Source: UNESCO, *Statistical Yearbook,* 1971, 1975, and 1981.
* Figures for 1977.
† Figures for 1978.
‡ Total for books and pamphlets.

rapid change. To implement radical changes in medium of instruction as well as new and more sophisticated curriculum and to integrate curriculum renewal with teacher training and the production of appropriate materials, state facilities may be required. Between 1975 and 1979, Malaysia's Dewan Bahasa, for instance, produced 743 titles for schools in Malay (472 elementary and 271 secondary), printed 35 million copies, and is credited with making the effective shift to a national-language-based education possible. Some foreign aid projects, such as the World Bank-assisted schemes in Indonesia and the Philippines, inevitably lead to greater government involvement in providing curriculum materials.

Within the Third World, particularly Asia, innovative projects, which involve teachers in their preparation and evaluation and which are closely tied to teacher training, are under way to produce more interesting, relevant, low-cost educational materials. The Asian Program of Educational Innovation for Development (APEID), Bangkok, has played a particularly important role in this transformation. The Program's brief is innovation in general, yet it has made important progress both in convincing educators to see beyond the textbook and in promoting and demonstrating the viability of low-cost indigenously produced educational materials. These materials are complimentary to the textbook and range from models, charts, puppets, educational toys and games to science and mathematics kits and laboratory equipment.

Pakistan is an example of this. The National Educational Equipment Centre produced a primary teachers' tool kit covering science, mathematics, social studies, and Urdu and consisting of 100 items complete with teachers' guides and supplied these to 50,000 schools. In addition, the center trained 2,200 master teacher trainers, who will in turn train 200,000 more teachers in the use of the kit. In Bangladesh, Nepal, and Korea various educational equipment bureaus are using local low-cost resources and materials to produce equipment for science and technology instruction. In India the National Centre for Educational Research and Training produces core instructional materials for translation, adaptation, and adoption. Singapore has established the Curriculum Development Institute of Singapore (CDIS) to prepare instructional materials, and recently the Institute of Education, a teacher-training organization, has been asked to help produce school curriculum materials. In the Philippines three curriculum centers were established to coordinate and produce new textbooks. It is clear that in these countries curricular materials have come to mean more than the usual textbook, and the pride of place commercial publishers once enjoyed has now been replaced by a more national effort, incorporating the Ministry of Education, curriculum development centers, and teacher-training institutes.

In producing and distributing textbooks both Indonesia and the Philippines have faced severe problems and both have benefited from major international, cooperative projects. In the early seventies the World Bank embarked on an eight-year US$39 million project in Indonesia to develop curricula, train teachers, and produce 138 million copies of texts in core subjects for grades one to six. Indonesia's second Five-Year Development Plan, 1974–78, envisaged that a total of 180 million copies of new primary-level texts and 52 million secondary-level texts would be printed. Though no extensive evaluation of the project is available at this stage, it is claimed that in 1974–75 over 13 million primary school textbooks were printed along with nearly half a million for secondary schools and one-quarter million for people in nonformal educational programs.

In the Philippines, preliminary World Bank studies indicated that in the early seventies there was only one book for every 9.8 pupils in grades one to four, one for every 11.5 pupils in grades five to six, and one for every 8.5 pupils in secondary schools. A lack of adequate curricular materials was responsible for both low and uneven achievement and high repetition rates. With Bank support a Textbook Board was created to supervise a US$52 million credit. The project's aim was to produce and distribute some 75 of the 109 new textbook titles and thus reduce the pupil-textbook ratio from 10 : 1 to 2 : 1. A recent assessment notes that "during the period, eighty-four textbooks and corresponding teachers' materials were developed and tested, over 33 million copies of the new textbooks were contracted for printing and 247 million copies actually distributed to the 40,000 schools throughout the country and more than 252,000 teachers and school administrators given orientation."[16] Already it is clear that the economies of scale have lowered costs between 50 and 70 percent. Pupil costs, as a consequence of this program have increased by less than 1 percent while student performance appears to have risen 14 percent. The World Bank has been so convinced of the program's utility that it has made available another loan of $100 million for the period 1982–85.

While valiant efforts are being made to provide basic texts in the poorer countries, there have been few studies that systematically compare the cost-effectiveness of newer forms of curriculum materials with the traditional textbook, and existing publishing structures and practices would seem to ensure the conventional textbook of a firm place. Only more massive government intervention in curriculum materials production and distribution can create the economies of scale that will make newer forms of curriculum materials viable.

At another level there have been efforts to move beyond the limitations of the textbook. Educational broadcasting has long been an instrument of curriculum enrichment in many countries, and recent developments in satellite and computer technology promise breathtaking advances. In August 1975, India launched a Rs20 million (US$2 million) year-long Satellite Instructional Television Experiment (SITE), simultaneously reaching a population of 3.5 million in 2,400 villages and aimed at assessing the potential of a satellite-based instructional television system. The educational component was designed to meet the needs of preprimary and primary children and to improve basic concepts and skills in numeracy, language, and technology.[17]

Not surprisingly, Japan has taken the lead in "technologizing" the instructional process in Asia. Several university departments of education have established educational technology centers within their teacher training programs, and in 1972 a Council of National University Centers for Educational Technology was established to facilitate research exchange and aid policy making. This has enabled Japan to explore systematically the uses of multimedia systems, teaching machines, computer-assisted instruction (CAI) and computer-managed instruction (CMI).

The unresolved issues and problems that will face educators in the eighties can be dealt with at two levels: new technologies and issues relating to the conventional textbook. The painful evolution of textbook publishing in some countries can be read as a development from dependence on overseas publishers and book imports to greater autonomy and control over books in national school systems. Just as this autonomy is being consolidated, new technologies in information processing and distribution are being offered to the Third World with the promise of enhancing learning, overcoming the problems of poor teacher supply, and being more cost-effective. These new technologies bring both opportunity and risk. If fully realized, they will lead to more flexible and more individualized instruction; pocket calculators are likely to be accompanied by electronic language learning aids, but their relative simplicity could mean incorporation into existing systems without too much difficulty. More ambitious systems for technologizing instruction imply, at the present stage of Third World development, a dependence on the developed world for hardware and for high-quality software. To what extent software packages will be interchangeable between systems, who will produce them and under what conditions they will be marketed, how this will influence, if not dictate, their use, are questions with no clear answers. How much investment in this new technology will affect future scope and directions of investment in print materials is also unknown. Will there be support for low-scale ecologically appropriate technology paralleling the move to produce low-cost indigenously devised instructional materials? The high cost of quality software may necessitate incorporating total school systems within a single instructional mode, something that can be done only at the price of greater centralization.

Notes

1. S. Heyneman, J. Farrell, and M. Sepulvada-Stuardo, *Textbooks and Achievement: What We Know* (Washington, D.C.: World Bank, 1978), p. 2.
2. C. E. Beeby, *Assessment of Indonesian Education: A Guide to Planning* (Wellington, New Zealand: New Zealand Council for Educational Research, 1979), p. 58.
3. For a general discussion of the context of the publishing enterprise, see Philip G. Altbach, "Literary Colonialism: Books in the Third World," *Harvard Educational Review* 45 (May 1975): 226–236. For a discussion of textbooks in developing countries see *Prospects* 13, no. 3 (1983).
4. Philip G. Altbach, "Publishing and the Intellectual System," *Annals of the American Academy of Political and Social Science* 421 (September 1975): 1–13.
5. Keith Smith, "Who Controls Book Publishing in Anglophone Middle Africa?" *Annals of the American Academy of Political and Social Science* 421 (September 1975): 140–150. See also W. H. Patwardhan, "National Goals of Publishing" (Paper delivered at the International Seminar on World Publishing in the Eighties, New Delhi, India, January 1976).
6. The educational heritage of colonialism is complex and, of course, not entirely one-sided. School policies were made by the colonizers but were often influenced by the colonized. For a broad discussion of the colonial impact on education, see Philip G. Altbach and Gail P. Kelly, eds., *Education and the Colonial Experience* (New Brunswick, N. J.: Transaction Books, 1984).
7. *Ibid.*
8. S. Gopinathan, "Publishing in a Plural Society: The Case of Singapore," in P. G. Altbach and S. McVey, eds., *Perspectives on Publishing* (Lexington, Mass.: Lexington Books, 1976), 157–172.
9. See table 9.2, p. 114.
10. S. Gopinathan, "International Educational Publishing," in *International Encyclopedia of Education* (Oxford, England: Pergamon, forthcoming).
11. For a more extensive discussion of the role of the multinational corporations in knowledge distribution, see Anthony Smith, *The Geopolitics of Information: How Western Culture Dominates the World* (New York: Oxford University Press, 1980).
12. K. Smith, "Who Controls Book Publishing?"

13. I. Olian, Jr., "International Copyright and the Needs of Developing Countries," *Cornell International Law Journal* 7 (1974): 81–112.
14. Philip G. Altbach, "Literary Colonialism."
15. Ministry of Education, Government of India, *Report of the Education Commission, 1964–1966* (New Delhi: Ministry of Education, 1966).
16. P. N. Aprieto, "The Philippine Textbook Project," *Prospects* 13, no. 3 (1983): 351–360.
17. C. K. Basu and K. Ramachandran, "Satellite Instructional Television Experiment in India," in A. Howe and A. Romiszowski, eds., *International Yearbook of Educational and Instructional Technology, 1976–1977* (London: Kogan Page, 1976).

3. Copyright:
Where Do We Go from Here?
Edward W. Ploman

In the course of time we have erected a structure of legal rules and theories so elaborate that it is difficult to discern the different purposes and uses of copyright. The traditional reasons for the copyright system may be summarized as follows: On the grounds of social justice, the creator of an intellectual work should benefit from the fruits of his or her labor; thus royalties function as the intellectual worker's salary. This, it is assumed, will also result in cultural progress since copyright protection will encourage authors to create new works. On economic grounds, copyright protection is assumed to ensure that the investment necessary for the creation of works (film-making, architecture) or for their exploitation (theater production, record manufacturing, book publishing) will be readily available. The copyright system is also taken to ensure that the remuneration to the originator of a work is equitably shared by the ultimate users, such as the purchasers of books and records or the paying customers of the theater, concert hall, or cinema. On moral grounds, the author should be given the right to decide whether, when, and how a work may be reproduced or performed in public and also to prevent mutilation and changes.

Copyright is used to reconcile the partly shared, partly contradictory interests of authors who give expression to ideas, publishers who disseminate ideas, and members of the public who use the ideas, and as such is expected to regulate the economic and social relations between different interest groups in society. It is a legal mechanism for ordering socioeconomic and cultural life and a method to link the world of ideas to the world of commerce. Seen from another angle, copyright is used to organize and control the flows of information in society; the assumptions underlying copyright condition patterns of cultural and scientific life.

The concepts of organization and control make it obvious that there is nothing universal about copyright. All societies have evolved systems for organizing information flows, but these systems show many facets. Different societies have given very different answers to copyright issues.

Copyright evolved in response to specific challenges. Its origin is Western and its parentage multiple: the invention of the printing press and the advent of the Industrial Revolution, the philosophy of the marketplace and that of natural rights, the rise of bourgeois society and the spread of literacy, new social attitudes toward art and the artist. The resulting notion of intellectual property is a European invention but is now used in diverse economic and social systems to structure the flow of information and cultural products.

At present, copyright, as other branches of communications law, is in a state of crisis. The reasons are many and varied. The impact of new technology, of new methods for the production, duplication, storage, and dissemination of information and cultural materials is obvious. The flows of information within and between societies have reached new levels of density and variety: communications both express and contribute to the transformations of the international system. Changes in economic organization affect the conditions of the intellectual worker. Changes in social and cultural values are reflected in new policies for culture, education, and communications. Just as traditional assumptions for organizing and controlling the flows of information are called into question, so too are the economic assumptions on which the law of copyright is founded. The growth of the information sector has led to new ways of looking at national economies. In industrialized countries the concept of the information society is gaining ground while new strands in development thinking emphasize the need to integrate the cultural and information dimension into strategies for economic and social development.

Copyright has become one of the most complex, technically difficult branches of law, an arcane area populated by experts hiding behind an almost impenetrable jargon. The legal complexities and the language of the experts make it difficult for the general public, for policy and decision makers, for technologists and even for practitioners in communication to understand the wider implications of legislation and practices in this field. The resulting failure to formulate coherent policies is serious in a situation where new technologies and changing social patterns alter the conditions for the ordering of cultural life.

Copyright and its origins must therefore be set in the large context of cultural and economic life, the social attitude toward intellectual creations and their uses, and the position of the creator in society. It has emerged as one means of organizing and controlling the flow of information and knowledge, art, and entertainment in society.

Systems of Copyright

The emergence of copyright as a method for organizing economic and cultural life was conditioned by a set of specific attitudes and circumstances. Its distinctive character is well encapsulated in the concept of "intellectual property," a uniquely Western idea conditioned by two interlocking prerequisites: the sociocultural attitude toward intellectual and artistic creation and the Industrial Revolution. In comparison with other cultures, the Western system for organizing cultural life and the attendant position of the artist in society is the exception rather than the rule.

The first prerequisite for copyright is a tradition of individual creation and art in which one goal of the artist is to attain recognition and fame. In a competitive system with direct economic benefits, a class of professional authors and artists can be established. This market-oriented attitude is directly related to the second prerequisite for modern copyright: the Industrial Revolution. The printing press was the forerunner and later technical methods transformed publishing into an industry for mass production. These two circumstances combined in the concept of immaterial rights, of intellectual property that could be bought and sold. It is significant that intellectual property has been divided into two main branches: industrial property (patents, etc.) and copyright, or authors' rights which in a general sense also include the so-called neighboring rights (particularly the rights of performing artists).

Given its origin, it may appear as a surprise that copyright has gained such widespread acceptance. Even though countries are organized under a variety of political and economic systems, the majority of nations possess statutes that establish policy and regulation in the area of copyright. These nations represent a broad spectrum of political, social, economic, and cultural ideologies; thus the popularity of copyright cannot be accounted for simply by a meeting of minds on this subject. Instead a contributing, though underrated, factor would appear to be the ability of copyright to be integrated into a wide variety of economic structures and to be moulded in a way that advances differing national priorities. "The underlying arguments in favour of copyright contain elements of thought which appeal to governments and legislators of almost every political complexion. Copyright can be seen as beneficial both to public policy and to private profit; as a boon to individual freedom and as an aid to State intervention; either as an expression of natural justice or as an assertion of property rights."[1] The flexible nature of copyright allows it to serve different functions and combine with other methods for the financial support of intellectual creation. While most countries would maintain that they apply basic principles of copyright, the results may vary considerably from one to another. The high degree of international cooperation in this field would seem to foster a greater uniformity among national copyright laws than would otherwise be the case. But since the international conventions have been drafted so as to achieve a maximum agreement on common principles, these principles yield different results when they are applied in various economic and social systems.

In an overall cultural perspective, the stated purpose of copyright is to encourage intellectual creation by serving as the main means to recompense the intellectual worker and to protect his or her moral rights. In an economic sense, copyright is a method of regulating trade and commerce. Copyright thus serves as a mechanism by which the law brings the world of science, art, and culture into relation with the world of commerce. In a social sense, copyright is an instrument for the cultural, scientific, and technological organization of society. Copyright can also be analyzed in terms of the different interests involved. It is possible to distinguish four major interests: those of the creator; those of the publisher, distributor, or other user of works; those of the ultimate consumer (i.e., the public at large); and those of society as a whole.

While varying greatly in detail and emphasis, most national laws on intellectual property deal with copyright under two distinct aspects, property or economic rights and personal rights. Among the property rights are the rights to authorize the publication, reproduction, performance, exhibition, translation, or dissemination of a work. Included among the author's personal rights, or what in many countries are called moral rights, are the right to prohibit distortions, mutilations, or modifications of the work and a right of "paternity," which is a right to prevent some other person being named as the author. These moral rights are taken to exist independently of and even after the transfer of the economic rights.

The relative emphasis given to these two aspects indicates differences in the philosophy of copyright which have been the subject of doctrinal controversies and debates, often conducted with great passion. Since the end of the eighteenth century numerous legal theories have been advanced and attempts made to describe and categorize the different copyright systems used in the world.

According to one doctrine which was dominant until some twenty years ago, a distinction was made between three main copyright concepts: (1) the essentially individualistic European approach, (2) the essentially commercial Anglo-American approach, and (3) the essentially societal approach in socialist countries. More recently the differences between the European and the Anglo-American concepts have not been emphasized since they are expressed less in the level of protection provided than in the formulation of rights. The theoretical basis for these new approaches is the social role of intellectual property rights. One version provides for a distinction among three groups: regimes in countries with a market economy, in countries with a socialist economy, and in developing countries.[2]

The legal regimes in all countries with a predominantly market economy share certain basic guiding principles. In the marketplace of ideas, the relationship between the author and society is regulated mainly by economic factors. The major feature of copyright is thus the exclusive character of the author's rights which provide for a property in the technical sense of the term. The creator thus has a monopoly with regard to the use and exploitation of a work, whether this monopoly derives from a recognition of a natural right or from a legally defined privilege. It follows that authors may dispose of their work as they wish, through the right to grant exclusive contracts or licenses by which they can authorize third parties to exercise all or part of their rights.

However, the ideal marketplace is no more a reality in the copyright field than in other economic relations. The ideal of the individual creator being able to sell his or her work to the highest bidder in the marketplace was probably always more the exception than the rule. Except for famous creators, the author is often in a weak negotiating position with publishers or other users of the work and would thus benefit only imperfectly from the results of his or her intellectual labor. Moreover, when works are produced in an employment situation or as the result of teamwork, the adaptation of traditional copyright concepts poses a series of new issues. Since copyright is based on an abstraction, countries with a market economy experience great difficulties in evolving concepts and methods to adapt copyright to rapidly changing economic and social circumstances.

In countries with a socialist system, which in this context refers mainly to those of Eastern Europe, the principles underlying copyright legislation are based on a different conception of the interrelationship between the author and society. This has been expressed as harmonizing the general interest and the special interests of the author. The creation of an original work depends on the individual creative activity of the author, but only within the given social framework which provides the sources of insight and experience expressed by the author. It is in the general interest to stimulate creative activity which contributes to the improvement of cultural life and the building of a socialist society. The relationship between author and society cannot be ruled by economic aspects only, but as much or even more by the cultural policies of the socialist society. Copyright has therefore been described as "an instrument for the management of cultural processes."[3] Within this overall framework, the legislation enacted by each of the socialist countries differs considerably in terms of adherence to the international conventions and the levels and nature of copyright protection provided.

Even less homogeneous as a grouping is the large number of developing countries. Here the distinction between domestic and foreign copyright policy is of even greater importance than in the other two groups. The major reasons are the special requirements of economic and social development and the fact that most developing countries are net importers of intellectual property. Since these countries have to design copyright policies suited to their particular needs, their large participation in the multilateral copyright conventions that have originated in the industrialized world might appear.

Several explanations account for this high degree of international cooperation. First, many of the developing countries were colonies of European powers which introduced the principles of copyright into their domestic laws. Second, although most developing countries must import a large proportion of the intellectual property they utilize, they are anxious to promote endogenous intellectual production. A widely accepted means of achieving this goal is a copyright law intended to provide the necessary incentive for authorship as well as to protect fledgling cultural industries. Third, in order to bridge the economic gap between themselves and the developed countries, it is important for these countries to have access to intellectual property at costs they can afford. However, a rejection of copyright protection for foreigners might jeopardize progress and would undoubtedly produce a backlash in the industrialized countries, particularly from private enterprises in the intellectual property field. In addition, technological developments in the communications field such as satellites and computer data networks offer the possibility of much faster assimilation of intellectual property than had been possible in the past. The basic objectives are therefore twofold: to encourage domestic production of intellectual works and to gain access on reasonable conditions to foreign works.

The governments of the industrialized countries have, to a certain extent, been sympathetic to the needs of the economically disadvantaged nations. The unions of intellectual workers and the commercial enterprises of these countries engaged in intellectual property have been less generous. While not opposed to the advancement of developing countries, they object to an economic burden being shifted onto them through a dilution of copyright protection. Despite the conflicts which have arisen, compromises have been made which, while not completely satisfying any one interest group, have at least preserved large-scale international cooperation between the developing and industrialized countries.

Issues of Copyright in Modern Legislation

Copyright concerns a wide range of activities and interests in society and is used to perform an increasing number of different and not necessarily concordant functions. From its origin in the print media it has been extended to cover totally new situations. The crucial issue in theory and practice is therefore the definition of copyright, the delimitation of what can and should, cannot or should not, be included in copyright protection.

The simplest definition would be that copyright is the individual right of an author to dispose of his or her work in return for remuneration. There are, however, numerous difficulties and contradictions, not the least of these being that expressions used in the copyright field are given meanings different from those in ordinary language. This is true for the expression "work," as the object of copyright, for the concept of "author," as the presumed beneficiary of copyright, and for the concept of "publisher," as the user of protected works.

What should be regarded as a "work" appears with some stretch of the imagination reasonably clear in traditional forms of intellectual expression. Often national legislation and international conventions provide long catalogues of the literary and artistic works that are protected, even though they include objects no ordinary person would classify as either literary or artistic. However, with each advance in technical production methods, the definition of work becomes more elusive. Therefore, while most national laws protect works in the classical categories, they vary widely with regard to other, new forms.

Nor is it a simple matter to define the "author" as the originator of a work and supposedly the main beneficiary of copyright protection. The archetypal author is, of course, an individual who, unaided, produces the finished work by actually putting the paint on the canvas, the letters on paper, or the notes on the stave. Special problems arise in cases of collaborative work, joint authorship, and especially with the changing working conditions of the author, who may be an employee of a legal entity, whether it be government, university, or company. The more elusive the definition and nature of the work, the more difficult it becomes to locate the author. New technologies have led to new ways of producing works, so that both work and author only vaguely resemble the classical definitions and situations.

Similar difficulties have arisen over what is to be understood by "publisher" and "publication." When copyright applied only to books and other printed matter, it was fairly simple to determine the meaning of these words. New means of production and forms of expression have made it necessary to extend the scope of these concepts, to encompass such situations as when a sound recording or a film is "published" as distinct from its "public performance."

The nature of copyright and related rights is based on exclusive, more or less absolute, rights granted to the creator and any assignees. However, social reality is not abstract, and social intercourse is not conducted in absolute terms. Therefore, copyright cannot be dealt with in these abstract, absolute terms. Copyright is to some degree opposed to other social objectives: the requirements of cultural life and of collectivity, the needs of information and knowledge in modern society, and the protection of privacy. In order to satisfy these other requirements in the face of exclusive copyright demands, it has been necessary to limit copyright or to deprive the author of the control of certain uses (for example, duration of copyright, limitations in terms of certain uses, compulsory or legal licenses, and so on).

Changes in technology and thus in the production and dissemination of works have led to some difficulties in intellectual property rights. The same holds true with regard to the use of works. The introduction of various new methods of photo-copying, video-recording, and playback for private use has raised new problems and requires new solutions. The pressure on the traditional copyright concept is also shown in the need to adopt rules to cover an increasing number of special cases: library deposits and public lending rights, archives, protection of titles and fictitious names, classic works, cable distribution, computer programs and computer-origi-nated works, official documents and anonymous works (as in the case of folklore).

Another reason for the present crisis in copyright stems from the conflict between public and private interests, between the rights of the author or copyright-owner and the rights of the users. Both of these fundamental principles are expressed in Article 27 of the Universal Declaration of Human Rights:

(1) Everyone has the right freely to participate in the cultural life of the community, to enjoy the arts and to share in scientific advancement and its benefits.
(2) Everyone has the right to the protection of the moral and material interests resulting from any scientific, literary or artistic production of which he is the author.

It is a matter not only of preserving these two principles but also of finding a balance between them. This balance as well as the balance between the interests of the creator, the publisher, and the public has to be based on an analysis of the social role of copyright and neighboring rights. The legal policies that condition the norms applicable to these rights are intimately linked to political, economic, and social structures. They cannot be seen only in static terms. Because social and cultural developments in most countries have resulted in an increased need to use protected material for information and other forms of public service, policies in the field of intellectual property rights must be defined in relation to policies for education, culture, information, and communications generally. This wider perspective is re-quired at the national as well as at the international level.

The Uneasy Case for Copyright

There has been a steady trend toward the expansion of intellectual property rights. Nationally and internationally, rights and protection have been extended to cover new categories of authors, publishers, and works, to include new methods for the generation, reproduction, and dissemination of information, and to provide for even longer periods of protection. At the same time, there has been a concerted drive to extend territorial coverage by persuading nonadhering countries to ratify interna-tional conventions and to adopt high levels of protection in national legislation. This trend has become an accepted fact, even though there has been resistance to some aspects of international agreements or national legislation. These have mainly con-cerned the relationships between the directly involved groups and institutions. How-ever, there are also reactions of another kind:

More generally, it is arguable that copyright terms have now passed the reasonable limits of protection. Profit, as a possible return for risk-taking, is essential if entrepreneurs are to continue to flourish in the arts as in industry and commerce. However, there is no evidence that the present limits are any incentive to the production of works of art. If only because these limits tend to be extended as of right, and to embrace more and more only marginally creative activities, they deserve re-examination in the light both of economic analysis and of the public's right to enjoy art more widely, more cheaply and with more advantage to themselves.[4]

In this view one major dimension has been neglected in the evolution of copyright: the interests of the general public. Copyright is supposed to serve a number of social functions, but the emphasis has been on the defense of the—legitimate—interests of certain groups in society. Copyright is portrayed as the natural or only method to deal with a cluster of complex issues and as the guarantor of the rights of intellectual creators. However, copyright has been discussed mainly as a narrow professional matter among the various interest groups concerned and in terms of the balance to be struck between them. In recent years, though, the effects of new technologies and changing sociocultural attitudes have transformed copyright into a matter of wider social concern. It is no longer possible to avoid fundamental issues: does copyright as currently conceived and practiced fulfill the social functions it was designed to serve? In other words, what is the case for copyright?

Some of the traditional reasons in favor of copyright might be acceptable to all systems, whereas some of them would be applicable principally in countries with a market economy. Consequently, critical analyses arising from within these countries provide the most revealing insights.

An unease over copyright is not a recent phenomenon. When the House of Commons in England discussed a new Copyright Bill in 1841, the only alternatives were copyright and patronage: "the least objectionable way of remunerating them [the authors] is by means of copyright. . . . The system of copyright has great advantages and great disadvantages. . . . For the sake of the good we must submit to the evil; but the evil ought not to last one day longer than is necessary for the purpose of securing the good."[5]

A more extreme stand was taken by Sir Louis Mallet in his minority report to the Royal Commission on Copyright some thirty-five years later. He in fact stated the case against copyright:

Property exists in order to provide against the evils of natural scarcity. A limitation of supply by artificial causes, creates scarcity in order to create property. . . . It is within this latter class that copyright in published works must be included. Copies of such works may be multiplied indefinitely, subject to the cost of paper and of printing which alone, but for copyright, would limit the supply and any demand, however, great, would be attended not only by no conceivable injury to society, but on the contrary, in the case of useful works, by the greatest possible advantage. . . . The case of a book is precisely analogous to that of a house, of a carriage, or of a piece of cloth, for the design of which a claim to perpetual copyright has never, I believe, been seriously entertained. [However] in a matter which affects so large and valuable a property, and so many vested interests as have been created under copyright laws, it would be both unjust and inexpedient to proceed towards such a change as has been fore-shadowed, except in the most gradual and tentative manner.[6]

Stephen Breyer, in a provocative and famous essay, "The Uneasy Case for Copyright," comes to the conclusion that none of the traditional reasons in support of copyright is particularly valid. Following a detailed analysis, he concludes that "it is difficult to do other than take an ambivalent position on the question of whether current copyright protection—considered as a whole—is justified. . . . The position suggests that the case for copyright in books rests not upon proven need, but rather upon uncertainty as to what would happen if protection were removed."[7]

A similar point has been made, starting from the statement that "the promise of copyright protection has nothing to do with the creative impulse. It can never have been remotely responsible for a masterpiece, even if it does affect the output of writers, artists and composers whose work is intended specifically for the mass market."[8] An economic analysis should therefore begin by asking whether the extra price involved in copyright is necessary to secure the flow of output. The problem concerns the position of the artist in the economy: "Does the ever-lengthening term of copyright protection enter his calculations very much, or indeed at all? Is it an inducement to give up one means of livelihood and instead take up writing, painting, composing or design?"[9] Here is the same thought put another way: "For three, if not four, centuries the advocates of property in the right to copy have argued as though book production were the conditioned response of authors, publishers and printers to the impulse of copyright legislation."[10]

Such questions are obviously difficult to answer, and they also require an answer on the basis of the social efficacy of copyright, yet it is important that they be raised, if only to elicit a careful analysis of the problems involved and to initiate a search for the most adequate solution.

A very interesting analysis originated from within the copyright community itself. At a recent congress held in Paris, Michael Freegard, general manager of the British Performing Rights Society, spoke of the future of the author's copyright, which he intended to cover most neighboring rights. He professed his faith in copyright: "My experience has led me to become increasingly aware, and more convinced, of the fundamental desirability, for the sake of society as a whole, of the protection and encouragement of authors." Nonetheless, he raised the question "Is there, in the long term, a future for the author's right at all?" The reason for this heretical question is that in Freegard's opinion it would be unrealistic to suppose that copyright would go unchallenged "in the ferment of change that affects every aspect of contemporary life."[11]

Freegard lists the challenges to copyright under three broad headings: technological, economic, and social. The technological factors relate to the evolution of new means for the reproduction, transmission, and use of works. While these advances present opportunities not dangers, all the new media share one central characteristic: they involve the use of protected works on a scale and in a manner that precludes the possibility of individual control. Freegard mentions the extension of state intervention and the trend toward trading blocks (COMECON, EEC, and so on) as the most important economic developments influencing copyright.

There is also an unresolved conflict between the principle of the free flow of information and the exclusive rights assigned to authors and performers. The often-heard argument that copyright promotes free flow hides the problem but does not resolve it. A similar conflict arises between official policies favoring cultural exchanges and attitudes expressed by holders of rights, in particular performers who resist the dissemination of their performances as being detrimental to employment opportunities.

The demands for greater access to cultural and intellectual works create conflicts with copyright at national and international levels. Domestically, issues of access arise with new educational and cultural policies. More flexible and open educational patterns presuppose a widespread and flexible use of educational and cultural products. Similarly, policies of democratizing and decentralizing cultural activities may collide with the principle of exclusive rights assigned to authors and other creators.

The conflict between protection and access is a major issue for developing countries. This dilemma is also present in another form: the protection and encouragement of national culture versus the need to have access to protected works as a tool of development in education, science, and technology. The same dilemma underlies their relations with the industrialized countries in the copyright field.

International Agreement

Some of the earliest steps toward a modern system of international law and organization were taken in the field of communications. The first genuine international conventions were concluded in the 1860s for telecommunications and postal services. These were quickly followed by the Paris Convention for the Protection of Industrial Property of 1883 and the Berne Convention for the Protection of Literary and Artistic Works of 1886, two treaties that provide the basis for international protection of intellectual production.

The Berne Convention has known a permanence and relative stability that few international agreements can match. Even though the ideal of one universal treaty has not proved feasible, it is the foundation of the elaborate international structure that has grown up in the area of copyright and related rights. This structure is both complex and complicated, consisting of a series of interlocking international conventions and structures with partly similar, partly different, intentions and varied memberships.

This international structure is subject to increased stress caused by technical developments and by changing policy attitudes in the communications and information field. A major reason for the evolution of this system has been the impact of new communications and information technologies, new ways of producing, reproducing, and exploiting intellectual works. The creators and performers, the enterprises that publish or otherwise use and disseminate protected works, and the legislators have attempted to keep pace with these developments by extending the scope and adapting the nature of copyright rules. Revisions of existing international conventions and adoption of new treaties prove the dynamic nature of intellectual property rights. However, the tension between the changing interests of the copyright owners and of society remains one of the key issues in copyright. Another major question is to what extent amendments and additions are adequate to deal with the new challenges, which herald not only quantitative but also a qualitative change in the information environment.

The international copyright system has also been subject to stresses of a different kind. In the late 1960s it was shaken by a serious crisis concerning international copyright relations between industrialized and developing countries. In 1966 the General Conference of UNESCO concluded that "the conventions at present governing international relations in the matter of copyright should be partially revised to take account of the economic, social and cultural conditions obtaining in the developing countries." The main issues concerned the demands made by these countries for access to protected works for teaching, study, and research.

Copyright relations between developing and industrialized countries continued to be a major issue throughout the 1960s and the early 1970s. A series of conferences concerned revisions of the major international copyright conventions in favor of the developing countries. It proved to be an arduous task to arrive at rules that could satisfy both groups of countries: developing countries felt the final revisions bore the stamp of the industrialized world, while some groups in the industrialized countries reacted against what they saw as sacrifices by one section of society—authors and publishers—on behalf of the developing countries and the dilution of the level of protection. Other observers emphasized the central goals of the revision conferences: establishing an international legal mechanism for permitting the developing countries a greater degree of access to protected works while respecting the rights of authors. The result of the revision conferences has been described as "a balance of interests which has regard to the legitimate concerns of developing countries, without expecting unjust sacrifices from authors and publishers. The need to arrive at a compromise, even wholly new questions, has resulted in more complex arrangements than those originally contemplated."[12] It is an open question whether there is general agreement on the first statement, but there is no doubt about agreement on the second. However, more stable international copyright relations have been achieved, at least for the time being.

Policies for the Information Age

It has become a truism to speak of the communications revolution or the information explosion. However, the expressions themselves are significant in that they point to a profound change in our attitudes to the entire communications/information complex. Throughout history communication and information were largely taken for granted and seen as processes functioning in support of more fundamental social activities and goals. Only in recent years have communications per se become an issue in society.

So far, efforts to deal with communications and information issues in a comprehensive, coherent manner are rare at all relevant levels: in terms of the development of technologies and the introduction of new services, in terms of policy, in terms of the institutional and legal framework. One effect of recent technical and social developments is the beginning of a breakdown, or rather break-up, of the traditional, mainly technology-bound, legal and institutional categories of systems and services. This is reflected in the recurrent, sometimes continuous, changes in legislation which are not so much an expression of coherent public policies as temporary reactions to insufficiently understood technological and social pressures.

Characteristic of the present situation is the absence, at the national and international level, of an agreed-upon conceptual framework. Not only do conceptual approaches vary according to political, socioeconomic, and ideological differences, but engineers, social scientists, communications practitioners, and lawyers operate with different concepts and without a common language. Even within the legal field there is no shared discourse since telecommunications, copyright, computer, or information lawyers have each developed a separate, specific universe of discourse.

One obvious cause for this is that legal concepts in the communications field generally have been linked to a particular technology or level of technology. Consequently laws and law-making institutions are often inadequate when faced with a rapidly changing technology. In general, the legal framework antedates the communications revolution. Concepts developed for one mode of communication, such as the press, are stretched to cover new situations. The adaptation to changing circumstances is mainly patchwork. This piecemeal approach has resulted in legislation covering limited aspects of communications, often in the interest of particular institutions or social groups and without due consideration of larger policy issues.

Consequently, the present image of policy, structure, and regulation in communications is one of rapid change and great confusion. Communications systems and information services have generally developed without coherent policies or overall planning. Neither national legislation nor the international legal framework provides for a coherent communications law. Such law is pluralistic, uncoordinated, and based on certain limited, functional objectives. Communications and information are the concern of various branches of law which are of varied origin and separate evolution, drawing upon different concepts and approaches, and resulting in legal rules that are, to varying degrees, deficient and contradictory.

The lack of consistency and coherence in legal concepts is also conditioned by historical circumstance: important branches of international communications law, particularly telecommunications and copyright, first developed in the mid-1800s, while others are based on more modern legal concepts. In early areas such as telecommunications law and copyright law, the original concepts were formulated by a limited number of mainly European nations; other applicable branches of law, such as space law, have evolved in a wider international context.

Some current challenges are an expression of the changing international system. The struggle for political independence has been followed by demands for a new world information order. The concepts of freedom of information and free flow of information are attacked by the developing countries as instruments of maintaining dependence and dominance in communications and information. In particular, they have reacted against the imbalances in the international flow of news and cultural products whether in the form of magazines, books, films, radio, or television programs. To a large extent, the demands for a new international information order can be expressed in terms of access by developing countries: access on reasonable terms to technology and services; access to the mechanisms of international information flows to make their views better known; and access to the information and knowledge required for development purposes. Copyright is both directly and indirectly affected by these issues.

The debates on the new international information order, even though conducted with a great deal of conceptual confusion, are one attempt to reach a more coherent approach to the communications/information complex. There are others.

Some consider the advent of electronic communications to be a fourth communications revolution, equal in importance to the three earlier ones: the invention of speech, the invention of writing, and the invention of printing. Other analysts postulate a new communications and information environment, whose invisible and largely transnational networks will radically change economic and cultural life. The changes in the information environment to go beyond the increase in the quantity of data and information and include qualitative transformations which affect fundamental aspects of society.

The changing modalities of communication have a crucial impact on cultural forms and identities. The traditional paradigm of linear communication from sender to receiver is shifting to multimodal, interactive, and more participatory modes of communication. The fusion of technologies amplifies the relationships with the social and physical environment and, more important, reshapes the information content and perceptions of society.

These approaches concern all forms, processes, and products of information, knowledge, and communications, and thus include the arts and other forms of cultural expression. They represent a new way of perceiving not only communications but society as well.

Another perspective focuses on economics. The computer, telecommunications, and other electronic information industries have become increasingly important. According to one evaluation, this complex of industries has become the third largest in the world economy. Related analyses point to the shift from an industrial to a postindustrial society. In economic terms there are two fundamental questions concerning information: should it be dealt with as a commodity or as a resource, or, rather, in what circumstances should the emphasis be on one or the other of these approaches? Each of these attitudes has different implications for policy and regulation.

The concept of information as a commodity has, as could be expected, evolved in countries with a market economy. Even though the concept was not formulated in the terms we now use, it represents one of the fundaments on which copyright legislation has been constructed and emphasizes the privatization of informational products. According to another economic analysis, the production and transfer of information is not only a commodity, but can almost be likened to a burden—indispensable to be sure—that has to be supported by the rest of the economy. Information, in one perspective, has a market price; in another perspective, it constitutes a growing part of the national economy. In this kind of approach, copyright as traditionally perceived has a given place, whichever way its role is defined.

A different perspective is that of information as a resource in society. This attitude is supported by the argument that information and organized knowledge, which includes the arts and other forms of cultural expression, have several unique properties. The first unique property is that all other resources depend on information and knowledge: the perception and evaluation of resources make their use possible. Thus the use of information determines the use of other resources. The second unique characteristic is the concept that, as a resource, information is not reduced or diminished by wider use and sharing. On the contrary, its value in both economic and social terms tends to gain in the process. A further aspect concerns the use of communications and information resources, in particular electronics, to reduce or replace the consumption of other resources. This has not been sufficiently explored and remains controversial. However, there is already an obvious trend toward replacing paper with electronic methods in public and private administrations and in information enterprises such as newspapers and news agencies.

The resource concept of information emphasizes a wide and unhampered dissemination of information as essential for the economic, social, and cultural activities of a society. This concept raises a number of fundamental issues which go beyond the market approach and involve wider social and political aspects: How should this resource be allocated in order to respond to social requirements and individual needs? Who controls and retains power over this resource? Which policies, structures, and rules are the most adequate in this perspective?

Thus far these analyses and observations have been mainly concerned with industrialized societies which are in a transitional stage of becoming "information societies." It is recognized, though, that areas such as informatics, defined as the fields related to the construction and use of mainly electronic information processing systems as well as to their social impact, are of equal importance to industrialized and developing countries and will play an essential role in achieving a new international economic order.

Recent changes in development thinking have led to a reappraisal of the role of communications and information in developing countries. The trend is toward comprehensive approaches similar to those developed for industrialized countries.

Analyses of the so-called basic needs model have resulted in relevant conclusions. The basic human needs approach grew out of the search for a development strategy that could deal more effectively with the problem of continuing poverty in the world. It constitutes a direct attack on world poverty by meeting the basic needs for food, nutrition, health, education, and housing, as well as through employment and income-generating activities among the lowest income groups. The basic needs model requires an appropriate macro-policy framework for development and a reallocation of total investment in favor of the lowest income groups. It also means a balance between centralization and decentralization and a commitment to development from the bottom up, to local self-reliance, community and grassroots organization, and participation in planning, decision making, and implementation.

This approach requires an unprecedented inflow of new information to the village—information that will reach even the poorest villagers. It will be necessary to develop programs designed to increase agricultural production, to stimulate and guide adjustments to new production methods and to new consumption patterns. Programs that increase farmers' and villagers' understanding of their dependence on and responsibility for environmental quality and of changing world social and economic circumstances are also needed.

Thus "what is essentially called for is the transformation of the village from a traditional society to an information community capable of acting and responding creatively to relevant information reaching it, capable also of reaching out for that information."[13] This thought has been expanded into one of the few concepts that includes both developing and industrialized countries; the concept of an information society in a wider perspective than that of an information economy can be applied to all countries.

Today all societies face the challenge of adjusting to rapid technoeconomic, sociocultural, and political changes on a large scale. A nation's capacity to manage this adjustment depends crucially on its ability to generate, to ingest, to reach out for, and to utilize vast amounts of new and relevant information. Soedjatmoko has called this capacity for creative and innovative response to changing conditions "the learning capacity of a nation."[14] The need for this capacity for social transformation requires all societies to become information societies in this larger and deeper sense.

What about the required policies in an information age, particularly as they relate to intellectual property rights? These concepts are very recent and still evolving. They have not yet penetrated policy. Communications or information policy exists only in isolated sectors, for specific media or in response to limited problems. Only a few countries have developed coherent policies in the telecommunications sector. Most countries are grappling with policies for their media but have generally concentrated on each medium in isolation. All recent reports in the field of informatics decry the lack of national policy; the basic list of issues includes the development of systems, the procurement of hardware and software, trade, the impact on employment, education and training, research, government applications, transborder data transmission, and international cooperation.

Copyright issues are one aspect of information issues; protected works are one element of overall information flows and processes. Two issues are particularly relevant: copyright in relation to the organization of information flows and copyright in relation to the control over information. The organization of information flows has become one of the most controversial—and one of the most confused—issues facing national societies and the international community. To a large extent public debate has crystallized around freedom of information, the free flow of information, and demands for a new international information order. The debate on these issues is controversial through the clash of different and often opposing concepts, ideologies, and interests and is confused by the lack of common conceptual framework and even an agreed-on subject of discussion. There is more reaction than analysis.

It is revealing that the debate on a new international information order is conducted without any clarity as to what is to be covered by the expression "information." Much of the debate has focused on "news," the journalistic dimension of information often conceived in a relatively narrow manner. It is clear, though, that we deal differently with news of political events, of commodity movements, or of the weather. In discussing information in a larger sense, we encounter a series of different information flows with a diversity of patterns in terms of purposes, content, structures, and legal regimes. It is therefore necessary to relate copyright issues to these diverse flows of information.

Copyright is a method for providing regulation and control over information flows and must be seen in the context of other methods of achieving such control or regulation. The question of control over information immediately raises the question of fundamental attitudes toward the role of information in society. Is information a resource, a commodity, a right, a duty? Or rather, in what circumstances should information flows be organized and controlled according to each of these criteria?

There is no one answer. Each kind of information flow requires its own organization. Disaster and health warnings are a public resource and not a commodity. Other categories are less clear-cut. Different societies have decided differently on the relative weight to be given to the resource and the commodity aspects, to the balance between the public sector and the private sector. The focus on the issues involved thus varies with different socioeconomic systems.

Communications systems develop in relation to the information flows between the individual and the total environment, physical as well as social. The emergence of a more systemic approach to communications and information has led to a new interest in communications policy and planning as an area of study, reflection, and action. These new developments provide the only possible framework for evolving a coherent approach to copyright: to consider the various networks and services of the total communications system available in a given society. The application of this systemic approach implies an analysis of how works, in various guises and transformations, flow through the available channels within the total communications system.

A flow- or process-oriented approach based on a systemic conceptual framework provides a new method for dealing with a number of almost intractable problems relating to copyright. First, it could identify the works in their different transformations and locate, in the communications processes, the points where mechanisms for the protection, authorization, and remuneration can be placed.

Second, it could identify and locate, in the production/manufacturing/multiplication/distribution chains, the contributions and functions of the author, performer, manufacturer, and publisher. A new approach in this area is particularly important as the functions traditionally ascribed to each of these categories are changing. It would, therefore, be possible to analyze the nature and role of the new kinds of authors/creators/contributors and publishers/producers/distributors as participants in the creation/production/distribution and flow of works.

Third, it could help solve the issues raised by changes in the nature of performance, publication, and making public in a situation where the traditional distinctions between public and private are no longer adequate.

Fourth, this method could be used to determine the flow of money within the communications system: the nature of financing and remuneration at different stages in the flow and transfer of works, how added value is created as supplementary "exchange value" in this process, the way in which this added value is redistributed and paid for, and what benefits accrue to authors, performers, and other participants in creation/production.

Finally, it could provide a means for clarifying the conditions for increased access by individuals who make up the public but also need to be participants. The unprecedented problems that now face all countries demand support for widespread creativity and for new levels of knowledge throughout society.

Notes

1. Michael Freegard, "The Future of the Author's Copyright," in *Performing Right Year Book* (London, 1977), pp. 42–43.
2. Marie-Claude Dock, "Radioscopie du droit d'auteur contemporain," *Il Diritto di Autore* 45 no. 4 (1974).
3. Heinz Püscher, "Copyright in the German Democratic Republic," *Copyright Bulletin* 10, no. 3, (1976): 10–19.
4. Denis Thomas, *Copyright and the Creative Artist* (London: Institute of Economic Affairs, 1967), p. 46.
5. Arnold Plant, "The Economic Aspects of Copyright in Books," *Economica* (May 1934), pp. 170–171.
6. *Ibid.*, pp. 193–194.
7. Stephen Breyer, "The Uneasy Case for Copyright: A Study of Copyright in Books, Photocopies and Computer Programs," *Harvard Law Review* 84, no. 2 (1970).
8. Thomas, *Copyright*, pp. 21–22.
9. *Ibid.*, p. 21.
10. Plant, "The Economic Aspects," p. 167.
11. Freegard, "The Future of the Author's Copyright," p. 2.
12. Eugen Ulmer, "The Revisions of the Copyright Conventions," *EBU Review*, no. 130B (November 1971), p. 98.
13. Soedjatmoko, "National Policy Implications of the Basic Needs Model" (Slightly revised version of paper presented at seminar on Implications of the Basic Needs Model organized

by Dutch National Advisory Council for Development Co-operation, The Hague, February 24, 1978), p. 13.

14. Soedjatmoko, *The Future and the Learning Capacity of Nations: The Role of Communications* (London: International Institute of Communications, 1978).

4. Distribution:
The Neglected Link
in the Publishing Chain*
Amadio A. Arboleda

Surveys of publishing in the Third World tend to be narrow for two basic reasons: publishing in the Third World is narrowly aimed, and data on it are noticeably lacking. Distribution is consistently neglected in surveys of Third World publishing. Many statistical overviews present a plethora of numbers on manufacturing and production, but there is almost nothing on what happens with the product. This is paradoxical because, as a number of book experts have pointed out, a book does not fulfill its purpose until it is read, and to be read it must reach a reader. This is where distribution becomes all important. Distribution is difficult in the industrialized countries as well as in Third World countries. The major difference is that distribution problems in Third World countries often take on the proportions of a crisis.

The difficulties of distribution stem from the very craft of creating and producing the written materials of communication in the form of books. The craft is a complicated one, far more complex than many of the processes that give us some of the well-known products of modern society. Marshall Lee writes that "the bookmaker has two basic tasks: (a) to facilitate communication between author and reader, and (b) to make the book a successful commercial product. Publishers," he points out, "often have cultural or personal objectives when they accept a book for publication, but the object of publishing as a business is to *sell* books."[1] Although Lee's view of

*This chapter is an expanded version of an article written for my column "Writing about Books" in *Asian Book Development,* "Distribution: The Neglected Factor," 14, no. 4 (1983).

a book as a commercial product is somewhat restrictive because it does not spell out the social and cultural roles of publishing, he tries to show us that the intricate process of facilitating reader-author communication involves both the shaping and creation of a book *and* getting the book into the hands of a reader. He also points out, nevertheless, that "it is only in the profit motive that book publishing resembles any other business. It is much more informal, complicated, and hazardous than most."[2] This business aspect and the hazardous nature of the publishing enterprise in general is recognized in the Third World, but there is very little awareness of its creative role, particularly in relation to culture and education.

Lee then goes on to show the essential difference between publishing and other economic endeavors by making a comparison between books and a very necessary and standard consumer product, toothpaste. The process of creating and selling a consumer product involves "manufacturers [hiring] people to create a few products to their desire [after considerable market research], [standardizing] their manufacture, and [turning] them out in large quantities year after year."[3] The accompanying promotion campaigns, he points out, are set up to encourage buyers to purchase the product. Once the campaigns are effective they can be used over and over again. "The products are sold in stores accessible to virtually everyone and their production can be geared to their sales—or at least to an estimate of sales based on thorough research. Most important, a satisfied customer is likely to continue buying the same product more or less indefinitely."[4]

A Peculiar Product, the Book

In contrast to other enterprises, the products that publishers sell are not standardized. Each book is unique. This means that a publisher, unlike the toothpaste manufacturer, has many products to sell, each one different and each one "a unique creation by an independent individual who has determined personally what the products shall be."[5] In addition, the sale of a book does not insure that the buyer will remain a steady customer of the publisher. This is quite unlike other commercial endeavors wherein a customer, if satisfied, will often continue to patronize a certain product and its producer. It is incumbent, therefore, on the publisher to try to cultivate as many distribution outlets as possible including, in addition to the usual channels of bookstores and wholesalers, government institutions, educational institutions, libraries, and book clubs.

Distribution is further hampered because publishers in Third World countries are often not well versed in the intricacies of consumer demand and, therefore, do not know how many people will buy a book. As a result they tend to produce uneconomically small quantities. Their limited production quantities are, of course, based on other factors: experience with low sales because potential buyers cannot afford to purchase books or do not consider books a primary need; high cost of raw materials, such as paper and printing ink; the limited number of available sales outlets, particularly in rural areas; and inadequate transportation systems. The distribution outlets are located mainly in major urban areas. The disadvantages are compounded because the sales outlets, if they are not part of the publisher's organizational setup, can return books that do not sell well.

Distribution in any business undertaking where products are intended for a large number of users must be well developed because it can mean the difference between success or failure of the enterprise. One of the main defects of book distribution in the Third World is the assumption that what is published will be sold. Curtis Benjamin, writing about indigenous publishing in Third World countries had this to say: "There is much more to the development of indigenous publishing than the availability of suitable facilities and materials and capital for the printing of books." In his estimation "far too many book-development programs had failed because they had concentrated on production and neglected distribution and utilization." He points out that "in too many cases, after thousands of desperately needed books had been produced, it was discovered that far too many copies were left sitting in warehouses—that there were no suitable mechanisms or facilities for effective movement of the books into the gaps where they were needed." Book gaps, he continues, cannot be filled by books alone—the supply of books, no matter how plentiful, will not fill a country's need unless adequate marketing mechanisms and sufficient distribution channels have been provided and unless rewarding use of the books is assured in the end.[6]

Roger Kirkpatrick's assessment of distribution is far more blunt and to the point. "Any book is dead until read, when it becomes alive," he writes, pointing out further that, "usually it is only read when bought. It is only bought if distributed from author through publisher to reader."[7] In his estimation a literate society is as dependent on its ability to distribute books widely as it is on the authors who write the books. No publishing industry can adequately serve a nation's needs without the support of a sound and efficient network of competent wholesalers and retailers. Yet in most developing countries little attention is given—even by publishers—to the essentiality of such a distribution system.

The difficulties of distribution are also formidable for publishers in industrialized countries. In a speech at the annual meeting of the Book Manufacturers Institute in 1983, Brooks Thomas, president of Harper & Row, pointed out that rising costs could be attributed in part to an "inefficient distribution system" in the United States. Of course, this statement must be qualified by the context in which it was made. What is inefficient in the U.S. is different from what does not work in the Third World. Another example is Japan where, despite a very well-developed and unique distribution system, readers, served by over 4,000 publishers, 60 distributors, and 20,000 or more bookstores throughout the country, are sometimes neglected by the sophisticated automation of the system that is not geared to meet special requests outside the distribution pattern.[8] Keeping in perspective the overall state of publishing in Third World countries, it is not difficult to recognize the monumental tasks facing them. Even meeting the *basic* needs for achieving mass distribution, i.e., adequate book manufacturing equipment, distribution equipment, display equipment, a distribution system and plan (including transportation), necessary capital, an adequate editorial and production staff, and tax relief, is beyond the capabilities and capacities of publishers in most developing countries. Datus Smith has pointed out that even Third World countries capable of developing a satisfactory distribution system have to recognize the role of mass distribution in helping to develop an educated citizenry. Educators and decision makers, he shows, readily accept that the advancement of development depends on a well-developed educational system and a nationwide system of libraries. They fail, however, to recognize that these must be supported by a nationwide system of distribution and sale of inexpensive books. A major reason for this flawed thinking, Smith opines, is that publishing, and particularly book distribution, is viewed as "just business" rather than part of the basic makeup of a country's educational system.[9]

Other Factors

The fault does not lie entirely with publishers in Third World countries. The problems of mass distribution are inevitably exacerbated by a combination of political, economic, resource, and organizational problems that are often beyond the control of local publishing enterprises. Even though the demand for books may exist on a large scale, the nature of local trading patterns and the prevalent bazaar-type economy may not be conducive to large-scale distribution of books. In addition, large bookstores in urban centers may concentrate on selling imported books or books in the languages of former colonial masters because of high profits from middle-class clientele. All these factors can lead to a chicken-egg syndrome that prevents publishers in Third World countries from increasing distribution: although production unit costs could be kept low with larger print runs, distribution problems limit the size of printings thereby resulting in high printing costs and ultimately high distribution costs. Distribution is also dependent upon the concentration of buyers in a location, the distance of outlet location from the source, demand for the product, and nature of the product. In many Third World countries, where populations are primarily rural and widely dispersed, prospective book buyers are difficult to reach. Even when they are accessible, however, their priorities are often necessities: food, clothing, medicine, and so on. Books are not foremost in their consideration.[10]

Each region, country, language or ethnic group has its particular problems affecting distribution. Still, there are some common difficulties. These are linked primarily to the sheer size of many Third World countries, which has implications for transportation and postal services, both of which are often poorly developed, unreliable, slow, and expensive. In addition there are a limited network of bookstores or other outlets, most of which are in large cities; few libraries, which are usually poorly stocked; and vast rural areas with few sales outlets and scattered populations with low purchasing power.

Many assessments of marketing strategies consider the problem primarily from the publishers' viewpoint of business, the government's position of policy and planning, or the scholars' empirical analysis approach. The cultural and social dimensions of the book buyer or reader are seldom studied.[11] However, these dimensions, which are dependent on local economic systems, cultural biases, and educational attainment, often determine effective approaches to distributing books in rural areas. Publishing systems in Third World countries have been invariably inherited from colonial masters. They almost always have continued to follow the operational patterns of industrialized countries, which often are not suited to the peculiarities of local conditions and, therefore, cannot adequately address local needs. Ideally, each Third World country should, on the basis of the universal principles of publishing as a business, develop its own approach to publishing as a cultural asset. This is seldom done. In recent years, there have been laudable efforts in a few countries to develop publishing that is more immediately adaptable and responsive to their situations. Publishers in Malaysia, India, Singapore, and Egypt, for example, have made great strides in tailoring local publishing, including distribution, to answer the particular needs of their citizens.

Asian Efforts

Even though the general picture of distribution in the Third World is the same everywhere, the actual situation varies with each country and region. In 1981, Asia, with a total population of over 2.6 billion inhabitants, accounted for about 20 percent of the total world production of 729,000 book titles. The industrialized world accounted for about 80 percent with only 25 percent of the world's population. There was an absolute increase in number of book titles produced in Asia from 1970 to 1981, from 75,000 to 147,000. However, population increases, from 2.09 billion in 1970 to 2.6 billion in 1981, reduced the number of titles produced per million inhabitants from 63 to 56 for the same years, respectively.[12] Of course, since the figures for Japan are also included here, the final total for the rest of Asia is much lower.

As more and more countries in Asia begin to recognize that education is fundamental to development, there is a parallel realization of the importance of publishing and, thereby, the need to improve distribution systems. There are, nevertheless, a number of obstacles. Among them, Abdul Hasan stresses, are the great number of languages within many countries, the lack of endogenous authorship, copyright problems, the lack of paper, the high cost of production, and the difficulties of promoting and maintaining the reading habit in rural areas where most of the population live.[13]

Some Asian countries have begun to develop networks of printing/publishing facilities in rural areas as a means of overcoming distribution problems, at least as it affects the literacy of rural populations. One such program is Indonesia's mobile printing *Micropu* units. By providing printing facilities to local communities, reading material produced by the people themselves is made available. Inevitably, this will enhance reader interest. This does not, however, solve the problem of getting a wider range of books to rural areas from the urban centers. Other efforts have concentrated directly on distribution solutions. There are mobile and community libraries in Korea, India, Thailand, and Pakistan. Home libraries, which have been vigorously promoted in Korea, are being considered by other countries in the region. There are also the traveling bookshops of the government publishing house Balai Pustaka that now reach twenty-six provinces in Indonesia. Balai Pustaka has also set up 2,453 library clubs in provincial cities. Following the lead of Korea, Thailand has organized a national book distribution center with twenty-nine participating publishers to help distribute books more widely throughout the country. China has a highly developed centralized distribution system which is run by the Xin Hua Book Store Agency with more than 5,000 retail outlets throughout the country.

Distribution in Asia is generally handled by wholesalers, retail bookstores, book clubs, and in a few instances kiosks, newspaper stands, and supermarkets. Libraries are responsible for the lending form of distribution. Although wholesalers are important for stimulating book circulation and are the main source of books for retailers, there are comparatively few wholesalers in Asia, particularly if one does not count those in Japan. This is still a new concept in the region. A few wholesalers exist in Korea, Malaysia, India, and Singapore. Hasan thinks that it will be "rather difficult to achieve a real breakthrough in book distribution in Asia without national wholesale distribution agencies." He feels that they could "act as a catalyst in the movement of books to every corner of a country."[14]

There are very few bookstores in most Asian countries and these are almost always concentrated in cities and large towns. They suffer from lack of ready credit and high overhead. In addition, publishers often bypass small bookstores to supply books directly to libraries and educational institutions. Many governments have not recognized the importance of publishing's role in development and its ability to enhance the country's intellectual level. Thus they tend to overlook the benefits publishing could derive from preferential treatment. This includes the role of bookstores in the distribution makeup.

With the exception of India, book clubs have not developed extensively in Asia despite the apparent advantages they would have in bringing books to a wider range of readers.

The future of distribution in Asia is bound to improve because many countries are more aware of the far-reaching implications of its advantages. This awareness has been cultivated and encouraged by subregional publishers organizations, national book councils, and two regionwide organizations that are linked with UNESCO: the Regional Book Development Center for Asia in Karachi, Pakistan, and the Asian Cultural Centre for UNESCO in Tokyo, Japan.

The Vastness of Africa's Problem

The vast continent of Africa, with 10 percent of the world's population, produced a meager 2 percent of the global output of books in 1981 or 14,000 titles in total.[15] William Moutchia, director of the Regional Center for Book Promotion in Africa South of the Sahara, characterizes Africa's book industry as young. Africa remains behind other parts of the world, he feels, because no colonial powers made a deliberate attempt to introduce education or publishing. "Publishing," he points out, "was accidental and occasional, with a religious objective"; religious missionaries set up the first rudimentary printing facilities to produce religious books and pamphlets. When the colonial powers left Africa many took the infrastructures of publishing with them. Comparatively speaking, Africa has achieved a lot because it started with nothing and developed something.[16]

Distribution, he admits, is still in dire straits, particularly because transportation systems are poor, government action is ineffectual, and interference is excessive. In one country, the Ministry of Education could not get needed syllabi to remote provinces because it had not devised an effective means of transporting the books. These books piled up in provincial educational offices but never reached the schools. Even now books prescribed by the Ministry tend to reach their destinations after the exams have been given. Because they can no longer be used, the books then remain in booksellers' depots or in the provincial educational offices.

Since much of the distribution in Africa is concerned with educational books, the government usually handles it. The remainder is handled by trade outlets and, to a lesser extent, by church bookshops, pavement "bookshops" (bazaar type), and newspaper stands. A representative government distribution setup, the Kenya School Equipment Scheme, has been described by Henry Chakava. It supplies equipment to the nearly 10,000 primary schools. In 1977, 60 percent of the $5.5 million allotted to the Scheme was spent on the purchase of books. After school book requirements from each school are approved, based on a list of titles drawn up by the Ministry of Education, tenders from publishers are received in the middle of the year, and finished supplies are available for delivery before the next school year begins. This ten-year-old arrangement is aimed at ensuring that book supplies reach rural areas on time and at reasonable cost to the government. Before the Scheme came into effect, schools dealt directly with bookstores.[17]

The Scheme, however, is not without its critics. Chakava stresses that it has led to the demise of many small rural bookstores. This, in turn, threatens a healthy and active book industry with bookstores as key distribution and marketing outlets. These bookstores played an essential role in the educational and cultural development of the country by providing, in addition to school books, general books which could help improve the reading habits of rural people. Among other difficulties, the transportation problem is a tremendous one because the Scheme owns the trucks used for distribution, yet it does not have the know-how for using them efficiently or the manpower and expertise for their care and maintenance.

Kenyan distribution problems are representative of the situation throughout most of Africa. The trade outlets in Kenya are located mainly in the major cities and large towns. Nairobi has the largest number of outlets and the largest bookshop in the country, the Textbook Centre, which controls approximately 20 percent of the total book market. Other major outlets are also located in Kakamega, Kisumu Meru, Momoasa, Nakuru, and Nyeri.

The defunct East African Literature Bureau, which operated in Kenya, was instrumental in setting up a book access scheme for African readers, particularly in rural areas, which included establishing libraries, postal borrowing, and mobile book vans. The Kenya National Library Service has eleven branches throughout the country. In addition, seven mobile libraries travel throughout the remote areas. There are also city libraries, university libraries, and numerous school libraries with an average of 1,000 volumes each. In Chakava's estimation, libraries to most Kenyans symbolize the elite and are not used by ordinary citizens. Book clubs have been tried in the past, but not with much success. For example, Heinemann established a Spear Books/Joe Magazine Book Club in 1976, but this did not arouse much interest. Nor did the Textbook Centre's club which offered mainly imported paperbacks. The lack of a functioning national book development council, although a council has been established in principle, is also hampering activities in Kenya.

Latin America: Potential but Little Power

Latin America, with 8.1 percent of the world's population in 1981, produced 5.2 percent of the global total of titles, giving it the greatest number of titles per million inhabitants among the developing regions.[18] Most of the large-scale publishing is concentrated, however, in Argentina, Brazil, and Mexico, with Colombia, Chile, Cuba, Peru, Uruguay, and Venezuela publishing on a smaller but adequate scale.

Alberto E. Augsburger points out that, as in the other developing regions, Latin America's main publishing problems are caused by illiteracy, with about 75 percent of all illiterates living in rural areas, and the lack of adequate marketing and distribution facilities. At present the following types of book distributors exist in the region: (1) *nonexclusive*—works with a number of publishers, usually not more than ten, on exclusive or nonexclusive basis (They are capable of reaching even the small buyer and, therefore, play an important role in distribution.); (2) *exclusive*—deals with one publisher; (3) *dependent*—branch office or warehouse of foreign publisher; (4) *combined*—deals some books in addition to main line of newspapers and magazines; (5) *occasional*—sporadic transactions; and (6) *specialized*—specialized books.[19]

In many Latin American countries a publisher may have to have several arrangements for distribution. In addition to distributors there are outlets that sell books as well as other types of merchandise (such as supermarkets, drugstores, or stationery stores), and there are traditional bookstores. This has some implications for the role of traditional booksellers in the intellectual and cultural milieu, for the competition of the marketplace often forces them to concentrate on the stocking of "popular" books. Other channels of distribution include kiosks, schools, house-to-house sales, libraries, mail-order sales, and book clubs.

The problems of distribution in Latin America are ostensibly not as complicated as in other Third World regions, mainly because Spanish is spoken in most Latin American countries. The movement of books across borders, particularly from larger publishing nations such as Argentina, Chile, or Mexico to nearby countries, should, theoretically, be simple. The realities of governmental restrictions, however, are one impediment. Tax barriers, customs laws, cultural protectionism, and political pressures restrict the free flow of books into and out of a country and, inevitably, throughout a country. The difficulties in distributing books across national borders explains, in part, why Latin America produces the highest number of book titles produced per million inhabitants in the Third World.

A 1974 seminar in Costa Rica, "The Role of the Book in Change Process in Latin America," highlighted some of the difficulties faced by publishers. One finding was that there is no communication among Latin American publishers. Many do not know what their counterparts in other countries are producing. This failure in communication, says Helbert Guevara Mayorga, is one reason for a decreased demand for books in the region. Another finding was that low productivity hampered large-scale production. Other problems mentioned at the conference included inadequate marketing infrastructures, monetary problems hindering free trade between countries, small editions of titles, and increased costs and higher prices.[20]

It is estimated that by the year 2000, when over 600 million Latin Americans will require a more advanced educational system, books will have to play a more active role. Mayorga reported that looking toward this eventuality, a number of steps have been taken. "In September 1969, for example, the 'Experts' Meeting for Increasing Book Production in Latin America' was held in Bogotá, Colombia, under the auspices of UNESCO, attended by representatives from the entire area, and from which emerged positive results."[21] One result was the creation of the Bogotá-based CERLAL (Regional Center for the Promotion of Books in Latin America) to study publishing problems of the region. In November 1971 it held the first course on Latin American editorial and production administration, stressing the importance of books in economic development. The Regional Office of Central America and Panama (ROCAP) was created by the Organization of Central American States (ODECA) for the purpose of printing school books for the area. "Although this experiment has not lived up completely to expectations due to local idiosyncracies," Mayorga says, "a great gap has been filled with the publication of millions of textbooks that are already being used throughout the area. These books, printed in large runs and exempted from taxation, are very valuable material produced at low costs."[22]

What Does It Mean?

The problems of distribution are generally the same in almost all Third World countries: illiteracy, large rural populations far from publishing centers, lack of professional know-how, inadequate transportation or postal systems, government publishing competing with commercial publishing, and low print runs of titles. At the same time, distribution is subject to the influences of each locale whether it be a large urban bookstore in Nairobi, a small bookshop in rural Indonesia, or a provincial government distribution center somewhere in Latin America. A. A. Read points out some of the major distribution problems unique to developing countries: "woefully inadequate" storage facilities that expose book stocks to physical damage and pilferage; inadequate transportation systems that cause loss, damage and delay; and inadequate trade outlets.[23]

The elements that constitute the distribution mix include textbooks as a mainstay, newspapers and magazines as bread-and-butter items, and, where available, general books, scholarly books, and reference books. The role of textbooks in distribution, and in publishing in the Third World in general, is overwhelming. As Curtis Benjamin points out, the market for educational books is almost "everywhere not only the largest but also the most profitable" for indigenous book publishers.[24] Textbooks occupy a place of primacy in a nations' cultural development because they serve educational needs and provide potential markets for Third World publishers. The development of this market is of vital importance in the development of a book industry, especially if the industry can also be geared to provide general books to the public. In order to develop an effective market demand, the educational system must, of course, be organized to encourage the use of books as basic tools of instruction and to instill lifetime reading habits in students. The book component must be carefully planned and integrated into the total educational system.

This demand for books is one factor that has a profound impact on distribution because what is not sought will not be bought. Another factor is level of literacy. The rate of literacy will be high if the educational system is well set up and encourages reading beyond school requirements and beyond school completion. This will in turn contribute to a high demand for books and will help keep the distribution process in high gear. Continual and well-developed distribution, based on an adequate selection of book titles, will, in turn, support a high literacy rate. Naturally, all of the foregoing will take an opposite turn if the educational structure does not contribute to improving literacy in a country.

The publishing process is already somewhat hampered by the nature of its products; a nonstandardized commodity that changes and must be reevaluated each time a new version appears. Unlike products such as clothing or food which can be produced in vast quantities in the same mold or model, books are *always* different. The normal process of supply and demand that exists for the average commercial enterprise does not exist for publishing because the product is constantly changing. Thus conditioning the buyer to accept the product *before* it is actually produced is a crucial facet in the publishing process. Book reading has economic, cultural, social, and educational implications. Once the buyer accepts books as enhancing each of these aspects of life, he will be receptive to book buying. If this can be accomplished on a nationwide scale, book sales and distribution will improve.

What Direction for Distribution?

The direction is obvious. The problem is: can Third World countries make the turn? All evidence indicates that there will be a tremendous increase in educational needs, both qualitative and quantitative. Increased populations will put a strain on outmoded educational systems and on the mechanisms that support them, particularly culture awareness, development, and books. Or will it be books? We are not certain of the continued role of books in light of new electronic information techniques that are becoming available. The scope of education expansion was described in an article by Christina Barbin in *Development Forum* in which she says that "between 1960 and 1980, the rate of school attendance in secondary education in Africa quadrupled. In 15 countries, over 70 per cent of all children between the ages of 6 and 11 attend school. . . . At the same time, illiteracy among adults has substantially declined."[25] Datus Smith also recognized, however, that in spite of the increasing availability of education "book-publishing [had] not kept up with [this momentum]."[26]

Alvin Toffler describing the next major economic-social revolution, what he calls the Third Wave, for humankind, says that "it [will make] us look at education . . . with fresh eyes. . . . All our conventional assumptions about education need to be re-examined both in the rich countries and the poor."[27] He asks telling questions, which have also been asked by education experts, about the meaning of literacy in light of new communications technologies which may make reading unnecessary for illiterate people in Third World countries. He quotes specialists who question the need to know how to write in the face of upcoming advancements in communications and those who feel that a return to oral traditions may benefit some societies.

Another study by Ithiel de Sola Pool confirmed that society is "in the middle of an information explosion" that is changing the pattern of human work endeavors.[28] The amount of information that is being produced is increasing at a tremendous rate, but the amount actually being consumed is not keeping pace. This is causing information overload and a decline in productivity of print media (although there is an actual increase, in absolute terms, of words produced). The shift away from print media to nonprint media particularly exacerbates the trend toward lesser consumption.

These phenomena are being looked at in industrialized nations which have, or are developing, the capacity to cope with the trend. What of the Third World countries that are only now beginning to find their way through the maze of educational needs facing them? How will they manage to use the rapid advancements in technologies and educational techniques while trying to balance their meager and often dwindling resources with their overwhelmingly large needs?

Some information has been given here and many questions posed. The formulation of answers is not easy because real analysis is not possible. Statistics to do in-depth studies are often not available. This chapter has attempted to pull together existing research; it does not guarantee solutions. One thing is clear: most Third World publishing sprang from and continues to emulate the systems inherited from industrialized countries. Studying local conditions might suggest mechanisms for improving distribution in each country. Eduard Kimman's study on Indonesian publishing which looks at the economic setup throughout the country is an example of this approach.[29] The reality is that the Third World, having done much to develop publishing from the editorial, design, and production aspects, must now improve distribution. Whether the communications revolution is around the corner or not, existing publishers, expectant readers and buyers, and educational planners need the tools that are available now. These are books, and moving books from producer to buyer means distribution. Book development programs have tended to neglect distribution in favor of editing and production. The conclusions are clear, for as Roger Kirkpatrick lamented "there is now a very real danger that as society develops those who publish and distribute books will lose the race to match the greatly stimulated expectations of immediate availability."[30]

Notes

1. M. Lee, *Bookmaking* (New York: R. R. Bowker, 1979), p. 10.
2. *Ibid.,* p. 10.
3. *Ibid.,* p. 11.
4. *Ibid.,* p. 11.
5. *Ibid.,* p. 11.
6. C. G. Benjamin, *A Candid Critique of Book Publishing* (New York: R. R. Bowker, 1977), p. 120.
7. R. Kirkpatrick, "Distribution - General," in P. Oakeshott and C. Bradley, eds., *The Future of the Book - Part 1. The Impact of New Technologies* (Paris: UNESCO, 1982), p. 57.
8. H. R. Lottman, "The Distribution Dilemmas," *Publishers Weekly,* October 16, 1978.
9. D. C. Smith, *A Guide to Book Publishing* (New York: R. R. Bowker, 1966), p. 15.
10. A. A. Arboleda, "A Giant Step in Tokyo," in S. Minowa and A. A. Arboleda, eds. *Scholarly Publishing in Asia, Proceedings of the Conference of University Presses in Asia and the Pacific Area* (Tokyo: University of Tokyo Press, 1973).
11. A. A. Arboleda, "English Language Scholarly Publishing in Japan," *Scholarly Publishing* 6, no. 3 (1975).
12. UNESCO, *Statistical Yearbook* (Paris: UNESCO, 1983).
13. A. Hasan, *Promoting National Strategies in Asia and the Pacific: Problems and Prospectives* (Paris: UNESCO, 1981), p. 19.
14. *Ibid.,* p. 20.
15. *UNESCO Statistical Yearbook,* 1983.
16. William Moutchia, interview in *Asian Book Development* 13, no. 4 (1982).
17. Henry Chakava, *Books and Reading in Kenya* (Paris: UNESCO, 1982), pp. 21–22.
18. *UNESCO Statistical Yearbook,* 1983.
19. A. E. Augsburger, *The Latin American Book Market: Problems and Prospects* (Paris: UNESCO, 1982), pp. 61–62.
20. H. G. Mayorga, "Publishing in Latin America: Present Status," in S. Minowa, A. A. Arboleda, and N. Raj, eds., *International Scholarly Publishing, Proceedings of the Second International Conference on Scholarly Publishing* (Tokyo: University of Tokyo Press, 1976).
21. *Ibid.,* p. 39.
22. *Ibid.,* p. 40.
23. A. A. Read, "Problems of International Book Distribution," in P. Oakeshott and C. Bradley, eds., *The Future of the Book - Part 1: The Impact of New Technologies* (Paris: UNESCO, 1982), p. 76.
24. Benjamin, *A Candid Critique,* p. 122.
25. C. Barbin, "Present and Future," *Development Forum* 11, no. 3 (1983).
26. Smith, *A Guide to Book Publishing,* p. 150.

27. A. Toffler, *The Third Wave* (New York: William Morrow, 1980).
28. I. de Sola Pool, "Tracking the Flow of Information," *Science* 221, no. 4461 (1983).
29. E. Kimman, *Indonesian Publishing: Economic Organizations in a Langganan Society* (Baarn: Hollandia, 1981).
30. Kirkpatrick, p. 55.

Countries and Regions

5. The Book Industry
in Africa, 1973–1983:
A Decade of Development?

Eva M. Rathgeber

In December 1973 the Ife Conference on Publishing in Africa in the Seventies ended in a burst of enthusiasm. The key problems facing African publishers had been identified. Strategies had been devised for coping with and eventually overcoming them. Bonds among publishers, authors, and booksellers from various countries had been forged. It had been agreed that the similarities in the problems of publishing in various African nations were greater than the differences. Delegates left for home determined to make efforts to develop the still fledgling book industries in their own countries.

Ten years later, a conference about publishing in Africa in the eighties could point to many of the same problems that were identified at Ife. Relatively little progress has been made toward building up strong, independent, indigenous book industries in most countries. To some extent, the optimism of the seventies has been replaced by wariness and even pessimism in the eighties. Ten years of struggle, disappointments, and failures have taken their toll.

This chapter will review the recommendations of the Ife conference, discuss efforts to implement them, and examine some of the obstacles that hinder the establishment of strong indigenous publishing industries in most African countries. Then the experiences of two new indigenous African publishers are examined in an effort to identify the problems they face.

Publishing in Africa in the Seventies

The Publishing in Africa in the Seventies conference was held at the University of Ife in Ile-Ife, Nigeria, in December 1973, and resulted in the formulation of recommendations on a wide range of book-related topics.[1] A few are summarized below.

The printing industry and paper manufacture. The pool of competent, well-trained printers in most countries was found to be inadequate for the needs of growing book production industries. It was recommended that associations of master printers which would draft uniform entry requirements and training courses be formed. Further, it was suggested that employees of smaller presses be given opportunities for brief periods of attachment to larger presses where they would be exposed to more modern equipment and practices.

The publishing sector. It was suggested that indigenous publishers be willing to gamble on young and unknown authors at least once. When such authors were published first by expatriate houses and later became better known, they tended to remain with their original publishers. A commitment to publish unknown authors was seen as a vital element in building strong indigenous book industries as well as in developing indigenous literature. It was also suggested that state participation in publishing could effectively ensure access to sufficient capitalization. State participation was seen as being particularly important in publishing in the vernacular languages and in educational publishing. However, entirely state-owned publishing was not desirable since it could potentially lead to problems with excessive bureaucratization, corruption, and the possibility of political interference.

To alleviate the dearth of trained book production people at all levels it was recommended that African publishers consider exchanges among their staff and especially that small publishers send staff members for periods of attachment and training to larger, longer-established publishing houses. This should be done not only with editorial staff but also with marketing, promotion, and distribution staff.

Readership for books in Africa. Illiteracy is a major problem in the African context, and it was suggested that publishers become actively involved in campaigns to eradicate illiteracy. Publishers were urged to produce low-cost books while still maintaining high standards in editing, printing, and binding, as well as books in local languages and books for the newly or semi-literate. It was recommended that books on health, sanitation and nutrition, simple how-to-do manuals on farming practices and various trades and skills, as well as books for leisure reading be produced for potential readers. It was recommended also that African writers consciously turn their efforts to home audiences rather than to overseas ones, sometimes writing in indigenous languages and always addressing topics of relevance and interest to local people.

Distribution, marketing, and promotion. The conference recognized that although there were many booksellers in most African countries, the majority ran small operations, selling mostly school textbooks and only at profitable times, i.e., at the beginning of the school year. These booksellers rarely had much interest in or knowledge of books, and they did little to foster a love of reading in their clientele. It was suggested that booksellers form professional associations and cooperate to improve the business expertise and experience of members of the trade, with staff of small shops visiting larger ones to learn business methods. Booksellers were urged, also, to take their books to the potential buyers: to display them at conferences, meetings, and public lectures. Book clubs were seen as another method of attracting readers.

Book development. The important role of libraries and teachers' organizations in fostering an interest in books and reading in children was discussed. Establishing national book development councils with a wide spectrum of representation—publishers, printers, booksellers, librarians, teachers—was seen as an effective means to increase government interest in the development of vigorous indigenous publishing industries. The reluctance of most African governments to commit funds to book development was seen as a grave miscalculation. Undercapitalization remains an important cause for the failure of many indigenous book publishing firms, and it was recommended that governments give encouragement, both in financial and policy terms, to such ventures. Book development councils could also advise governments on the importance of relaxing restrictions which hinder the importation and increase the costs of printing materials; encourage research into and the eventual founding of local industries for the production of these supplies and equipment; support the formation and strengthening of associations of writers, publishers, booksellers, printers, and librarians; encourage the examination of children's and other library services; and initiate and lend support to all forms of research on the kinds of publishing needed. Such councils would help integrate book development into overall national development planning.

Regional and pan-African cooperation. The necessity for cooperation was stressed, beginning at the national level, proceeding to the regional level, and eventually resulting in pan-African organizations. Regional organizations would be able to sponsor training institutions, annual conferences, journals, exchange of personnel between publishers, exchanges between libraries, and exchange of overstock between bookshops.

This, then, was the general state of African book publishing at the beginning of the 1970s. There was a feeling, shared by many book personnel, that the industry was on the verge of taking off, that problems had been identified, and that systematic efforts would be made to tackle them. This feeling of positive expectations was further heightened by the fact that many African governments were emphasizing the eradication of illiteracy and the provision, as far as finances allowed, of universal primary education. Moreover, international organizations like UNESCO and UNICEF and national donor agencies of various metropolitan governments were concentrating large amounts of money on literacy programs and on the development of educational infrastructures in Africa. It seemed likely that the potential market for locally published reading and educational materials would continue to expand and that the future for indigenous African publishers was bright.

Development of an African Book Publishing Industry

Despite the earnest intentions articulated at the Ife meeting and the general emphasis placed on eradication of illiteracy by most African governments during the 1970s, in the 1980s book production in Africa is for the most part still at a neophyte stage. Africa accounted for 1.1 percent of the number of titles published worldwide in 1955, but by 1975 the number had increased only to 1.9 percent and in 1977 it fell to 1.7 percent.[2] For the world as a whole, the increase in book production between 1955 and 1977 was on the order of 43 percent.[3] UNESCO figures indicate that by 1977, the developed countries were producing annually 449 titles per million inhabitants.[4] The developing countries, in contrast, were producing 46 titles per million population and African countries were producing 26. It is clear, therefore, that Africa was producing considerably fewer books than the other developing regions of the world, notably Latin America and Asia.

When the African figures are examined in detail, the state of the book industry on the continent looks even bleaker. For example, UNESCO figures report that in 1973 an estimated 6,800 titles were published in Africa, but 2,673, or 39 percent, were published in the Union of South Africa. UNESCO figures for 1975 indicate that South Africa published 46 percent of the total number of titles for that year.[5] During the 1970s, Nigeria emerged as the only black African country with what could be described as a substantial book publishing industry.[6] Almost 1,200 titles were published annually in Nigeria by the late 1970s and a number of indigenous publishers had established strong presences, including Onibonoje Press, Progresso Publishers, Ilesanmi Press, and Tabansi.[7] The Nigerian share of the total African book publishing industry during the late 1970s stood at just below 20 percent.[8] The UNESCO figures are crude, of course, since they do not differentiate between books and pamphlets and because the criteria used to judge what constitutes a book or publication vary from country to country. Furthermore, the figures are based on self-reporting and thus are even more prone to error and unreliability. Many African countries do not have depository laws, and there is no way of knowing what has been published. However, the figures do give a general indication of the decline over the past decade.

Table 5.1 presents figures on general African book production during the late 1970s. From these figures, incomplete as they are, it is clear that book production is at an extremely low level in most African countries. Figures for Latin America and Asia are much higher. For example, in 1977 Peru produced 910 titles, Chile 387, and Argentina 5,285. India produced 12,885, Korea 13,081, and Sri Lanka 1,201.[9] Kenya is sometimes described as a country with a fairly vigorous publishing industry,[10] but it is conspicuously absent from the UNESCO figures quoted in table 5.1. Other countries, such as Tanzania, Liberia, and Zimbabwe that also have publishing industries, small though they undoubtedly are, also are not mentioned in the table.

The majority of books published in Africa are produced for the educational market. The thrust toward universal primary education in many countries, the less rapid but equally steady development of secondary and tertiary education, and the establishment of many forms of nonformal education in the context of rural development programs, have led to a burgeoning demand for educational reading material. Much of this demand has been and continues to be met by the multinational publishers, which have a long history dating back to the colonial period. However, the rapid expansion of this market also has offered opportunity for the establishment and growth of some indigenous publishers throughout the past decade. In Nigeria, where it is estimated that more than 80 percent of the publishing market lies in textbook sales,[11] indigenous publishers such as Onibonoje and Ilesanmi have established strong presences in the educational market.

In other Anglophone African countries, the major multinationals—Longman, Oxford, Heinemann, Thomas Nelson, and Evans—still maintain control over educational publishing. In Francophone African countries, the Paris-based giants like

Table 5.1. Book Production in Africa.

Country	Number of Titles		
	1977	1978	1979
Angola			43
Benin		13	
Botswana	71	103	
Congo	127		
Egypt	1,472	353	
Gambia	113	81	
Ghana	135	251	72
Ivory Coast	125		
Libyan Arab Jamahiriya		481	
Madagascar	211	219	
Malawi	133	96	96
Mali		6	
Mauritania	40		
Mautitius	40	20	84
Niger			18
Nigeria		1,175	
Reunion	76		
Senegal	48		64
Seychelles	11		
Sierra Leone	61		
Sudan	104		138
Tunisia	85	85	118
United Republic of Cameroon		54	22
Zaire	154	109	
Zambia	32	123	

Source: UNESCO, *Statistical Yearbook,* 1981.

Hachette have an even greater influence on book production and marketing, although some indigenous houses like Editions Clé of Yaoundi in the Cameroon and Les Nouvelles Editions Africaines of Senegal and the Ivory Coast have had some success in satisfying local book needs. However, aside from local publishing carried out by multinational firms, most African countries still import a considerable number of their educational books, particularly at the secondary and tertiary levels where locally written and published material usually is unavailable.

Table 5.2 presents an overview of educational book production in a number of African countries in the late 1970s. It is clear that, with the possible exception of Nigeria and Egypt, most countries were still importing the majority of their school textbooks. The implications of using old textbooks containing examples of little relevance to African children and presenting history from a perspective which favored the former colonial powers in particular and the developed western countries in general have been discussed elsewhere.[12] Again, the African situation with respect to local production of school texts is more desolate than the situation in other parts

Table 5.2. Production of School Textbooks in Africa.

Country	Year	Books	Pamphlets	Total
Egypt	1977	414	41	455
Ethiopia	1978	118	1	119
Gambia	1978	20	–	20
Ghana	1978	27	2	29
Ivory Coast	1977	8	13	21
Kenya	1976	26	–	26
Madagascar	1978	37	1	38
Malawi	1977	2	–	2
Mauritania	1977	21	22	43
Mauritius	1977	–	2	2
Nigeria	1978	583	298	881
Senegal	1977	7	–	7
Sierra Leone	1977	2	–	2
Sudan	1977	88	–	88
Tunisia	1978	69	–	69
United Republic of Cameroon	1978	54	–	54
United Republic of Tanzania	1976	52	19	71
Zaire	1977	15	–	15
Zambia	1978	31	–	31

Source: UNESCO, *Statistical Yearbook*, 1980.

of the world. Figures for school text production in Latin America and Asia, as with overall book production, are somewhat higher. In 1977 Peru produced 24 titles, Chile 84, and Argentina 339. India produced 462, Korea 1,708, and Sri Lanka 74.[13]

In general, the African book industry has grown relatively little within the last decade. However, in some respects, the book industry has become better organized and systematized since 1973. National bibliographies, or the equivalent, now are published in Botswana, Ethiopia, Ghana, the Ivory Coast, Madagascar, Malawi, Mauritius, Nigeria, Senegal, Sierra Leone, and South Africa.[14] The Library of Congress has published its *Accessions List: Eastern Africa* out of its Nairobi field office on a quarterly basis since 1968, listing many local publications. The first edition of *African Books in Print* appeared in 1975, two later editions followed, and a third is due soon. *The International African Bibliography* has been published from London on a quarterly basis since 1971, and the *African Book Publishing Record,* a quarterly journal issued from Oxford, England, has appeared since the mid-1970s, with lists of new titles published by African publishers, comprehensive book reviews, and informative articles about the African book scene.[15] At the same time, concerted efforts have been made by some African publishers to break into the metropolitan market. They distribute announcements of new publications to overseas journals, send out books for review, and mail catalogues and bulletins to libraries and individuals who have expressed an interest in their publications. On the whole, then, although the actual number of titles published in Africa has remained more or less stable over the past decade, the book industry has not remained static. Improvements have been made in distribution, and the industry as a whole has acquired a greater sense of cohesion.

The Ife Recommendations in Retrospect

It is clear from the broad view of African publishing which has been presented that there have been a few important changes in the structure of the publishing industry in Africa, most notably an increase in the number of successful indigenous publishing houses. However, in order to get a more thorough idea of the extent of these changes, it is useful to reexamine some of the recommendations that were made at Ife to see how successfully they have been implemented and to assess the potential for greater changes and/or further improvements within the next few years.

The Printing Industry and Paper Manufacture

The printing industry in the developed countries is going through a period of rapid technological change. Although the full impact of these developments is not yet being felt in the African book industry, it is inevitable that this will occur. New computer- and microprocessor-based equipment is being used, including terminals, direct-entry photosetters, electronic cameras able to produce halftones, and word processors. The original letterpress printing process is being phased out and letterpress machines no longer are being produced, although efforts still are being made to extend the life of existing equipment.[16] Despite the advantages of the computer-based printing technologies in the developed countries, they are not necessarily equally advantageous in the African context. Computer-based printing is labor saving but requires a level of infrastructural support (e.g., a steady source of electricity, air-conditioned offices, ready access to spare parts and skilled repair services) which often is not available in the African context. In contrast, labor is cheap and plentiful. Moreover, Datus Smith estimated in 1977 that African composition and presswork costs were still most economical using the traditional linotype and letterpress methods for print runs of 10,000 or less.[17] These considerations certainly qualify the overwhelming acceptance of new printing technologies by African publishers, but it generally is conceded that the new technologies are the way of the future and that they eventually will be introduced in Africa.

The supply of printing paper has been and continues to be a problem for many African publishers. Limited local paper industries, escalating paper prices, fierce competition in world markets for scarce supplies, and heavy import duties on paper which is not imported expressly for educational uses have made the acquisition of paper a tiresome and expensive undertaking. Relatively few countries are self-sufficient in paper supply. According to UNESCO figures, only 42 percent of the paper needs of the African book industry were met locally in 1976.[18] Mills producing paper for book publishing purposes existed in Algeria, Angola, Egypt, Ethiopia, Kenya, Madagascar, Morocco, Nigeria, and Tunisia. Other countries were dependent on imported supplies, and often countries with paper industries only partially met the demands of the local book industry. Paper costs in Africa were higher than in other regions of the world; UNESCO estimates in the late 1970s indicated a higher per unit cost for paper in Africa than in other regions (Table 5.3). These relatively higher paper costs added to the cost of books, often removing them from the financial reach of the poorest segment of society and strengthening the tendency to buy books only for essential utilitarian purposes, i.e., for school but not for pleasure.

To some extent the inadequacy of local printing facilities has remained a deterrent to the development of strong indigenous publishing industries. In a country like

Table 5.3. Paper Costs.
(U.S. dollar cost of paper for one copy)

	In Editions of 1,000 Copies	In Editions of 5,000 Copies	In Editions of 10,000 Copies
Asia	$0.18	$0.16	$0.16
Latin America	0.19	0.19	0.19
Middle East	0.31	0.29	0.28
Africa	0.50	0.43	0.43
All Areas	0.24	0.23	0.23

Source: UNESCO, *An International Survey of Book Production During the Last Decades,* Statistical Reports and Studies, no. 26 (Paris: UNESCO, 1982), p. 81.

Nigeria, for example, there are a number of modern, well-equipped, reliable printers, such as Caxton Printing Press in Ibadan, Academic Press in Lagos, and New Nigerian Press in Kaduna, but all of them have heavily committed printing schedules and the time lag between placing a manuscript with them and having the print order filled often is quite lengthy. It has become common during the past decade for African publishers, particularly multinational ones, to send their manuscripts overseas for typesetting, especially to printers in Singapore and Hong Kong where service is efficient and turnover is rapid. The disadvantages of this solution are obvious: it entails the use of scarce foreign exchange which usually is difficult and time-consuming for a small publisher without significant overseas sales to procure. Secondly, it involves reliance on sometimes inefficient postal systems, and corrections and changes are time-consuming and bothersome.

Most African countries need reliable, efficient local printers. Local printers must be adept at realistic estimations of job time and costs and at making optimal use of plant facilities as well as have access to essential spare parts and technical assistance to ensure that their operation continues to run smoothly. Again, this involves the question of foreign exchange. Printing facilities in a country like Nigeria often are crippled for weeks and even months while a crucial spare part is ordered from overseas, causing huge backlogs.

On the whole the printing industry in most African countries is still faced with a number of constraints. New technologies, while present, have not developed as quickly as in industrialized countries. Printing costs, using traditional methods, are still relatively high. Paper is expensive and sometimes difficult to obtain. The best equipped and most efficient printers are heavily committed and long waits for the filling of print orders are common.

The Economics of Publishing

A number of factors make book publishing an unattractive form of capital investment in most African countries. Banks are reluctant to give loans to would-be publishers. Book publishing is a little-known or understood form of entrepreneurship; it is seen as a risky undertaking and as fairly capital-intensive for relatively small returns. A warehouse full of unsold books is poor collateral for a loan. African entrepreneurs who start publishing ventures often do so with only their own resources and those of friends and relatives. Consequently, they usually are chronically undercapitalized and unable to invest adequate amounts in important areas like promotion and distribution. Largely because of this undercapitalization, publishing houses have high rates of business failure. The start-up capital required to establish a publishing venture can be high, especially if printing facilities are set up in conjunction with the publishing program. Heavy investment in prepublication activities, i.e., editorial costs, also is common. Publishers often have to wait as long as three years before realizing a profit on their titles, and in the interim they usually have to pay production costs. The initial investment is high; the returns are slow to accumulate. Since banks are reluctant to lend to unknown publishers, the financial resources of a fledgling house are bound to be stretched to the limit. Not uncommonly, publishing houses operate at a loss for several years, and even when they begin to make a profit, it is usually in the range of 5 to 10 percent of the initial investment.[19]

High rates of business failure are influenced by the tendency toward undercapitalization. In many African countries there is no book production infrastructure, and so publishers are forced to undertake tasks which normally would be contracted to outside firms, such as composition, presswork, and binding. This places further financial burdens on the publisher.[20]

Pricing is another problematic area. The increased scarcity of paper on the world market during the past decade has made it difficult for small indigenous publishers to accurately estimate paper costs. Thus, it is difficult for a publisher to estimate the cost of a book until paper for it has been procured. Most indigenous publishers are too small to import their own paper stocks from overseas, and they do not have access to sufficient foreign exchange. Multinational firms, in contrast, often do import their own paper for local publishing. By importing paper directly for educational purposes (i.e., book publishing as opposed to the manufacture of paper towels or other utilitarian items), the multinational publishers are able to avoid the import tax levied by some countries. The smaller, indigenous firms tend to buy directly from printers or paper importers and are forced to pay fluctuating prices which often include the cost of the tax.

In the area of pricing the indigenous publisher starts with a considerable handicap. Very little research has been conducted into the pricing structure of the book industry in various African countries. Datus Smith's 1977 study published by UNESCO remains one of the few attempts to examine costing patterns in a number of countries in Africa, Asia, Latin America, and the Middle East. He gives an indication of pricing structures in developing countries, although he is not specific about the African case.

The relatively high profit margin indicated for publishers in developing countries is explained by the fact that such enterprises tend to be family owned; management expenses and interest on loans are likely to be taken out of profits rather than listed as overhead. Peter Newman has made a comparative study of the profit margins of American educational publishers, and his conclusion, based on an examination of his own and Smith's data, is that the costing structure of the book industry in the developing countries and in the U.S. is surprisingly similar.

Smith also found that the manufacturing cost and nonmanufacturing cost incurred in book production in developing countries are in the range of 29.3 and 70.7 percent, respectively.[21] Nonmanufacturing costs include costs incurred in selling a book, such as royalties to author, discounts to wholesale and retail dealers, promotional costs, and overhead charges. These charges, generally categorized as "mark-up," tend to be lower for some types of books than others. Textbooks, for example, can be sold at a lower per unit cost because publishers have more of an assured market for them, and there is little chance of their remaining in the warehouse for indeterminate lengths of time. In many African countries, textbooks are published in response to requests from Ministries of Education and the market for them is assured.

The costs of producing a book have been carefully itemized by a group of Indian researchers. Based on a cost survey of the Indian book industry, they found that the profit margin for publishers was even lower than that quoted by Smith—in the area of 5 to 10 percent.[22]

Book publishing is not a particularly lucrative business. Publishing houses fail with regularity, often because of a lack of business expertise and experience on the part of their initiators but also because of the vagaries of the conditions under which they are forced to operate, paying high prices for required services and recouping small profits for completed work.

Publishing Personnel

In Africa there is still a shortage of trained and experienced editors, graphic artists and illustrators, and promotion and distribution professionals. Book publishing remains a little-understood profession. A survey of faculty members on two university campuses in Nigeria in 1978 revealed a general ignorance about the kinds of expertise required to establish and efficiently operate a book publishing house.[23] Training programs for book publishing professionals are rare although a few efforts have been made. For example, the Zimbabwe Publishing House in Harare recently has organized a number of seminars on editing and book production for local participants. In most cases, however, the best a small publishing house can do is to place its staff with larger houses for short periods of time; larger houses, especially the multinational ones, sometimes send staff overseas for a few months of training. Somewhat ironically, the multinational firms have performed an invaluable service in training staff. The multinational publishers have a long history in many African countries, sometimes dating back to well before independence. Oxford University Press, for example, has had an increasingly prominent presence in Nigeria since the 1920s, passing through various stages of dependency on the British headquarters until the mid-1970s when it became completely indigenized. Over the past three decades, many African publishing professionals have started their careers as junior trainees with multinational firms. Some moved into positions of authority as the multinational houses were Africanized; others have left to establish their own publishing houses or to develop state publishing ventures.

Language

The question of publishing in indigenous languages has received little concerted attention from African publishers over the past decade. At a 1983 seminar on children's book publishing in Freetown, Sierra Leone, which attracted publishers and librarians from all over Africa, the issue did not receive much interest.[24] On the other hand, some authors have begun to write in indigenous languages. The Kenyan author and social critic Ngugi wa Thiong'o in recent years has written first in his native Gikuyu. His work is now more directed toward Kenyan readers, and he has declared his intention to write in the language of his people, thus ensuring that they are the first to have access to his novels, plays, and social commentaries. He also is ensuring that the rural folk about whom he writes much of his work will not be denied access to a modern Kenyan literature because of their lack of literacy in English. Other well-known African authors such as the Ghanaian Kofi Awoonor and the Nigerian Chinua Achebe, for example, also have focused on the need for the development of literature in indigenous languages.

Despite the support for indigenous language publishing, African publishers, both multinational and locally based, have been slow to develop lists in local languages. Many of the big houses include some indigenous language titles on their lists, but the emphasis is on English or French language publishing. The reasons for this are not difficult to discover. The market for most indigenous language titles is small. The book buying capability of the rural poor, who would be a potential market, is limited; disposable income is scarce and books are bought only for educational or other specifically utilitarian purposes. Moreover, the number of indigenous languages in Africa is large. In Nigeria, for example, more than 350 languages are spoken by ethnic groups ranging in population from a few thousand to several million. However, Yoruba, Hausa, and Ibo all are spoken by huge population groups, and Swahili, in East Africa, is spoken across national boundaries and has the potential of offering a sizeable regional or international publishing market.

The bulk of the African book market still lies in educational publishing. Since education beyond the primary, or sometimes the secondary, level is usually in English, French, or Portuguese, the profitability of indigenous language publishing is further reduced. In Africa the emphasis has been more on the development of indigenous publishing houses rather than on publishing in indigenous languages. In some Asian countries there has been a strong move to publish in local languages, but indigenous language publishing is fraught with difficulties despite the large book markets. In India, for example, almost one-half of the books published in 1976 were in English, the remainder being in the other fifteen recognized national languages.[25] Even in a country like Malaysia where the national language, Bahasa Malaysia, replaced English as a medium of instruction in the schools soon after independence in 1957, there continues to be a problem with the production of textbooks at the secondary and especially the tertiary levels. Commonly such books are translations of English works. The country does not have a cadre of authors able and willing to write teaching materials for a wide range of university courses. Finding competent translators for university textbooks sometimes has been a problem for Malaysian publishers. This deficiency probably is due in part to lack of knowledge about book writing, translating, and publishing as a career choice for an educated person. University students venture into book writing and publishing rarely or by accident rather than as an actively exercised choice.

Perhaps the most persistent efforts to publish in indigenous languages have been made by the religious publishing houses. By the early 1970s the United Bible Societies in Africa had published religious texts in 561 African languages.[26] Moreover, many of the Christian publishing houses have published school texts, fiction, and other materials, often concentrating on books for new literates, as well as religious literature. Christian societies have expended a great amount of time and energy in organizing small-scale, local literacy programs in contrast to the grander efforts sponsored by national governments and international agencies. Despite the undeniable contributions made by Christian societies and publishing houses in many African countries, however, the literature they provide, whether in English or in indigenous languages, tends toward an ideological and cultural perspective which does not necessarily reflect the viewpoint of non-Christians or even of less committed Christians. As such, it must be regarded with a certain detachment by some readers.

African Book Publishing in the Eighties

While some of the Ife recommendations have been accepted and implemented, the growth and development of the African book industry during the past decade has not met the expectations of the 1973 meeting. Literacy rates on the continent are still low, especially in metropolitan languages and among females. The Sierra Leonean writer Talabi Aisie Lucan recently estimated that English literacy in her country was only 15 percent.[27] Perhaps most important, books and the development of publishing have been overlooked by many African governments. Book development is not an integral part of development plans. Book development councils, when they have been formed, have been more figureheads than effective, active organizations promoting the industry, and their pronouncements have been more platitudinal than pragmatic. Distribution networks throughout the continent are shaky at best; it is easier to get a West African-published book in London than in Nairobi. Copublication ventures among African publishers have been rare.

There are a few positive developments, however. Many new publishing houses have been founded and some are surviving quite well. Nigeria has experienced a surge of book publishing entrepreneurship over the past decade, influenced, no doubt, by that country's relative financial security during the late 1970s, its emphasis on universal primary education, the size of the population, and, especially, the ever-growing size of the book-buying market. In Nigeria there is also a history of reading for pleasure. The Onitsha Market Series pamphlets which were quite well known in the 1960s always found large audiences anxious to learn about *How to Get a Girl in Love and Keep Her* and similar homilies.

Some of the Nigerian publishers who came to prominence during the 1970s were Fourth Dimension Publishers, which has published numerous well-known local authors such as Chinua Achebe, Cyprian Ekwensi, and Chinweizu[28]; Tana Press, which has produced a number of interesting children's books; New Horn Press, with an emphasis on literacy works; and Spectrum Books, which is bringing out educational books as well as popular fiction. For the most part, their lists are small and their markets are predominantly local—it is difficult to obtain their books outside Nigeria or sometimes even outside their region—but they are evidence of an active and vigorous, if small-scale, publishing industry in the country.

Outside Nigeria there also has been some activity. Two relatively new firms in East and southern Africa illustrate the kinds of problems new publishers face in Africa.

Bookwise

Bookwise is a relatively new publishing house in Nairobi, Kenya, founded by Leonard Okola, formerly chief editor at the East African Publishing House. According to Okola, the government is the main market for books in Kenya since it purchases vast quantities for educational purposes. Since many more Kenyan children attend primary than secondary schools, the aim of most Kenyan publishers is to produce books for the primary school market. The school textbook market is dominated by three giants—the parastatal Jomo Kenyatta Foundation, the Kenya Literature Bureau, and Longman, one of the most successful multinational publishers operating in the country. Okola started Bookwise in 1978 to bridge what he saw as a gap in the trade book market. He has produced a number of primary school readers, some plays and poetry, history and geography books. He also has published a few scholarly titles, concentrated mostly in the social sciences and relying heavily on subsidies.

According to Okola, there is a substantial reading and writing public in Kenya. His house, small and relatively new though it is, receives many submissions from prospective authors, for the most part unsolicited. Most of them are not of a publishable quality, but he sees it as a strong indication of interest in writing activities among Kenyans and he rejects the notion that "Africans don't read except for educational purposes." He cites the success of David Maillu's Comb Books which published simple, sensational, and often sexually titillating novels like *My Dear Bottle* or *Unfit for Human Consumption* which became overnight bestsellers and sold upward of 50,000 copies to a cross section of Kenyan and East African society. Transafrica Book Distributors of Nairobi profitted with the same formula in their Afroromance series which features easy-to-read, descriptive, highly romantic, and often moralistic love stories. Just as there is a mass market in America for the romances of Harold Robbins, Marie Corelli, and James Hadley Chase or the wildly successful Harlequin Romance series published in Winnipeg, Canada, there is a growing African market for similar simple romance stories. In Nairobi, a number of the multinational houses now are publishing literature of this genre, including Macmillan, Heinemann, and Longman. According to Okola, however, none of these publishers have had the same success as Comb Books, perhaps because their works tend to be a little less sensational. Comb Books went bankrupt in the early 1980s, although David Maillu, its founder and most active author, still writes.

The main problems faced by Kenyan publishers in the 1980s, according to Leonard Okola, are essentially financial. Kenyans are buying books, and, he is convinced, there is less of a tendency now for one book to be bought and shared among many readers; instead, individuals buy their own copies. However, book prices must be kept very low—fifty Kenyan shillings (or approximately US$4) is a high price for a book. Thus publishers are unable to recoup their full expenses, much less make a profit, unless their sales for a particular title are extremely high. The key problem for a general interest publishing house like Bookwise is small sales and small potential market. Before the Kenyan border with Tanzania was closed, it was possible to sell books in Tanzania. Uganda has long ceased to be a lucrative market in view of that country's political and economic troubles. The Kenyan government, due to financial stringencies which have grown increasingly tighter since the beginning of the 1980s, is buying fewer books. Thus the market for Bookwise's titles is growing smaller while production costs are rising. Initial print runs of novels are usually 3,000 copies or, in exceptional cases, 5,000. Still, it is difficult to ensure sufficient cash flow to cover production and storage costs until stocks are sold.

Distribution is a major problem for small Kenyan publishers. Overseas distribution is almost impossible without access to international networks. Participation in international book fairs and exhibits is expensive, involves foreign currency, and places further burdens on small and overworked staffs.

Local distribution also is a problem. Transportation to the rural areas is difficult and at some times of the year impossible. Booksellers outside the urban centers often are reluctant to stock books not related to educational needs. Their shelf space is small and rapid turnover is necessary for them to make a profit.

In Okola's view, the Kenyan publishing industry has been going through a crisis for the past three years. It has suffered greatly from the recession which has crippled the economies of most developing countries. Further, the Ministry of Education has tended to favor the school texts published by its long-standing publishing house clients; it has been difficult for small, new, indigenous houses to break into the lucrative educational market. Not only does the government prescribe the texts which will be used but it also distributes them directly to schools, thereby eliminating the role of booksellers in primary school book sales. At the secondary level, except in government-aided schools, parents buy books from booksellers, but again they have been recommended by the Ministry of Education and thus it is impossible for publishers whose titles have not been recommended to sell their books. They in turn don't publish many "risk" titles. At times this government intervention has worked against some of the giant multinationals. Recently Longman in Nairobi found that instead of the expected fifty-two titles being on the government's list, less than twenty had been recommended that year. As a result the company was forced to reduce its sales and editorial staffs and almost closed its Nairobi operations.

Whether the Kenyan government should continue to allow foreign or multinational publishers to dominate the educational book market is a subject of heated debate. The Kenya Publishers Association is dominated by multinational publishers and local indigenous publishers have made a move to form their own organization because of what they see as a basic conflict of interest with the multinationals.

According to Okola, the future for small publishing houses like Bookwise is bleak but not hopeless. He is convinced that they will not be able to survive without a share of the government market and he is focusing on producing a few secondary-level textbooks. The one advantage small firms have over the multinationals, he thinks, is their willingness to accept payment in local currency. Government might find itself increasingly hard-pressed to pay for school textbooks in foreign currency in coming years and, if this is the case, then there will be a more important role for publishers like Bookwise. However, the government also will have to make a commitment to developing local book publishing. Local resources are relatively small, the pool of experienced editors and production personnel is tiny, and sometimes the quality of work is lower than that of the more experienced and better-endowed large companies.

Zimbabwe Publishing House

One of the most exciting and innovative publishing ventures in Africa at the present time is that of David Martin and Phyllis Johnson who started Zimbabwe Publishing House (ZPH) in Harare, Zimbabwe, in April 1981. Former journalists of British and Canadian background, they served as war correspondents during the country's struggle for independence from Ian Smith's Universal Declaration of Independence government, and their book, *The Struggle for Zimbabwe,* published in 1980 by Faber and Faber in the U.K., was the first analysis of the fight for Zimbabwean independence. They reprinted the book in paperback under their own imprint in September 1981, and sold out their first print run of 60,000 copies within a year. At the same time, they exported 19,000 copies under their own imprint—10,000 to Ravan Press in South Africa; 5,000 to Monthly Review Press in the U.S.; and 4,000 to Faber and Faber in the U.K.

The book needs of a newly independent country like Zimbabwe present a special challenge. Not only is there a hunger for books such as *The Struggle for Zimbabwe* which document and analyze the long struggle which the country endured, but also there is a need for new texts at all levels of the education system which present history, literature, social studies, and a multitude of other subjects from the perspective of an independent people and a predominantly black population. Moreover, there was a need to promote a local African literature which had been stifled or discouraged during the long years of colonial rule. Thus, when ZPH burst upon the scene in early 1981, it was greeted with enthusiasm and excitement. The energy and creativity that Martin and Johnson brought to the enterprise was matched by the dedication, interest, and imagination of their Zimbabwean colleagues.

One of the first publishing tasks ZPH undertook was to reprint a number of important books that had been banned in white-ruled Rhodesia. The first of these was Walter Rodney's classic *How Europe Underdeveloped Africa*. The book had been available before independence only through an underground network. When it was reprinted in April 1981, the first print run of 7,500 sold out within five weeks and booksellers around the country clamored for more. Thus, ZPH began its career with an emphasis on reprint publishing. Its aim was to save foreign currency by reprinting important foreign books, especially ones of a radical political nature. Making available books such as Rodney's and literature published in other African countries was its first priority. ZPH next began to publish textbooks written specifically for the local market, using local examples and interpreting recent history from the perspective of the newly independent state. Children's literature was a third area of emphasis. With support from a number of churches and from the Canada Book Centre, ZPH has established *Ants,* a unique magazine for Zimbabwean children which features stories, illustrations, and quizzes in English, Ndebele, and Shona and is written and edited by a staff of ten local children, aged seven to fourteen (with advice, when required, from an adult ZPH staff member). Response to *Ants* has been highly positive, not only because of the entertainment and educational value it has for Zimbabwean children but also because of its efforts to forge links among the country's main ethnic and linguistic groups.

Despite ZPH's interest in publishing books for children and in promoting African literature, the financial future of the company will be tied to its ability to break into the educational market. In the past Longman has been the most prominent publisher of primary school texts in the country, and the new government, faced with massive expansion of the primary school system, has continued to use books from the former regime. In 1982 more than 140,000 students were enrolled in Form One, and the government is committed to providing individual copies of textbooks for each child. The life of a school textbook in Zimbabwean schools is about two years, and it will be some time before ZPH and other indigenous publishing houses are able to commission and publish new or relevant textbooks to replace all of the old ones. The company published a lower primary school history text, written in a cartoon style, in 1981 and immediately sold out the 70,000 copies of the initial print run. By mid-1983 it was being reprinted. However, the thrust to publish relevant textbooks for the educational market is not being undertaken solely by indigenous houses like

ZPH. The multinational publishers are commissioning new school texts to reflect the current political, cultural, and social realities of the country.

ZPH was registered in April 1981 as a nonprofit publishing venture. It pays no fees to its directors nor dividends to its shareholders (who are allowed a maximum of two shares each). Profits made by the company's sales go into further development and diversification of the publications program. Staff has grown from Martin, Johnson, and a driver in mid-1981 to twenty full-time employees and an additional fifty-one part-time. The company has not undertaken a readership survey but according to Martin they now, through experience and instinct, have a fairly accurate idea of what kinds of books will sell outside the educational market. The areas in which they plan to concentrate their efforts over the next few months are: children's literature; African drama (Kenyan dramatist Ngugi wa Thiong'o worked in Zimbabwe and consulted with ZPH for a short time recently); women's development studies; and historical scholarship.

Initially the company invested considerable effort in publicity to ensure that its books were brought to the attention of potential readers. Because of the press connections of Johnson and Martin, the first few titles received much newspaper coverage. This example is being followed by other Zimbabwean publishers, leading to lively book review sections in some local newspapers and journals.

As a new company, ZPH has faced slightly different problems than Bookwise in Kenya. The Zimbabwe Publishing House was the first indigenous house to appear during the euphoric days right after independence; there was an immediate demand for the kinds of books the company was publishing; there was little competition from other publishers; and it was endowed with government support, both verbal and, to some extent, financial. According to Martin and Johnson, ZPH's major problem has been its inability to ensure that its publications reach the rural areas. Illiteracy is still a problem, perhaps more so in Zimbabwe than in many other African countries because access to primary education became a reality for most Zimbabweans only after independence. It has been especially difficult to sell children's books. Fathers are reluctant to spend their hard-earned money on books for children; mothers, even if they are more sympathetic (which is not necessarily the case), tend to have little of their own income or control over family income. Yet Martin and Johnson believe it is important to make an impact in children's literature.

On the positive side, the printing infrastructure in the country is good. Printers have had access to foreign currency, enabling them to import modern equipment. There is a fairly high level of local expertise in the industry. There is one paper mill in the country which produces about 18,000 tons of paper per year and the country's current need is in the range of 25,000 tons, but the government has given ZPH a generous allocation for importing paper from countries like Brazil and Sweden.[29] The company has established good links with some of the multinational publishers, some of which had particularly difficult periods of adjustment as they found themselves overstocked with books they were unable to sell to the new government. ZPH has entered into a copublishing arrangement with Heinemann Educational Books. The two companies have set up Zimbabwe Educational Books, of which ZPH owns a 60-percent share and Heinemann a 40-percent share. This new company will concentrate on meeting the educational market needs of the country over the next few years.

On the whole, the future for book publishing in Zimbabwe looks bright according to Johnson and Martin. There is a shortage of professional book people, but the company is attempting to create a cadre of experienced editors and production people by running a series of training workshops locally. They are convinced that a pool of competent, well-trained African staff will emerge within a few years. Unsolicited manuscript submissions to ZPH are already high, and there have been many from scholars outside the country. In view of all this, it seems likely that with the imaginative, energetic, and aggressive beginning that ZPH has made during its first two years of existence, it soon will become a major presence in African publishing.

Conclusion

This overview of African book publishing during the past decade has discussed some of the recommendations of the Ife meeting in 1973, describing the enthusiasm and optimism with which they were made, and it has examined the current status of book publishing on the continent. Perhaps one of the most important lessons of this examination is the fruitlessness of making predictions about the future of anything in Africa. The continent has been torn by internal wars, plagued with years of famine, unsettled by frequent coup d'états, and preoccupied with liberation struggles. These internal factors have had a generally destabilizing influence in many countries. External factors have also contributed to destabilization. Africa, perhaps more than any other part of the world, has felt the brunt of the oil crisis of the 1970s. Countries with fragile economies, small reserves of foreign exchange, and limited means of increasing their export earnings had little to buffer them against the world inflationary cycles of the 1970s. It is hardly surprising when faced with shortages of essential commodities that most African governments have invested little funds or attention in developing strong national book industries. Literacy programs have continued throughout the decade, often with support from external sources, but book development usually has been assigned a low priority. There has been relatively little innovation and creativity in the publishing industry in Africa during the 1970s and early 1980s. The new developments that have occurred have often come from outside. The decade was more a struggle for survival than a celebration of growth and development.

The problems the industry faces in 1984 are similar to the ones it faced in 1973. There still is difficulty with communication. Efficient sales and distribution systems rarely exist within countries and almost not at all within or between regions. The multinational publishers remain the most successful, the best organized, and the most prolific producers of books in most African countries. The majority of books are published in metropolitan languages, and the African share of the world book market still is dismally small. There are relatively few professional editors, production people, and book illustrators. Good printers are rare and those that exist are overcommitted.

Despite all of these problems, the industry struggles on. Many mistakes have been made, and enthusiasm and optimism has often turned into tedium and pessimism. But there is a growing nucleus of African authors, publishers, and booksellers who continue to try to write, publish, and sell books of relevance to African readers— literature, textbooks, self-help manuals, instruction books, cram books. The variety and scope of book production is becoming more varied as the number of readers continues to grow. The fact that this group of dedicated book people exists and that new conscripts are joining their ranks portends well for the future of African publishing. The other favorable factor is the dramatic increase of literates on the continent. As more and more Africans read, the demand for reading materials will continue to increase. And, if there exists a market for books, then ways will be found to publish and distribute them.

Perhaps the past decade can be seen as one of maturation. The euphoria and energetic efforts toward self-assertion in political, social, and cultural forums of the early post-independence days in most countries has settled into concern with predominantly economic issues. No one suggests in 1984 that book publishing will make a great deal of difference in solving the fundamental economic and political problems of Africa. Nonetheless, books are recognized as useful tools—for education, for entertainment, for forging national consciousness. This recognition and the commitment of a small group of African book people to act upon it bodes well for the future of African book publishing.

Notes

1. For a detailed account of the conference see Edwina Oluwasanmi, Eva McLean, and Hans Zell, eds., *Publishing in Africa in the Seventies. Proceedings of an International Conference on Publishing and Book Development Held at the University of Ife, Ile-Ife, Nigeria, 16–20 December 1973* (Ile-Ife, Nigeria: University of Ife Press, 1975).
2. UNESCO, *An International Survey of Book Production During the Last Decades,* Statistical Reports and Studies, no. 26 (Paris: UNESCO, 1982).
3. *Ibid.*
4. *Ibid.*
5. *Ibid.*
6. Eva Maria Rathgeber, "Africana Acquisitions Problems: The View from Both Sides," *Library Acquisitions Practice and Theory* (1982), pp. 137–148.
7. S. O. Olanlokun, "Textbook Publishing in Nigeria," *International Library Review* 14 (1982): 83–90.
8. UNESCO, *International Survey.*
9. *Ibid.*
10. Harry M. Kibirige, "Bibliographic Control in East Africa: State of the Art," *International Library Review* 10 (1978): 313–326.
11. Ruby Essien-Udom, "The University Press as Publishers in Africa," in *Publishing in Nigeria* (Benin City, Nigeria: Ethiope Publishing Corporation, 1972), pp. 34–43.
12. See, for example, Keith Smith, "Books and Development in Africa—Access and Role," *Library Trends* 26 (Spring 1978): 469–487.
13. UNESCO, *International Survey.*
14. Rathgeber, "Africana Acquisitions Problems."
15. *Ibid.*
16. M. Yuri Gates, "Technological Developments in the Printing Industry from Now until 1990," in *The Impact of New Technologies on Publishing.* Proceedings of the Symposium organized by the Commission of the European Communities, Directorate-General for Scientific and Technical Information and Information Management, Luxembourg, 6–7 November 1979 (London: K.G. Saur, 1980).
17. Datus C. Smith, Jr., *The Economics of Book Publishing in Developing Countries,* Reports and Papers on Mass Communications, no. 79 (Paris: UNESCO, 1977).
18. UNESCO, *International Survey.*

19. R. J. Taraporevala, "The Nature and Financing of Publishing," in *Priorities and Planning for the Provision of Books,* Report of the Commonwealth Asia Pacific Regional Seminar held at the India International Centre, New Delhi, India, 21 February to 1 March, 1973 (London: Commonwealth Secretariat, 1973).
20. Philip G. Altbach and Eva Maria Rathgeber, *Publishing in the Third World: Trend Report and Bibliography* (New York: Praeger, 1980).
21. Datus C. Smith, Jr., *The Economics of Book Publishing.*
22. National Council of Applied Economic Research, *Survey of Indian Book Industry* (New Delhi: National Council of Applied Economic Research, 1976).
23. Eva Maria Rathgeber, "The Establishment of an Intellectual Elite in Nigeria" (M.A. thesis, McGill University, Montreal, 1978).
24. Hans Zell, "Writing Wrongs for Children," *West Africa,* March 7, 1983.
25. UNESCO, *Regional Seminar on Book Publishing in National Languages. Karachi, Pakistan, 20–24 January 1980* (Karachi: UNESCO, 1980).
26. Modupe Oduyoye, "The Role of Christian Publishing Houses in Africa Today," in Edwina Oluwasanmi et al., eds., in *Africa in the Seventies* (Ile-Ife: University of Ife Press, 1975).
27. Hans Zell, "Writing Wrongs for Children."
28. Hans Zell, "Publishing in Africa," *West Africa,* August 22, 1983, p. 83.
29. The bookselling industry is fairly well established; Zimbabwe has approximately 80 bookshops, a high proportion of them concentrated in Harare. Portugal, in contrast, has 250.

6. Publishing in Ghana:
Aspects of Knowledge and Development
Amu Djoleto

Historical Overview

The publishing phenomenon in Ghana, like that of most Anglophone countries of Africa, had its beginning in a variety of sources: Christian missionary activity; educational development; the expansion in government business; the increase in the number of printing houses and book production expertise; the slow but sure rise in endogenous authorship, publishing firms, book manufacture, and distribution, as well as a steady growth of social consciousness. For over two centuries Ghana has had a tradition, naturally minuscule at first, of a society that took the book seriously. Acquiring knowledge through books is in itself admirable; the more learned a person is, the more he or she is looked up to as an informed citizen whose considered opinions are worth taking seriously. Furthermore, successful book study, which has been the main weapon of formal education in Ghana, has also been the most dependable means to economic and social well-being.

Sustained reading after formal education reinforces the resolve to forge an independent lifestyle in a society that is unevenly literate, that was subjected to extreme conformity, and in which old and new ideas and practices coexist uneasily. Notions of correctness are still in flux, yet the bibliophiles display an easy grasp of the role they have decided to play in society with an optimism that baffles and impresses at the same time. The book, reading, and independent thinking are effective instruments in helping individuals define and chart their lives in an environment under rapid and often confusing pressures. In a country where social classes have not coalesced and statuses rise and fall within a lifetime, the book provides a stabilizing self-awareness against destabilizing political and social uncertainties.

Finally, the growth of government has had a tremendous effect on the development of printing in the country, which in turn has been a prerequisite to the rapid expansion of private printing houses, indigenous authorship, publishing and book manufacture, and mass reading. The foundations were laid long before but were most noticeable during the nineteenth century when missionaries were active and the central government expanded its control over the southern portion of the country.

During the first half of the nineteenth century, the Basel and Bremen religious missions investigated three Ghanaian languages for religious and educational purposes: Twi, Ga and Ewe. By 1850 they had published four Twi spelling and reading books. These were followed by several other books by expert writers like Johannes Zimmermann, J. B. Schlegel, J. G. Christaller, D. L. Carr, and I. P. Brown. In the meantime, the Methodist Mission had established a modest printing press at Cape Coast which the Basel Mission utilized as early as 1851. Although newspapers such as the Accra *Herald* continued to be handwritten up to 1858–1859, this difficult process was soon eliminated as evidenced in the printing of the bimonthly paper, *The Gold Coast Times*. Between 1859 and 1874 printing in Ghana produced mostly newspapers and periodicals with a few books thrown in here and there for local schools and for religious use.

There was, however, tremendous growth in the printing industry from 1907 to 1928 and between 1932 and 1940, corresponding to the growth in government business, education, and commerce. Between 1940 and 1960 many private printing presses were set up, but most of these were not used for book production. The presses that were established by religious bodies, such as the Presbyterians, the Seventh Day Adventists, and the Catholic Church, specialized in and continued to produce books and religious readers for schools.

The extraordinary expansion in education in the 1950s coincided with a new dimension in books and publishing in Ghana. First, it marked the beginning of the control of indiscriminate, mass importation of books, whether for education or any other use. Second, it initiated a new era of authorship, publishing, book production, and bookselling. Third, book content and illustration were no longer taken for granted. This period ushered in widespread reading augmented by the successes of the contemporary adult education programs.

By the 1950s the fact that most books were written in English had become a matter of valid national concern, for Ghana was a multilingual society. Accordingly, the Bureau of Ghana Languages was established in 1951, initially to provide easy reading material for new literates produced by the mass literacy campaigns of the national educational effort. The Bureau later began to publish and distribute, at reasonably low prices, books for schools and the general public in nine Ghanaian languages. This momentum has been sustained in both quantity and quality to the present day. The changeover from exogenous writing and production to endogenous authorship and manufacture of both text and trade books is an important process.

It is linked with the development of Ghanaians' bibliographic consciousness which in turn derives from their definition of cultural imperatives.

The quest for a fully integrated book industry involving conception, design, and manufacture began in earnest when the Ghana Publishing Corporation (GPC), a parastastal organization, was established in 1965. This was soon followed by the development of new, private, indigenous Ghanaian publishing houses, which have sought to realize an integrated national book industry.

Ghana today is capable of publishing both text and trade books. The eighty textbooks published for the nation's basic education program since 1974 (and which are still in use) were entirely conceived, written, and designed in the country. Organized by the Curriculum Research and Development Division of the Ghana Education Service under the aegis of the Ghana Ministry of Education, this program was partially funded by the Board of Trustees, Authorship Development Fund of the Ghana Book Development Council (GBDC). In addition to these texts for primary schools, efforts are currently being made to produce textbooks for secondary schools. The Ghana Education Service and the Ministry of Education, on one hand, and four private publishing houses in addition to the Ghana Publishing Corporation, on the other, have come together, with consultancy provided by the Ghana Book Development Council, to copublish school textbooks. Meanwhile, the private sector is active publishing popular supplementary textbooks and general books, mostly for children and young adults, many of high quality.

This current achievement is marred by two severe handicaps in the publishing chain: manufacture and distribution. The problem with book production in Ghana is not lack of technology or production know-how but the absence of a guaranteed paper supply. This makes book printing extremely difficult. The lack or inadequate supply of paper also affects print runs of new books, restricts reprints, and frustrates the enthusiastic authorship that now pervades the country. And since only a few text and trade books are available at any given time, distribution is a major problem.

Though Ghana could be said to be capable of writing, manufacturing, and distributing books to meet the national need, it does not have an integrated book industry that can cope easily with the demand. The absence of books in schools and shops is not due to the inefficiency of a national book industry, which is somewhat successful despite limited resources. The problem lies in a general characteristic of developing countries, that of not being able to ensure the full integration of a national industrial process before it is called upon to produce on a continuing basis. Nonetheless, it is encouraging that the need for books is at last being realized by national planners in Ghana who, happily, now rate the book as number six on the national priority list.

A Statistical, Quantitative, and Qualitative Picture

Though the Ghana Book Publishers Association has thirty-one members, the current number of active publishing houses is about fourteen, and eight are leaders in the industry.[1] The rest are small firms that publish a few titles each year. Of the several new publishing houses that were set up as a result of the Ghana Investment Policy Decree (1976), which indigenized, among other things, the publishing industry of Ghana, only three (Edupress, Sedco, and Adwinsa) have made a considerable impact on the country's publishing scene.[2]

Considering the present economic climate of Ghana and the insufficient supply of paper and other raw materials for book production, it should be no surprise that these publishing firms publish only a few titles each year. In 1981 Ghanaian publishers produced a total of twenty-five titles in the following subject areas: religion and social studies, two titles; politics and government, one title; economics and management, seven titles; education, one title; language (English), one title; creative literature, nine titles; and children's books, four titles. The initial print runs for these titles range from 5,000 to 12,000.[3] Publishers acknowledge that good manuscripts are not hard to come by and that occasionally they have had to turn down extremely good manuscripts for lack of paper. The extent to which book production is affected by the inadequate supply of paper and other materials is demonstrated by the following examples. The Bureau of Ghana Languages, the state publishing organization established in 1951 to publish in Ghanaian languages only, published forty-two titles in 1978 but only twelve in 1979 and ten in 1982. By the end of 1982, over thirty manuscripts were with printers, indefinitely delayed, and another lot of eighty manuscripts was waiting to be sent to press. Edupress, a private concern, was set up in 1979. In 1981 it published seven titles but had no title to show for 1982: publication dates for several books are long overdue and several other manuscripts have been held up.

The Ghana Universities Press was established in 1962 to publish scholarly works, most of which were printed in Britain. It can no longer do this because hard currency is unavailable for payment. On the other hand, capable local book manufacturers cannot help significantly because of inadequate supplies. In the last five years, 1978–1982, GUP published only three books and fifteen monographs. In 1981 and 1982 it did not publish a single book; its output for the two years was four monographs.

At the Ghana Publishing Corporation a chronic shortage of production materials delayed publication of some titles for five or more years. The Tema Press, the main book production press of the Ghana Publishing Corporation, had a backlog of over 150 manuscripts to clear by 1980. The Press therefore placed an embargo on new manuscripts from the Publishing Division. The 1980 embargo on processed new manuscripts meant that reprints of thirty-one titles, if not given to private printers, would wait indefinitely; some of these titles could have been bestsellers, guaranteeing not only break-even but outright profitability. The result was that after publishing twenty-nine titles in 1978, the Division could publish only seven in 1980, one in 1981, and three in 1982. Notwithstanding these problems the Division has published a number of splendid titles including educational, academic, general, and children's books.

These houses—Ghana Publishing Corporation, Afram, Sedco, Adwinsa, and Edupress—are known to publish uniformly high quality books, especially over the past five years. The Noma Award for Publishing in Africa has been won twice by Ghana, in 1982 and 1983. Besides this achievement, UNESCO declared Meshack Asare's *Tawia Goes to Sea,* published by Ghana Publishing Corporation, the best children's book produced in Africa in 1981.

Overall, however, the quantitative production of books in Ghana according to the Ghana Research Library on African Affairs has shown a steady decline for the past five years: 1978, 300 titles; 1979, 310 titles; 1980, 209 titles; 1981, 115 titles; and 1982, 140 titles.

Publishing Prospects

This section considers publishing in Ghana in relation to books for all levels of the formal and nonformal education system—books for general reading, children's books, scientific and technical books, translations, and copublications. Some historical background is necessary to understand Ghana's book situation in 1951 when the *Accelerated Development Plan for Education in Ghana* was published. By 1948, a form of internal self-government was in place, paving the way for full independence in 1957. During these years of ferment, new ways for genuine, political, social, intellectual, cultural, and economic independence were being explored.

The content and slant of textbooks and general books were an issue of some concern. There was considerable dissatisfaction with most books previously and contemporarily published on and for Ghana. The switchover from what had been to what was now desired could not be a one-day affair; all the textbooks were authored and manufactured by expatriate multinationals outside Ghana and distributed in Ghana through local agents. Oxford University Press, Evans Brothers, Macmillan, Longman, Cambridge University Press, and the University of London Press were the major multinational publishers.

The publishers, taking a cue from the mood of the times, took an important, far-reaching first step by commissioning African or Ghanaian authors to write textbooks, either alone, in groups, or in collaboration with non-Ghanaian coauthors. These textbooks were based entirely on new syllabi designed by the pioneer unit of the present Curriculum Development and Research Division which represented national educational goals. This was phase one of the publishing renaissance in Ghana.

Phase one worked well for a decade, and a number of books produced under it are still in use. A second phase began with the introduction of the Free Textbooks Scheme for primary and middle schools in 1963. Under this Scheme the Ghana government became solely responsible for the writing, design and illustration, production, and distribution of textbooks to the basic level of the educational system. Overseas multinationals were effectively dispensed with; some of their titles were still allowed in the system, but the books had to be manufactured in Ghana under license. In 1965, when the Ghana Publishing Corporation was established, it had the mandate "to print, publish, distribute and market books and other educational materials for schools, higher educational institutions and the public." It now became even more possible for textbooks, at least for elementary schools, to be written and published entirely in Ghana; secondary and tertiary institutions continued to depend on the older order of expatriate, local, or mixed authorship, overseas publishing, and local distribution.

However, large-scale production of seventy or more textbooks for over one and a half million children was not an easy undertaking for a developing textbook industry. The rushed circumstances under which the Scheme was announced and undertaken made some problems inevitable. The volume of work at the Ghana Publishing Corporation's printing press at Tema, the sole printer, became too great, and by the early seventies some of the titles published by the Ministry of Education had to be contracted to Far Eastern Press of Singapore for manufacture. This improved the textbook supply to the schools considerably, though several schools still are undersupplied.

Phase three was ushered in when the Ghana Investment Policy Decree was passed in 1976. Among its provisions was a ban on overseas publishing houses engaging in publishing and/or distribution in the country. These firms, though they were no longer active at the basic education level, still had a substantial hold at the secondary and tertiary levels. Their local branches were transformed into indigenous publishing houses owned and manned by Ghanaians with a good deal of expertise and experience. The Noma Award for Publishing in Africa for 1982 and 1983 was won by firms whose manpower had its genesis in these multinational book firms.

Most of the Ghanaian publishing houses established in the late sixties and particularly in the seventies were founded by individuals with publishing skills that enabled them to produce books, textbooks especially, for all levels of education and all age groups. The field of educational publishing, however, is not wide open to Ghanaian publishers. The government has a virtual monopoly on elementary textbook publishing; only the government can publish the mandatory textbooks used in the primary and middle schools. These books are distributed practically free of charge as the fee paid by each pupil under the Free Textbooks Scheme does not meet the cost of a single textbook. Consequently, the Ghanaian publisher can do a profitable business at the basic educational level only by publishing supplementary textbooks with strong terminal examination bias that appeal to the market.[4]

The multinationals still have a considerable, if not a major, hold on supplies to secondary and higher institutions. Indigenous publishers are making steady headway in these areas despite the preponderance of overseas publishers, some of whom have recently emerged from India and the U.S.S.R. The Ghanaian publisher tends to produce textbooks for which there is a reliable mass market, including the popular "aid" book to help the student pass critical examinations.[5]

General adult books have not fared as well as textbooks for three main reasons. The first is that most well-known Ghanaian writers began their careers with overseas publishers, not only to catch a worldwide readership but also to enjoy the protection and benefits such established firms could provide. Second, these overseas publishers were in fact more interested in the kind of work these authors were producing.[6] The third reason concerns profitability. Even the parastatal Ghana Publishing Corporation cannot take risks with general books whose market potential is uncertain. Firms are invariably poorly capitalized, and they have been operating in an economy that has been subject to high and unpredictable inflation and lack of foreign currency and other resources. Naturally they are wary of publishing general books even when there are lot of good manuscripts about. In these circumstances, it is encouraging that the Ghana Publishing Corporation, Waterville Publishing House, Adwinsa Publications, Sedco Publishing Limited, the Bureau of Ghana Languages, Three Brothers and Cousins Publications, and Mfantsiman Press in particular have consistently published a number of adult general books.

The area of children's books is one where Ghanaian publishers find considerable outlets for their publishing ingenuity and expertise. Also the financial rewards encourage them to expand their efforts. They are not likely to be disappointed if the Free Textbooks Scheme whets the appetites of Ghanaian elementary school children without providing supplementary readers to sustain their newly acquired literacy. The child is therefore eager to read these generally fine-quality, extracurricular books to make up for what formal education fails to provide.

By and large, the few up-and-coming publishing firms of Ghana have concentrated on publishing large print runs of textbooks, fewer books for general reading (unfortunately the very area in which new Ghanaian authors are writing most right now), and substantial quantities of children's books. Though they publish scientific and technical books, they have so far restricted publication to textbooks for secondary schools, teacher training colleges, universities, schools of nursing, and technical institutes.

The same modest production goes for translations from and into Ghanaian languages. Here the pioneering efforts of the Bureau of Ghana Languages, Waterville Publishing House, and Mfantsiman Press are noteworthy.[7] The Ghana Book Development Council is seeking to have some of the popular Ghanaian children's books translated from English to Akan, the most widely spoken language in the country. Like copublication and regional cooperation, translation remains an underdeveloped publishing area. It thus requires deliberate policies and concerted efforts to promote it.

Controversial Issues in Ghanaian Publishing

Ghana's copyright law protects the legal status of the book as an intellectual creation and of the author as owner. This act is a general legislative instrument that defines literary, musical, and artistic works, cinematography films, gramaphone records, and broadcasts as eligible for copyright.

The act provides that "a literary, musical or artistic work is not eligible for copyright unless: (a) sufficient effort has been expended on making the work to give it an original character, and (b) the work has been written down, recorded or otherwise reduced to material form, whether with or without consent." The term of copyright for an unpublished literary work ends twenty-five years after the end of the year in which the author dies. For published literary, musical, or artistic works the copyright expires at the end of the year in which the author dies or twenty-five years after the end of the year in which the work was first published, whichever is later.

This section of the act is the most controversial. While the law limits copyright to the creator's lifetime so that the fruits of authorship become universal property and easily accessible to all, there is little concern for the author, except during his or her lifetime. The publisher's investment also is not protected after this period, and the creator and popularizer suffer in favor of the consumer. Authorship in Ghana is not yet a full-time occupation, largely for financial reasons. Ideally the state would structure the copyright law to encourage the gifted and hard working to write full time, coupled with an assurance that income from their labors would sustain their families after their deaths. This would of course encourage authorship in the country and promote publishing.

As it is, part-time writing is becoming an unquestioned tradition; this legislation is obviously damaging to the prospects of writing in a developing country. The act has just been extensively reviewed and submitted to the Ghana government. It is hoped that the next legislation will settle the matter, making writing and publishing reasonably worth pursuing.

Another controversial area is the Free Textbooks Scheme, implemented in 1963, which led to a government monopoly of the large textbook market. Under the Scheme, the government provided textbooks to primary and middle schools, thus forcing the publishing industry to restrict publication at the elementary level to supplementary textbooks and general books. The market for these books is not guaranteed, because they are not yet used in the public system, although better-run private schools use them extensively. In essence, the government monopolized the lifeblood of the private sector.

The Scheme is expensive and the government can afford to provide only one textbook per subject. This, no doubt, may be justifiable in terms of national budgeting but is certainly educationally indefensible. Pupils are not allowed to take textbooks home since there is a concern for the longevity of the books; therefore, they have no books for homework. More seriously in terms of publishing, it forces curriculum researchers and developers, not to mention teachers, who are not trained as publishers, to combine the two professions to the detriment of both.

It is now felt that the state should team up with genuine publishers (the parastatal Ghana Publishing Corporation and four private firms) to copublish the textbooks. If this works, publishing of elementary texts should revert to the professional book industry, and this will surely stimulate both publishing and sales, because extra print runs could then be sold outside the Scheme. Extra copies sold on the open market would help ease public anxiety since a reliable supply of textbooks is what the Scheme should be about in the first place. It is important, though, to note that when the Scheme was launched the intention was not to monopolize textbook publishing in the country. The government wanted to ensure that it could successfully operate the Scheme without relying on the private sector, over which it did not have full control.

The role of the Ghana Publishing Corporation has actually been more catalytic than monopolistic. Undoubtedly, its very organization and size could easily lead to the impression that private book publishing, printing, and selling would have no place in the country. In practice, however, its achievements and operations have spurred the private sector to better performance. The real issue is that for ten years or so, textbooks for the Free Textbooks Scheme have been manufactured outside the country in spite of the substantial state and private investments into the book industry of the country.

A switchover of textbook production from international publishers to indigenous publishers amounts not only to transfer of skills and technology but indeed of very real wealth. When a large proportion of a multinational publisher's income derives from overseas distribution, it does not easily accept curtailment. When Ghana or any other African country takes over parts of the textbook industry as a prelude to the subsequent takeover of other levels, it should be on the lookout for the enticing offers of assistance made by previous multinational suppliers. Such offers delay industrial integration and could be very risky to the steady development of an integrated, viable, national publishing industry.

Further, they raise the specter of monopoly of the publishing market by the African government and a single private overseas firm at the expense of all other overseas firms, and, worst of all, local, state, and private publishing firms. International cooperation and aid need not be a means of keeping developing countries permanently developing. Nor should it be used to impede the free flow of information, knowledge, and culture to the Third World.

Problems Facing Ghana's Book Industry
Economics

The economics of the Ghana publishing industry cannot be divorced from the general economic condition of the country, although there are considerations peculiar to the industry. Almost all Ghanaian publishing firms started with low levels of capitalization, including the parastatal Ghana Publishing Corporation. The initial capital covers only 5 to 10 percent of the operating cost per year. For the past five years the bank rate has been exceptionally high, between 15 and 18 percent, and this makes the financing decision for some titles, especially those with an uncertain profitability, a difficult one.

Unfortunately the government has a monopoly on elementary textbook publishing, for this could easily have been the financial mainstay of the local publishing industry. The reasons for and against this practice are complex and include issues of political doctrine, educational policy, who can best supervise and ensure delivery of books and stationery to primary schools, and what the state's role should be in providing free books. These are important issues, but they jeopardize the economics of the publishing industry which are circumscribed by a lack of adequate capital and a restricted textbook market.

The selling prices and pricing policies for books are subjects for concern. The Ghana Book Development Council, the Ghana Book Publishers Association, the Ghana Booksellers Association, and the Ghana Printers and Paper Converters Association have all been concerned in recent years with the problem of inflation and the consequent reckless retail pricing. Though book prices are subject to approval by the Prices and Incomes Board, this does not mean that the average wage earner can afford a book currently produced in Ghana. The tax on imported books and raw materials for local book production is so high, roughly 900 percent, that the retail price is prohibitive (particularly since April 1, 1983). No doubt, this situation cannot continue indefinitely.

Language

Of the estimated 1,200 languages and dialects in Africa, some fifty-four are spoken in Ghana. A few of these such as Twi, Ga, and Ewe have been reduced into writing, and there are now nine officially recognized written languages: Akan, Dagaare, Dagbani, Dangme, Ewe, Ga, Gonja, Kasem, and Nzema. These are the languages studied at the specialized languages teaching institution for teachers, the School of Ghana Languages, Ajumako, and in other educational institutions. The Bureau of Ghana Languages has been producing its books in these languages.

In addition, there are a few more written languages, especially in the north of the country, and more are being created. On the other hand, there will always be several Ghana languages such as Ahantan that, for a variety of reasons, will be insignificant, bibliographically at least. They are spoken by only a few people, and market forces would not permit profitable publishing in them. The average Ghanaian now has to learn the mother tongue, possibly the language of the area where he or she resides, English, the national official language, and French, if possible, for better African solidarity and international employment opportunities. Ghana clearly has a national language problem which affects book production and reading. It is likely that Akan, which now dominates the scene, will emerge as the national language and this could be turned to good account.

In publishing, profitability, which in turn depends on potential market size, is a crucial factor in determining whether or not to publish, and this is why the ordinary Ghanaian publishing firm has not published much in the local languages. In terms of population and the national literacy rate of 40 to 50 percent, only Akan, Ewe, and possibly Ga or Dangme could sustain print runs of up to 75,000 copies over a five-year period for a bestseller in Ghana. An author tends to write in the language in which he or she is most proficient. The Ghanaian author has to choose carefully between the community language and the official foreign language because very few write equally successfully in both. The language factor further hinders publishing in Ghana if the author is not proficient or literate in the language chosen. Many good writers make an effort to contribute to the bibliographic development of their community languages.

The Accelerated Development Program for Education in 1951, which led to mass enrollments in schools, also resulted in the withdrawal of religious bodies, who had paid considerable attention to Ghanaian languages, from direct management of schools. The state hastily established several new teacher training colleges to meet its educational needs, but the inability of these emergency colleges to ground teachers well in the learning and teaching of Ghana languages created unintended but disastrous consequences: Few Ghanaians under thirty are able to read and write tolerably in their own mother tongue, even though good textbooks and literature may be easily available today. On the other hand, the quality of English language teaching has so deteriorated over the years that there would have been linguistic catastrophe, had it not been for efforts in language teaching in secondary and tertiary institutions.

There is, consequently, a large, talented, and young generation of Ghanaians who, if the quality of their short stories, novels, plays, and poetry is any indicator, are unable to produce reasonably acceptable manuscripts because of poor literacy attainment in both their mother tongue and in English. Moreover, consciousness of this handicap by the individual discourages writing and inhibits authorship in Ghana.

Since one out of every two Ghanaians can read in a population currently estimated at 12 million, market size is not an immediate problem. A greater problem is that few Ghanaian publishers really know what the average Ghanaian wants to read. As S. I. A. Kotei and P. A. Twumasi have stated: "Every period has its own mentality and this tendency means that in a particular historical point in time people tend to want to read certain books and other reading material. In Ghana today the wish is to read books which can portray the present way of life. Specifically people want Ghanaian authors who can write about our society, its transitional phase, its institutions and the prospects we have for the future."[8] The list of publishing problems in Ghana would shorten if and when publishers confront this wish squarely.

Ghana Publishing and Regional and International Developments

Ghana's publishing industry has been relating to regional and international developments in three main ways: attendance at regional and international book fairs; book exports and offers of translation and reprint license or rights; and the Ghana Book Development Council's role through its promotional programs.

The Ghana Book Publishers Association has joined the Ghana Book Development Council in renting a booth for the exhibition of books published in Ghana at international book fairs. This does not prevent publishers from exhibiting individually, but it does save money; publishers are exhibited at Frankfurt, Bologna, Moscow, New Delhi, and, above all, Ife in Nigeria. At these international and regional fairs Ghana participates in seminars and symposia, shares ideas, and exchanges views with the international book world.

Books that are popular in Ghana tend to be liked in Anglophone West Africa. These are usually text and children's books, areas where Ghanaian publishers are doing a good job. The current effort is to get such titles into the book trade of these regional countries on ordinary trade or special terms.

Additionally, the Ghana Book Development Council has been working closely with the Centre for Book Promotion in Africa South of the Sahara (CREPLA) through attendance at its consultative meetings, seminars, and congresses. At the moment a regional copublishing venture is being discussed by the Centre, and Ghana is keen for this to succeed for there is more that unites Africa culturally and intellectually than divides it.

Notes

1. The fourteen active publishers are: Ghana Publishing Corporation (Publishing Division), Afram Publications (Ghana) Limited, Educational Press (Edupress), Waterville Publishing House, Adwinsa Publications, Ghana Universities Press, Bureau of Ghana Languages, Three Brothers and Cousins Publications, Asempa Publishers, Mfantsiman Press, African Christian Press, Curriculum Research and Development Division, Ghana Education Service, and Illen Publications.
2. These three, plus the Bureau of Ghana Languages, the Ghana Publishing Corporation, Ghana Universities Press, Waterville, and Afram Publications, all established earlier, constitute the eight leading publishing houses of the country.
3. In Ghana official statistics on book production are listed in the bibliography compiled by the Research Library on African Affairs (RLAA) of the Ghana Library Board. The Library Board has been compiling statistics since 1968. The *Ghana Current Bibliography* is published bimonthly and then cumulated into the *Ghana National Bibliography* which lists all books, pamphlets, and so on deposited at the Research Library by publishers.
4. The following are a random sample: I. D. Mensah, *Objective Exercises in Geography* (Accra: Ghana Publishing Corporation, 1976), Frank W. Mason, *Junior Aptitude Tests and Exercises: Verbal and Quantative* (Accra: Sedco, 1977), G. A. Manful, et al., *Afram Mathematical Handbook for Junior Schools* (Accra: Afram, 1976).
5. Examples are Margaret Kwakwa, *A Handbook for French Studies* (Accra: Ghana Publishing Corporation, 1975), E. O. Amah, *Exercises in Biology* (Accra: Ghana Publishing Corporation, 1975), and N. A. Essilfie, *Teaching Practice Tips* (Accra: Afram, 1976).
6. Exceptions are Hans W. Debruner, *A History of Christianity in Ghana* (Accra: Waterville Publishing Company, 1967), P. A. Twumasi, *Medical Systems in Ghana: A Study in Medical Sociology* (Accra: Ghana Publishing Corporation, 1975), and Mike Oquaye, *Politics in Ghana* (Accra: Tornado Publications, 1980).
7. Examples are Waterville's Akan translations of Plato's *Apology of Socrates* and Sophocles' *Antigone* both by L. H. Afosu-Appiah, 1979, published by the Bureau of Ghanaian Languages, the Nzema translation of Shakespeare's *Julius Caesar* by A. R. Blay-Morkeh, 1970, and the Ewe translation of Moliere's *Tartufe* by F. K. Adinyira.
8. S. I. A. Kotei and P. A. Twumasi, *Research Report for the Ghana Book Development Council on Reading Habits of Ghanaians* (February 1979), chap. 7.

7. Publishing in Kenya

Fred Ojienda Okwanya

Historical Overview

In 1925, a meeting of experts in Dar es Salaam, Tanganyika (now Tanzania), set the stage for establishing two important organs for publishing in eastern Africa, the Inter-Territorial Language Committee and the Central Publishing Committee.[1] Publishing in eastern Africa and in Kenya in particular has since undergone many changes. About eight years after the meeting, the East African Literature Bureau was established to serve as a central publishing committee; today the bureau is known as the Kenya Literature Bureau. At about the same time some notable British publishing firms started limited operations in eastern Africa.

In 1965, forty years after the meeting of experts, the East African Publishing House, the first indigenous publisher in the region, was established in Kenya under the auspices of the East African Institute of Social and Cultural Affairs. By this time Kenya had nine publishing houses, most of which were foreign owned with their professional and technical operations based outside Kenya. This meant that the bulk of publishing work done by these companies was carried out overseas, except for the actual printing. Even the printing was, more frequently than not, assigned to foreign printing houses established in Kenya. The Institute, a nonpolitical, nonprofit institution devoid of ideological orientation, had the specific objective of stimulating a cohesive cultural growth within eastern African. It was meant to embrace people of different intellectual, social, cultural, and political backgrounds and to enrich, synthesize, and enunciate their ideas of the different facets of life in eastern Africa. At the time of its founding, the people of the region were moving toward a way of life suited to their needs and aspirations. The Institute's main strategy in promoting cultural growth and cooperation was to encourage the concept of eastern Africa as a homogeneous society in which the interests and welfare of all its inhabitants were linked. Establishing the *East Africa Journal,* an academic journal for publicizing the views of East Africans on a wide range of social, cultural, and educational aspects of life in the region, was one of the Institute's earliest milestones. This journal ceased publication in 1973.

The new East African Publishing House emphasized the publication of educational materials because formal education was viewed as the greatest single factor in promoting learning and in providing the much-needed trained manpower for development. The success of education depended on the availability of books which hitherto had been supplied by foreign colonial firms. It was hoped that the publishing house would relieve the East African states from dependence on the foreign firms for textbooks. Another goal was to develop new (indigenous) authors who would write books tailored to the needs of the East African society. Its initial publishing program included plans for textbooks for primary and secondary schools, teachers' reference books, books for teacher training colleges, and books for university education, while supplementary readers and adult education books would be published during the second stage.[2]

Prior to independence, the only locally owned publishing house was the East African Literature Bureau, under the auspices of the East African High Commission. Headed by expatriates, the bureau employed a few Africans who were trained in publishing on a rudimentary level. These local personnel augmented the work of the Bureau as a clearing house for expatriate and foreign publishing houses in eastern Africa. Through the Bureau foreign authors and publishers learned which subjects were "appropriate" before colonial staff and interested expatriates began producing books. This role of the Bureau ended in the late 1950s as Kenya moved toward independence.

Education and Publishing

Kenya became independent in 1963 after almost eighty years of British colonial rule. A year later it became a republic and remained a member of the Commonwealth. The current population is estimated at 16 million, having increased by 40 percent between 1969 and 1979. The dramatic population increase compounds the problem of dependence—nearly 60 percent of the population is under twenty years of age and, due to universal free primary education, a large number of these youngsters require schooling facilities. The country's development plans have sought to give practical and appropriate application to Kenya's educational objectives which see education as being "much more of economic than social service . . . the principal means for relieving the shortage of domestic skilled manpower and equalizing economic opportunities among all citizens."

An independent Kenya inherited well-established printing houses, the most notable among the foreign ones being: Printing and Packaging Corporation Ltd. (formerly East African Standard); Kenya Litho Ltd. (formerly W. Boyd); English Press

Ltd.; and the (now defunct) International Aeradio printing department. The outstanding locally owned printing houses were: The Government Press; Central Printing Press; General Printers Ltd.; Afropress Ltd. (formerly the East African Institute
Press); and Colourprint Ltd. (formerly Colonial Times), all of which had operations
in Nairobi. These printing houses played a key role in training some of the personnel
who operate the printing and to some extent publishing services in Kenya today.

Publishing in Kenya gained considerable strength during the late sixties, and the
Kenyan Publishers' Association was formed in 1970. The fifteen founding members
agreed that the main objectives of the association were to further book publishing
in Kenya. This meant that an interdisciplinary approach to regional book promotion
was needed. Toward that objective, the association founded a regional prize award
in 1973, known as the Kenyatta Prize for Literature. Five publishers each contributed approximately 1000.00 Kenya shillings toward the prize fund, while the Kenya
Publishers' Association, as an organization, donated a further 5000.00 Kenya shillings.

The Kenyan Publishers' Association joined with other members of the Kenyan
book community to put on a book exhibition in 1971 which was followed by
another in 1976. The 1976 Book Exhibition was organized by a member of the
Kenya Booksellers Association, the Text Book Centre, which staged a paperback
exhibition in Nairobi, Mombasa, and Kisumu.[3]

Between 1973 and 1976, Kenya experienced promising growth in publishing with
the establishment of ten new indigenous publishing houses. These were: Pan African
Researchers, Ltd.; Comb Books; TransAfrica Publishers, Ltd.; Bookwise, Ltd.;
Shungwaya Publishers, Ltd.; Gazelle Books; Uzima Press, Ltd.; Evangel Publishing
House; Gakara Press; and Foundation Books, Ltd. These houses produced approximately 100 new titles in different fields and brought about dramatic changes within
Kenya's publishing structure which previously had consisted of twenty British publishing companies operating through eight representatives based in Nairobi. (The
number of British publishers represented later increased to sixty-two.) The British
publishing branches, with a stronger economic base and more experienced personnel,
were better prepared than the newly established houses and consequently the foreign
and indigenous publishing houses, instead of complementing each other, developed
a disadvantageous rivalry.

In Kenya there are two important book markets which a publisher has to satisfy
if he is to remain viable. The first is the educational market at both primary and
secondary levels. The second one is the negligible university-level market; Kenyan
publishers account for almost zero percent of this book market. A Kenyan book
publisher who wants to succeed must concentrate on the educational market at the
primary and secondary levels.

Kenyan publishers should be encouraged to play a positive role in producing
textbooks and educational materials, thus enabling them to acquire the requisite
financial base for promoting growth within the industry and ultimately reading
materials for all levels of the populace. Indigenous publishers in Third World countries cannot be expected to operate outside the educational system because of the
limited number of universities and library services in such countries. The scarcity of
libraries in Kenya has made it rather difficult for indigenous publishers to develop.

The Kenya Institute of Education chooses educational books and materials to be
used in schools and makes recommendations to the Kenya School Equipment Scheme

(KSES) in the Ministry of Basic Education. The KSES is charged with purchasing all supplies; it processes orders from school headmasters who make their choices from the list of recommended books.

Surveys of book purchases by two major urban districts of Mombasa and Nairobi in 1973 and 1982, respectively, provide useful insights. Of the 40,077 titles purchased by the Mombasa City Council in 1973, the overwhelming majority came from non-Kenyan publishing concerns.[4] Table 7.1 shows how British publishing houses in particular dominated Kenyan publishers. Of the 40,077 titles only 242 were authored by Africans. Of the approximately 95 titles authored by East Africans, (i.e., Ugandans, Tanzanians, and Kenyans), 5 titles were translated works from outside East Africa. Six titles were from southern Africa; 110 titles were from East Africa; and 31 titles were from the rest of Africa, of which 5 titles were translated major works from outside Africa. Of the 242 African-authored titles, 80 were in Kiswahili language, 22 were in vernacular languages of Kenya, and 140 were in English. Seventy-six of the titles were printed and published in Kenya, while the rest were printed and published outside Kenya. These statistics indicate the scope of publishing activities in Kenya.

Of the 52,043 purchases by Nairobi City Council in 1982, British publishers accounted for 48,871, Kenyan publishers and bookshops for 2,901, and church organizations for 265.

A survey of the 52,043 titles with regard to their authorship is similar to that of Mombasa City Council, except for the language position. In the case of Nairobi City Council the Kiswahili language accounted for 28 titles while the rest of the publications were in English. One hundred and twenty titles were printed and published in Kenya, while 572 were published outside Kenya.[5]

From table 7.2, it is important to note that books from British publishers accounted for 64.4 percent of the total government purchases through the Ministry of Basic Education, while Kenya's own publishing houses supplied 1,511,000 copies, or 31.8 percent of the total. Church-owned publishing houses and their organizations supplied 266,660 copies (5.6 percent), and privately owned Kenya publishers supplied only 5,000 copies, accounting for 0.1 percent of the sales. Most of the titles included in these statistics are not new; in fact, approximately 98 percent are reprints, with limited appropriate revisions, of works dating as far back as ten to thirty years.[6]

Table 7.1. Mombasa Primary Textbook Sales, 1973.

Publisher	Number of Titles
British Publishers	30,876
Kenyan Publishers	5,080
Kenyan Bookshops	591
Church Organizations	181
UNESCO	16
Others*	3,333
Total	40,077

* Includes institutions or individuals.

Table 7.2. Titles Supplied to KSES.

Publisher	Quantity
LOCAL	
Jomo Kenyatta Foundation	
(Kenya Government)	1,192,000
East African Publishing House	234,200
Evangel Publishing House	137,000
African Inland Church	89,500
Kenya Literature Bureau	
(Kenya Government)	77,800
Bible Society of Kenya	5,000
TransAfrica Book Distributors	5,000
UNESCO	1,000
Kenya News	
(Kenya Government)	5,000
Government Printers, Kenya	5,000
Total	1,747,500
FOREIGN	
Longman Kenya	1,414,000
Oxford University Press	1,186,000
Macmillan	112,000
Thomas Nelson & Sons	72,000
A. & C. Black	40,000
Evans Brothers	36,000
Collins	24,000
Allen & Unwin	21,000
Hodder & Straughton	16,000
Heinemann Educational Books	12,000
Hulton	6,000
Cambridge University Press	5,000
Edward Arnold	5,000
I.F.B.	4,000
Macdougal	3,000
G. Bell	1,000
Total	2,957,000

Problems in Kenya's Publishing Industry

Language

Kenya has at least forty-one languages, more than half of which have established orthographies. This was made possible by European missionaries during the last century. The large number of phonetical formulas currently in use in Kenya are based on what nationality first arrived at a particular geographical area of Kenya (or East Africa as the case may be). If the first missionary was Dutch, German, Danish, or British, that mother tongue formed the functional orthographical and typographical order for the area's native language.

As a local vernacular as the medium of instruction could not succeed beyond the primary school level, the obvious answer was to adopt a lingua franca. The Kiswahili language of some of Kenya's and Tanzania's coastal ethnic communities was chosen. Its proclamation as Kenya's national language in 1977 reflects the fact that over 85 percent of Kenya's population speaks the language, while only 15 percent of the population speaks English (Kenya's official language). Kiswahili is also the lingua franca of eastern and central Africa.

Technologically, the Kiswahili language poses difficulties for publishers and has not been accorded its rightful place in the national publishing programs in Kenya. It has not yet been possible for the publishing industry to formulate and standardize typographical and orthographical policy. Thus the publisher and printer of Kiswahili, or vernacular, books is confronted with a multiplicity of typefaces to suit the numerous phonetic and orthographic formulas. Local authorship in Kiswahili is accordingly stifled. Another problem is that any book published in the Kiswahili language (regardless of subject matter) is classified under "Kiswahili books" in the UDC classification system. As a result important reference material is omitted from the UDC "science books" section.

The limited number of Kenyans literate in languages other than English and Kiswahili makes it impossible to think of publishing in Kenya's other languages. The declaration of a "war on illiteracy" by Kenya's president with the target of eradicating illiteracy by 1984 prompted the Department of Adult Education to form a committee to study how books could be produced in these languages. The committee found that many books could be authored for new literates and that quite a number of the vernacular languages had sublanguages within them. For example, the Embu people of eastern Kenya, who had used Gikuyu as their medium of instruction, opted to revert to their own sublanguage for which they had to create a new orthography. The Embu people have since written at least six primary textbooks and two primers which are being used by adults.

The multiplicity of language groups, limited national publishing resources, and lack of skilled manpower in publishing will remain problems in Kenya in the near future. Even Kiswahili editors will be difficult to find for some time to come.

The medium of instruction in Kenya is still English. This is temporarily serving its purpose; however, in the long run there is the danger of creating a stereotyped authorship in a society whose culture will not be linked with its desired goals and aspirations. Kenya's situation cannot be compared with that of West African countries as Kenya is culturally disadvantaged in many respects. Kenya does not, as yet, have a well-defined language policy (a situation which must be tolerated in the short run). The scarcity of locally oriented scholars makes the situation more difficult, and this can be seen in all the cultural components of book production in Kenya.

Size of book market

By 1980 Kenya's literacy rate was 75 percent, which is a very reasonable position in Africa. Although its educational standards are not low compared to other developing countries, the postliteracy and postschool reading habit in Kenya is stagnant: the sale of several hundred copies of a Kiswahili title (apart from school textbooks) is a rare occurrence. A survey was conducted in the Nairobi area to determine who reads what in Kenya.[7] Twelve agencies were selected for case studies aimed at determining the accessibility of their materials to readers. They included government ministries dealing with adult education, church organizations, and publishers. The materials used had been produced and read by new literates to test their level, accessibility, and relevance. The thirty persons selected for this survey were exposed to various materials produced by different publishers and tested on their ability to read. The survey books were written in English and Kiswahili. Of the twelve publishers 76 percent published in both English and Kiswahili and 24 percent published in Kiswahili and vernacular. The percent of reading population for areas of reading matter is shown in table 7.3.

Two titles were selected to determine the readers' topical preferences. The same thirty persons were asked to read these two books: 30 percent read with very low comprehension, 5 percent could read only isolated words; and 65 percent could not read at all. This suggested that the market for books in this context was very limited. The results appear in table 7.4. Of the thirty people interviewed, 50 percent were subordinate workers employed by various local organizations; 20 percent were domestic servants; and 30 percent were factory workers. As table 7.4 indicates, people reading books to improve proficiency in English and Kiswahili had the highest scores. All the respondents said their jobs demanded that they speak and read these languages to some extent.

Are published works readily available to this community? Of the thirty people interviewed, 89.3 percent owned no books nor did they know where to find books and 10.7 percent had access only to some primary school texts. They all expressed their concern about the availability of books. It was impossible to determine whether a market for books exists. This study was conducted in an urban area where communication facilities are abundant and thus raises questions about the availability of books in rural areas and the market position countrywide.

Table 7.3. Spread of Reading Materials.

Subject Area	Number of Publishers	Percentage of Readers
Family Life Education	4	25%
Religious Education	3	18
Skill Improvement	3	18.7
Entertainment Reading	3	18.7
Civil Education	1	6.4
Reading Skill Improvement	2	12.5

Table 7.4. Reading Preference of Literate Persons.

Topics	Score out of 30	Percentage
English/Kiswahili	20	60%
Nutrition	13	36
Child Care	6	20
Number Work	25	82
Agriculture	2	7

Relationships with Regional and International Publishers

Indigenous Kenyan publishers have participated in some of the major book exhibitions outside Kenya. For example, they have continuously exhibited at the Frankfurt Book Fair, at the Delhi World Book Fair, and at book fairs in other African capitals.

In 1972, International Book Year, Kenya hosted a UNESCO regional seminar to follow up the African Publishing Experts' meeting in Accra, Ghana, in 1968. The Accra meeting recommended, among other things, that training in the book industry in Africa be encouraged to develop the African publishing industry significantly by 1980. The Accra meeting noted that lack of trained personnel prevented the continent from acquiring her rightful position in book publishing. Increasing the number of books of all types in African libraries in proportion to general supply from a one-to-four ratio in 1968 to a one-to-ten ratio by 1980 was suggested as a goal. However, by 1972 the level of books available in Africa was estimated at 24 pages per person, a figure far below expectations although it was a slight improvement over the 1968 census figure of 19.2 pages per person for educational purposes. Progress between 1968 and 1972 was negligible and very discouraging. By 1980 Africa had increased her book production to 120 pages per person, while her population for the same period was projected to increase by 12.2 percent.

As a member of the United Nations, Kenya has continuously contributed to agencies such as UNESCO for the growth of the book industry in Africa. Kenya's publishers are also proud that Kenya is a signatory to the Conventions and Agreements of a Normative Character adopted either by the General Conferences or by Intergovernmental Conferences convened solely by UNESCO or jointly with other international organizations. Kenya has a well-established National Commission for UNESCO, with approximately fifty member commissioners working through six major committees in which the book industry is well represented.[8] The commission chairman is the minister responsible for higher education in Kenya. The Communication and Culture Committee of the commission has in the past seriously considered the issue of regional cooperation in terms of publishing, recognizing and articulating the fact that indigenous African publishers must be encouraged. From this background of promoting African publishers Kenya welcomed the formation of the Regional Centre for Book Promotion in Africa South of the Sahara (CREPLA), one of whose principal aims is to encourage publishing relevant materials at a price affordable by the majority of the disadvantaged African children in Kenya and Africa south of the Sahara.[9]

In 1980 CREPLA, in conjunction with the Kenya National Commission for UNESCO, held a seminar in Nairobi sponsored by UNESCO on book distribution in eastern, central, and southern Africa. The underlying principles of CREPLA are based on the need to integrate book development into national development plans so as to increase public participation in the development. Books are a means of gaining access to fundamental human rights, in particular, the right to education, to a cultural life, and to communication.

Indigenous African publishers compete with the multinational giants in contracting authors as well as in promotion and distribution. This has meant that publishers with limited resources inevitably find their books have lower sales; hence, the collapse of indigenous publishing houses in the region. The challenge of promoting the small African publisher in part led Kenya to associate itself with the formation of CREPLA. Another CREPLA goal that Kenya supports is the copublication of works by African authors for distribution across Africa south of the Sahara.

Notes

1. Chiraghdin Shihabudin and Mathias Mnyampala, *Historicaya Kiswahili* (Nairobi: Oxford University Press, 1977), p. 58.
2. B. A. Ogot, "A Meeting Place for East Africans," *East Africa Journal* 1, no. 10, pp. 32–33.
3. Text Book Centre, "Bookfare Catalogue," 1976.
4. *Municipality of Mombasa, School Equipment Tender for the Year 1973* (Mombasa: Education Department, 1973).
5. Nairobi City Council, "Contract E/S/82: Text Books Educational Supply, 1982" (Nairobi: City Education Department, 1982).
6. Ministry of Education.
7. J. Wathika, "Action Research Workshop" (Unpublished paper, Institute of Advanced Studies, University of Nairobi, February 22, 1980).
8. Kenya National Commission for UNESCO, Minutes of October 1982.
9. The regional Centre for Book Promotion in Africa (CREPLA) was established in 1975 in Yaounde, Cameroon. It is an inter-African cooperation organization whose primary aims are book development and promotion. CREPLA itself does not publish books. It encourages and coordinates efforts of member states in book promotion. In 1978 the Centre became a regional (an African) center following the first conference of ministers responsible for book development. These are usually the ministers for education or ministers for culture in their respective countries. Kenya has been actively involved in CREPLA since the Accra UNESCO-sponsored consultative meeting in 1968 and the first Conference of Ministers of CREPLA in the same year.

8. The Book Publishing Industry in Egypt

Nadia A. Rizk
John Rodenbeck

Historical Overview

The earliest form of the book—in the sense of an easily portable collection of written documents—originated in the Egypt of the Pharaohs. To record writing on some more convenient material than stone or clay, the ancient Egyptians developed papyrus, a paperlike material processed from the stalk of *Cyperus papyrus*. This giant water plant once grew abundantly along the banks of the Nile, later became virtually extinct, and now occurs naturally only in Wadi Natrun. Papyrus was produced in rolls six or seven inches wide; writing was divided into columns of the same height and could thus be revealed, column by column, simply by unwinding the roll. Natural conditions gave Egypt a monopoly over this material. Its abundance was undoubtedly the basis of the intellectual activity that centered around the great libraries of the Ptolemies: the "Mother" Library of 500,000 papyrus rolls, with a catalog occupying 120 (burnt by the Romans during Caesar's invasion), and the "Daughter" Library in the Temple of Serapis (which remained a center for study until the temple itself was wrecked and the leaders of the pagan philosophical schools were expelled by Christian authorities in the last decade of the fourth century A.D.).

The use of papyrus outlasted the classical world and when it was replaced in Egypt, it was replaced not by vellum or parchment but by paper. Paper was introduced at least as early as the opening years of the ninth century; it probably came from

Samarkand, where Chinese papermakers captured in battle in 751 had set up paper mills. By the end of the ninth century paper had become more fashionable than papyrus, though still perhaps not as cheap. By the eleventh century it was so plentifully produced in Egypt that it was used for wrapping vegetables and spices; and it is thus most likely that the earliest extant European paper document, a deed of Roger of Sicily (1109) in Arabic and Latin, was written on Egyptian paper.

The adoption and manufacture of paper was accompanied by another development so extraordinary that until recently it has been either ignored or disbelieved by modern historians—the introduction of printing. Unlike paper making, the techniques of printing were probably brought to Egypt directly, by way of sea trade with T'ang China, rather than over the Great Silk Road; for this reason printing in Egypt antedates by at least two centuries any similar development elsewhere in the Arab world.

Printed papers found in Egypt were ascribed to the tenth, eleventh, and twelfth centuries on epigraphical evidence more than sixty years ago; this dating has recently been confirmed by archaeological evidence, which has linked them conclusively with the reign of the Fatimids. The Fatimids were a Shi'i dynasty that ruled Egypt, then a half-Christian, half-Sunni-Muslim country, from 969 until 1171, when they were deposed by Saladin, the champion of Sunni Islam. Basing their claim to sovereignty upon descent from the Prophet through his daughter Fatima, they acquired Egypt by force of arms but sought to consolidate and extend their rule by intellectual persuasion. The block printing of the Chinese, which allowed the publication of documents in multiple, identical copies served their purposes admirably, and it involved techniques that were in large part already familiar. The 100,000 volumes recorded as comprising the private library of the eleventh-century Fatimid Caliph Mustansir may possibly have contained printed books.

The Fatimids thus have claim to being the first modern publishers in the Middle East and among the first in the world. Examples of their block-printed texts may be found in several collections—most notably the Erzherzog Rainer Collection in Vienna, where the identification was first made—but in many cases have been ascribed to later dates, on vague grounds that the appropriate technology must have been introduced from the West. These misattributions have been encouraged not only by the fact that scholarship has taken more than sixty years to catch up with itself, but also by the fact that, after the Fatimids, printing on paper—though not apparently on cloth—simply disappeared from Egypt for several centuries. This interesting development may be due to a variety or a combination of political, religious, and cultural causes—Saladin made strenuous efforts to obliterate all trace of a dynasty widely regarded as heretical—and will undoubtedly be in itself the object of much further study.[1]

It is therefore true that Egypt's modern book industry did not begin until after 1798 and that it began as a by-product and aftereffect of Bonaparte's invasion in that year, which in many respects was a curious repetition of the invasion of the Fatimids. Believing that the way to the heart of the population, of which by now a large majority were Sunni Muslim, lay through their religion, Bonaparte set out to establish a puppet theocracy. A first step was to use a program of publication aimed primarily at the Muslim elite to identify the principles of the French Revolution with Islam. To carry out this portion of the project, he imported two presses and fonts for printing in both French and Arabic.

Two years later the expedition had failed and the French withdrew, taking their presses with them. Their brief presence had already made an impact, however. When Mohamed Ali Pasha, the Albanian soldier of fortune whose dynasty was to rule Egypt until 1952, subsequently established himself as undisputed head of state, he turned his attention to organizing Egypt along modern industrial lines. Of primary importance was the creation of a regular army, which needed administration and instruction. From this necessity arose the need for printed materials. By 1821 Mohamed Ali had sent a trainee in printing to Milan and imported a press, which he installed at Bulaq, Cairo's Nile port of entry, then in the process of being transformed into a commercial-industrial center.[2]

While the primary purpose of the Bulaq press was to provide translated and original materials for the use of the government, particularly the army, its secondary purposes included training printers and printing publications for private entrepreneurs. Though government-centered, the Bulaq press produced two kinds of publications: (1) government-sponsored printing, consisting mostly of Mohamed Ali's instructions for the army, textbooks for the use of his various new educational foundations, and translations for official use; and (2) literary and religious publications, produced mainly for merchants in the book market associated with Al Azhar University, the tenth-century foundation that has remained a major intellectual center for the Muslim world. From this production of materials for the private-sector market Egypt's modern publishing industry has emerged.

Mohamed Ali had looked to presses and their publications as major instruments of government and therefore extended governmental printing and publishing activity to Alexandria and the provinces. Under his immediate successors, however, his ambitious program for modernizing Egypt began to decline, thanks in part to increasing pressure from the Great Powers, who had already curbed his efforts to redraw the map of the Ottoman Empire and who were increasingly attracted by the very success of his reforms to interfere in Egypt's internal affairs. After his death in 1848, the educational institutions he had founded as the core of his program either faltered or closed, and industries that had depended, either directly or indirectly, upon successful military mobilization entered a period of recession. By the time of the accession of his grandson Ismail in 1863, the original staff of the Bulaq press had been reduced from 169 to 60.[3]

A large part of the work of Mohamed Ali had already been accomplished, however, as is demonstrated by the remarkable resurgence under Ismail (1863–1879). Both a corps of trained printers and a market of readers had been created, sufficient to justify offsetting the decline in governmental activity by the foundation of a number of private presses. Expanding on a pattern already established under Mohamed Ali and still prevalent in the Arab world, bookshops became publishers, while the government's share in printing and publishing continued to diminish. Due to the relative relaxation of censorship in Ismail's Egypt, several privately printed newspapers appeared: *Wadi el-Nil* (1867), *Al-Ahram* (1875), *Al-Tijara* (1878), *Mir'at al-Sharq* (1879), and *Misr* (1880), followed by *Al-Muqtataf* (1883) and many others, a significant number being founded by Syrian Christians who were to create publishing empires.

In 1881 Egypt was occupied by the British, who remained, exercising various degrees of overt and covert mastery, until 1956. Like Bonaparte and the Fatimids, they understood the political uses of technology: they brought larger printing presses with them and quietly subsidized several newspapers. Among the sizable foreign linguistic communities then resident in Egypt—Italian, Greek, Turkish, Persian, and Armenian, as well as British and French—special interests had meanwhile arisen in addition to those of the Arabic market.

During World War I Britain deposed the reigning Khedive, declaring Prince Hussein Kamel "Sultan" and Egypt a "Protectorate." This action severed the 400-year-old link with the Ottoman Empire. By the end of the war, three major new types of publishers had emerged: (1) private establishments motivated solely by the lure of profit, publishers of fast-turn-over books of dubious quality for an increasing mass market interested chiefly in religion and pulp fiction; (2) large-scale enterprises, publishing empires originally attached to newspapers, which now not only published books, but sometimes offered commercial printing as well; and (3) private intellectuals, such as those who comprised the Committee for Writing, Translating, and Publishing, who paralleled in their aims some of the scholarly presses of the West by undertaking publishing on a nonprofit basis to supplement what they felt to be the low cultural level of more commercial offerings.

Many booksellers continued to publish, as they do to this day, and the government continued to publish along official lines. A major foreign-language publisher had meanwhile emerged in the French Institute of Oriental Archaeology, which since 1900 had produced its own books on its own presses in Egypt and which was to acquire, during the reign of the highly cultivated King Fuad, practically an official status in connection with history and archaeology lasting up to 1956.

Cairo—the largest city not only in Africa, but south of Berlin, west of Bombay, or east of New York—had long been the cultural center of the Arab world, a role that remained undisputed until the short-lived challenge of Beirut, which emerged only in the mid-1960s. With such a cosmopolitan capital, relative commercial and financial strength, and a population that included a majority of all the literate Arabic speakers in the world, Egypt was destined to become what Robert Escarpit has defined as a "high-pressure" zone in publishing, an "anticyclone" to the "cyclone" of the rest of the Arab world.[4] Its own local market was based on an expanding public that was literate, could afford books, and could exercise its taste with relative freedom; these tastes, in turn, fell into patterns that allowed them to be largely predicted and thus built upon. Conditions in Egypt therefore favored mass production, while its Arab neighbors, with low demands and highly diversified needs, provided a market to which production beyond local requirements could be exported.

Post-1952 Developments

The leaders of the 1952 revolution, like the Fatimids, the French, and the British before them, recognized the potential of publishing as a powerful tool in attaining both internal and external political goals. These goals were defined in Gamal Abdel Nasser's *Philosophy of the Revolution* as a search for unity extending into the Arabic sphere, the Islamic sphere, and the African sphere. The Egyptian book undoubtedly contributed to the goal of unity in linking Egypt to other countries within the first two spheres. Books were important in achieving internal goals as well as helping to create a literate, culturally awakened society that would in turn speed economic development, thus making the transition to socialism, which was regarded as inevitable, easier and more rapid.

With such new ambitions assigned to it, the publishing industry in Egypt was laden with new and far heavier responsibilities, aims that required planning that could be entrusted only to an official body. The government under the monarchy had sponsored the publication of two educational series in the years preceding the revolution, the "Thousand Books" and "Popular University" series, both designed to raise cultural levels by supplementing formal instruction. Moving far beyond the scope of such modest undertakings, the revolutionary government sought to expand the governmental or public sector on a massive scale, necessarily reorganizing the publishing industry in the process. The result of this process, which included not only creating large public-sector printing and publication organizations but also nationalizing private publishing empires, was a radically diminished private sector.

Establishment of a public sector was characterized by trial-and-error organizational changes. At one time, for example, both the Ministry of Culture and the Ministry of National Guidance were publishers, a situation that led to duplication of effort, conflict of interest, and inefficient utilization of resources. In another phase the slogan "A Book Every Six Hours" was adopted, with the consequence that expansion and productivity took precedence over quality, demand, distribution, and sales.[5] By 1966 the government's Publishing Organization and its divisions, now an integral part of the Egyptian bureaucracy, had run up a standing deficit of 760,000 Egyptian pounds, equivalent to US$1,786,000. Presses were working at only 50 percent capacity, raising production costs, and only 10 percent or less of a typical press run "moved," leaving warehouses crammed with approximately 9 million copies of unsold books. Editorial confusion led to duplication—for example, the same works being translated by more than one person and published at government expense under different names—while administrative confusion led to such mistakes as purchasing in scarce hard currency vast quantities of paper that for technical reasons could not be used.[6]

The General Egyptian Book Organization

In 1969 the Organization became an Authority, a move that separated it from bureaucratic strictures, including wage scales, and thus allowed incentives for efficiency and a higher degree of administrative autonomy. Formerly, separate economic units were gathered into departments of a General Authority for Writing and Publishing, which was defined as a nonprofit service enterprise. In 1972 a further consolidation took place, when all book-related activities, including not only those of this authority but also those of the National Library, were united under a single new authority called the General Egyptian Book Organization (GEBO). Among its other activities, GEBO now sponsors the Cairo International Book Fair, held annually beginning in the last week of January.

On May 24, 1963, the large private publishing companies were nationalized by presidential decree, creating what is known as the "press sector," a term that correctly suggests a role lying somewhere between the public and private sectors. Ownership was nominally vested first in the National Union then in the Arab Socialist Union, the sole political party, which was defined as the agent of the Egyptian people and hence of the state. When the Arab Socialist Union was abolished under Sadat, the three political parties that replaced it did not lay claim to this role. Since 1980 the state has therefore been represented as owner of the press sector by the Shura Council, a two-thirds elected, one-third appointed body equivalent to a national senate.

The speaker of the Shura Council is chairman of the Supreme Council of the Press, the press sector's governing body, whose membership may by law include public figures concerned with the press, who are appointed by the Shura Council, in addition to members representing individual publishing organizations. Each such organization is governed in turn by its own general assembly (in which the Shura Council appoints twenty of thirty-five members), executive board (in which it appoints eight out of fifteen), and editorial board (of which it nominates the chairman). This elaborate arrangement assures that ultimate policy-making responsibility rests with appointees of the state, while day-to-day management is left, as before, in the hands of professionals.

Management of press-sector organizations from the beginning resembled those of an authority, but with a private-enterprise-style mandate quite distinct from the policies that governed the Publishing Organization or GEBO. Each former publishing empire retained managerial autonomy and control over wage and incentive structures and staffing levels. The result, on the whole, was efficiency and, for some years, impressive growth, as typified by Dar al Maaref and Al-Ahram, two giants of the Egyptian publishing industry. Sayid Abul Naga, the former controller of Dar al Maaref, has declared, for example, that profit is a major motive for publishing, rejecting the allegation that Dar al Maaref's role was to peddle a "message" that could not be delivered without government subsidy.[7] Planning within these companies is centralized, but functions fall into three separate departments—publishing, distribution, and printing—and responsibility for implementation is further divided. Departments are budgeted separately and are expected to perform separately. Printing, for example, may well be done on presses other than an organization's own. Performance is measured by a year-end balance sheet.

By the mid-1960s the Egyptian publishing industry had been reduced from five discernible sectors to three: the public sector, the press sector, and a diminished private sector, which included a variety of small publishers, most of them directly connected with bookshops. Separate from GEBO and therefore in addition to these three sectors, the government expanded other publishing activities, making available a vast amount of information not only for sale under the imprint of ministries or learned and scientific societies, as had formerly been the case during the monarchy, but also for free distribution through other means. The only bibliographic record for such publications remains the *Legal Deposit Bulletin* of the National Library.

In the mid-1980s this structure is unchanged. Through GEBO and other agencies the government is still the largest publisher in Egypt, followed by such press-sector giants as Al-Ahram, Dar al Hilal, and Dar al Maaref. The expansion of the private sector that was optimistically expected after the initiation of "economic opening" by President Sadat in 1974—a move accompanied by a general loosening of restrictions and the outright rescinding of some earlier socialist measures—has not materialized. Characteristic instead has been deeper penetration of the Egyptian market by Lebanese publishers, who have continued to produce and sell books successfully, despite nearly a decade of civil war and foreign invasion.

Problems in the Seventies

As late as 1974, Egypt was still the "anticyclone" to the "cyclone" of the rest of the Arab world, with exports accounting for 50 percent of sales. In that year, however, the Federation of Egyptian Industries drew attention to a 50 percent drop in title production and a decline in exports to Lebanon, Syria, Jordan, Saudi Arabia, and Tunisia.[8] The drop in title production was attributed to: (1) increases in the price of paper and its consequent frequent scarcity, as both paper merchants and publishers attempted to readjust themselves to the market; (2) the low quality and inadequate supplies of locally made ink, while high-quality imported ink was kept off the market to encourage local production; (3) the low capacity and outdated technology of the printing industry; and (4) a new tendency for Egyptian authors, who had been the intellectual mainstay of the Arab world, to look for publishers elsewhere. Three of these four causes are related to the technical side of book production, and two of the three suggest declining quality; the fourth meanwhile suggests an increasing prosperity elsewhere in the Arab world of precisely the kind that would make poor quality unacceptable, the more so if unjustified by extremely low prices.

A dozen years of experimental socialism had raised internal standards of living and isolated Egypt from the worst of worldwide inflation. But it had also isolated the country from a revolution in printing technology, from the wage scales of the rest of the Arab world, and from international standards of book production, even those that had come to characterize other developing countries. During the same period, moreover, the indefatigable entrepreneurs of Beirut had shown characteristic initiative: using immigrant expertise, some of it from Egypt, and the latest Western technology, the Lebanese printing industry expanded threefold; by 1974 the industry was performing at standards and prices that made Lebanese printers the rivals of Europe.

Cairo's decline, in fact, had provided Beirut with a golden opportunity. While Lebanese printers expanded and modernized, creating excess capacity that found a ready market abroad, Lebanese booksellers were becoming publishers and small Lebanese publishers were becoming large ones, ready and able to cater to a market that had formerly been almost exclusively Egypt's.

Within Egypt itself the drop in exports was blamed less on Lebanese competition than on Egyptian government regulations. In particular, a finger was pointed at an export regulation (symbolized by Form E-X, which all exporters of books were required to file) that virtually eliminated the possibility of selling books on consignment, the normal mode for Egyptian publishers selling abroad. Under terms of this regulation, exporters were held responsible for importing into Egypt the full net value of their exports in foreign currency at the official rate of exchange (then, as now, at considerable variance with the free market rate, which pegs the value of the Egyptian pound to the U.S. dollar at nearly 45 percent less than the official rate) within six months of the departure of a shipment. Even the press-sector giants were affected by this regulation, which forbade them to maintain consignment stocks abroad for longer than six months, even at their own branch outlets. Unable to hold stocks of Egyptian books, such outlets therefore had the choice of switching to non-Egyptian books or closing. Smaller publishers, many of them dependent upon the giants for foreign distribution, thus lost their outlets and the export game became a scramble for single orders.

The regulation was later relaxed to the extent of allowing a percentage of earned foreign exchange to accrue abroad for use in purchasing primary materials such as paper and ink, provided these materials were imported into Egypt and further provided that such importation was actually allowed. The most crippling proviso, however, the six-month time limit, remained unchanged until recently, when it was extended to three years. A book exporter is also now allowed to spend up to 100 percent of foreign exchange earnings on primary materials for importation. Such corrective measures have obviously come too late either to help recent export figures—those for 1983 are expected to take a further plunge—or to do much toward rebuilding the dominant position in Middle Eastern publishing that Egypt once enjoyed.

The second factor most frequently blamed for declining exports in the mid-seventies was piracy. This complaint may seem ironic to Western publishers, who have occasionally been concerned with piracy of technical and scientific textbook titles in Egypt. Especially in the period between 1977 and 1981, the chief culprits were not established publishers but "fundamentalist" student groups opposed to the Sadat regime, who used cheap pirated editions of textbooks as a recruiting device. If Egypt's own copyright law is rarely invoked, one reason may be fear of testing its extreme stringency, which extends protection not only to the work of publishers and authors but also to an author's idea or conception. Egypt has also become a signatory of the Berne Convention, though ratification of its signature and hence implementation has been delayed for several years.

No reputable Egyptian publisher is unaware of the meaning of international copyright or is inclined to violate it, whatever the temptations. Egyptian publishers and authors have not been violators to one-tenth of the extent to which they have been victims. Both have been pillaged by publishers in Beirut, where the model of scrupulosity offered by the illustrious firm of the Librairie du Liban has too rarely been followed. Such income as even famous Egyptian writers have enjoyed from the sale of non-Egyptian editions of their most important works has come to them only in a form tantamount to charity. The full scale of piracy was brought home to Egyptian publishers in the course of a recent Cairo International Book Fair, when a Lebanese publisher had the temerity to display and sell pirated copies of a major Egyptian reference work.

There are no literary agents in the Arab world, no functioning reciprocal copyright agreements, and Arab governments have been reluctant to invoke such national laws as may exist. The job of policing has been left to Arab firms large enough to operate on an international scale, who may theoretically prosecute within local statutes. This situation, reminiscent of the relationship between British and U.S. publishers before 1900, testifies to political and cultural disunities that a common linguistic, artistic, and (in large part) religious heritage cannot entirely conceal.

A third factor influencing Egyptian exports has been politics. During the last years of Nasser's life, for example, Egypt became alienated from Saudi Arabia and Tunisia, both of which bought books elsewhere until good relations were reestablished after the October War of 1973. A far greater disaster for Egyptian publishing was the Camp David agreements of 1979, which led to an immediate boycott of Egypt by every Arab country except Oman (where the fact that the first languages of a sizable portion of the elite are English or Swahili has led to a program of Arabicization, but where there is no prospect of there ever being a major book market) and Sudan. During the following year (1980) exports of books fell by more than 80 percent, exports of newspapers and journals by more than 85 percent, and the total value of exports to considerably less than a million Egyptian pounds. Libya alone had previously accounted for annual export sales of half a million. When exports momentarily recovered their value in 1981, they rose in volume to only half the 1975 level.[9]

Some ground has been won back recently. Saudi Arabia, Kuwait, Morocco, and Tunisia have allowed Egyptian newspapers to enter, and Egypt's support of its war with Iran has earned the good will of Iraq. The attitudes of such countries as Syria, Algeria, Libya, and the two Yemens are unlikely, however, to change. The export figures for 1981 and 1982 should not be taken as indicating a positive trend; in fact, there is some fear in Cairo that elsewhere in the Arab world the Egyptian book, like the gazelle and the ibex, may well be an endangered species.

Efforts to Reestablish Egypt's Publishing Preeminence

The recognition that the decline of Egypt's publishing prestige can no longer be wholly explained by external factors (hampering government regulations, the inroads of piracy, or the vagaries of Arab politics) but is also due to substantive internal factors, to the standards and conditions prevalent within the industry itself, has led to efforts to revitalize the industry. Although historically advantaged in the Arab world, this advantage has now largely disappeared.

No investment was made in printing technology, all of which must be imported from abroad, between 1966 and the institution of the Open Door—President Sadat's policy of "economic opening"—in 1974. During this period the Lebanese printing industry underwent its greatest expansion, swiftly accommodating itself to the offset revolution despite the fact that adequate photocomposition of Arabic was still in its developmental stages. Printshops in Cairo remained virtual museums of printing technology, spare parts—including such crucial items as matrices—ran short, production times lengthened, and quality declined as various economizing short cuts were taken. After 1973, flush with the extra wealth provided by skyrocketing oil prices, other countries formerly dependent upon Egypt set up their own printing industries, staffing plants with the skilled Egyptian labor that was made available by relaxed labor-emigration laws and was attracted by far higher wages.

The massive investment made by Egypt in the years since—much of it supported by USAID—has barely been sufficient to address minimum local needs, much less to provide the quality and capacity that would enable Egypt to recapture some of its lost foreign market. First-class color separation and four-color printing, for which there is a worldwide demand, are still unobtainable, as is high-quality cost-efficient typesetting in any language other than Arabic. Even the Lebanese civil war, which might have been expected to improve Cairo's sales at Beirut's expense, did not prove beneficial, due in part to Camp David but even more to Lebanese enterprise. Printing and publishing for the Arab world has not only continued in Lebanon itself but has now been carried by the Lebanese diaspora to England, Italy, and France, with some Beirut publishers extending their interests as far as the Netherlands, Spain, and the U.S.

Continuing Problems

Datus Smith has warned against the tendency in developing countries to seek "hardware" solutions to "software" problems.[10] It is obvious that technology alone offers no answer to Egypt's current publishing difficulties, a fact that the traditional linkage between publishing and printing tends to obscure. The decline in title production that was first officially observed in 1974 was discernible earlier and has continued irregularly but almost unabated since, despite any large-scale importation of machinery from the West.[11] The major reason for this continued decline—subsuming and thus clearly far more important than the three reasons connected with the technical side of book production that were officially given in 1974—was the collapse of the export market.

The fourth reason given in 1974—a tendency among Egyptian authors to look for publishers elsewhere—still holds, but with a new vengeance. An established Egyptian writer may earn as much as 1,500 Egyptian pounds from the first printing of a novel, assuming a typical maximum run of 3,000 paperback copies, a typical price of two pounds, a royalty of 25 percent (at the top end of the scale), and a complete sellout of the printing. The book may have taken two years to write, two more to sell out, and the author can expect nothing from the sale of subsidiary rights. Only famous writers like Naguib Mahfuz can expect their books to be kept in print, and thus by cumulative effort they might actually derive enough income to live as professional novelists.

From a single bestseller, however, the author's annual income from the inception of writing to sale of the last copy of the first printing will have been considerably less than the Egyptian GNP per capita (US$580 in 1980), one-fourth of the salary of a low-grade civil servant, and one-hundredth of what might be earned working as a teacher in Saudi Arabia, Iraq, or one of the Gulf States. For a single article in one of the Arabic-language journals emanating from London, Paris, or Kuwait, on the other hand, which might take no more than a week to write, an author can expect as much as 500 pounds sterling, or US$750, the equivalent of more than two full years of earnings from an Egyptian bestseller.

It is therefore not surprising that there seem to be few writers in Egypt or that they should prefer to publish abroad. Mahfuz himself, who worked as a civil servant until retirement age, has declared that he made no money from writing until he began to construct scenarios for the cinema. Nasser's experimental socialism, which eliminated many private incomes, and Sadat's Open Door policy, which gave entrance to waves of foreign inflation, have made writing more than ever a part-time occupation. No young writer can expect to try his or her wings at the expense of a publisher already beset by business problems, although a handful of them may hold titular responsibilities connected with the press sector, the only form of government subsidy to authors.

There is no subsidy of any kind for publishing, however, outside the public sector. Even the press-sector giants are expected to be self-supporting. The government's indifference to the industry in general, except as a source of revenue, can be gauged by the fact that the Committee for Publishing in the Supreme Council for Culture, the only official body where its role and needs might have been appreciated, has recently been abolished. Egypt maintains no public libraries, and purchases of books are not normally made by any public body; deposit copies for the National Library and other organizations are acquired gratis, sometimes direct from the binders. State schools formerly maintained libraries in each classroom, but the practice has been discontinued. In Kuwait and Saudi Arabia, on the other hand, governments purchase 1,000 copies of any title in Arabic by a citizen or resident professional and pay outright for the publication of theses, dissertations, and cultural material. This latter activity has drawn the attention of many publishers and "packagers" in the West. It is an activity, of course, from which Egypt has been excluded by Camp David, as well as by the fact that its printing industry, geared to a Third World product, is simply incapable of producing the usual kind of hardbound coffee-table book in four colors on high-quality paper, no matter whan the language of the text.

With a printing industry barely adequate to its task and authors in short supply, what of Egyptian readers? The consensus, both within the publishing industry and within the cultural establishment at large, is that despite a stable literacy rate and an all-too-rapidly growing population, readership of anything other than religious publications or textbooks is actually declining. Private libraries, common a generation ago, are now a rarity and their owners, the rich and respectable of the old regime, have been displaced in the economics of Egyptian society by what is referred to as the New Class, those who have made money either under the revolution or thanks to the Open Door policy and who notoriously do not read. In consequence of such social changes, reading bears a narrower *cachet de chic,* being typically regarded as a specialized activity—justified if pursued for religious or practical purposes but essentially antisocial. The mass media are not susceptible to this charge, making them preferable agents of instruction and entertainment even among the literate. The television set has excluded books from Egyptian households with more ease, rapidity, and thoroughness than in the West.

A survey conducted in 1966, at the outset of universal transistorization but long before TV had become pandemic, disclosed that the market for books and journals was already quite narrow, essentially an age group between twenty and forty, 60 percent of whom were university students, professors, or professionals, though it should be remembered that this group alone would have constituted a reading and buying population probably larger than that of all the other Arab countries combined.[12] Within this group the average disposable income available for books amounted to 44 piastres, then equivalent to one U.S. dollar, per month.

The smallness of this sum—then equal to the daily wage of a policeman and surpassing that of a factory or agricultural worker, testifies both to Egypt's poverty and to its low costs. It represents the relative privilege of an elite and would have purchased many books annually, especially those produced by the public sector.

No member of this former book-buying elite is likely to have acquired the riches of the New Class, except by owning rental flats or by working abroad.[13] Meanwhile the price of books has risen roughly tenfold and consumer goods that were unavailable in 1966 vie for the market. The increase is directly due to rising costs, which generally remain (using factors of three, four, and five) the sole basis for establishing prices. Half this increase is traceable to the cost of paper, the remainder to the inflation that Egypt has shared with the rest of the world since 1974. Before the Arab boycott publishers were occasionally able to subsidize Egyptian prices with sales abroad at world market (i.e., Western) prices—selling books at near or below cost in Cairo, for example, and at ten times cost in Jeddah or Riyadh—but only when their product could compete in terms of quality. Buyer resistance to increased prices in Egypt has proven very strong, especially among the book-buying elite, who either cannot afford Egyptian books or prefer to spend the money they have on books imported from Lebanon and the West. Many, of course, no longer reside in Egypt at all.

Foreign products, in addition to such sure-fire items as religious tracts and text-books, which need not be published except on demand, now provide the canniest Cairo booksellers with their profit. The only area of interesting growth within general publishing recently has been children's books. It hardly seems accidental that the three most successful firms in this field on the Cairo market—Dar al-Fata al-Arabi (Palestinian-owned, Cairo-based), Dar al-Shorouq (Egyptian-owned, with interests in Lebanon, Saudi Arabia, and the U.K.), and the distinguished Librairie du Liban (Lebanese-based, owner of the Arabic rights to the Ladybird series)—have produced their books in Beirut.

Meanwhile, Egyptian general publishers justifiably feel themselves to be under a serious threat. One of the most prestigious, the press-sector giant Dar el Maaref, is said to be supporting itself only with its commercial printing, while ESDUC, the successor to the Franklin Book Program in Cairo which once shared the distinction (with Tehran) of being the most thriving Franklin operation in the world, is reported not to have issued a single new title since 1981.

Newspapers carry daily editorial columns complaining of cultural crisis, citing the plight of publishing among their evidences of decline. It seems clear to many that Egyptian publishing must either completely change its character—or slowly die.

There are, however, obvious areas where improvement is possible and which could lead to larger change. The typical Egyptian book produced on the latest Western equipment is an unnecessarily shoddy affair by whatever standards are applied and certainly by Egypt's standards of twenty-five years ago. What excuse, for example, can be offered for perfectly paginated and well-printed sheets of an offset reprint that are haphazardly folded, without regard for visible registration marks? Such short cuts do not save money and lower the reputation of Egyptian books at home and abroad.

In partial consequence of low production standards as well as of political pressures, marketing vision has been limited, concentrating on the lower end of the market within the Arabic linguistic bloc, a concentration that has been further narrowed since 1979 by the effectiveness of the boycott. Little has been produced that would help satisfy the needs of Egypt's foreign-language tourist industry, for example, and well-illustrated up-market books on any aspect of Egyptian culture are, without exception, foreign-made and available only in European languages.

Government interference—which in publishing as in other Egyptian industries has frequently tended to kill the goose that laid the golden egg—has been plentiful and support nil, except in fostering the public sector, creating an atmosphere of discouraged improvization rather than one that allows rational planning.

To raise standards, expand market horizons, and change government attitudes will require a determination that perhaps the Egyptian publishing industry can no longer muster, encysted as it is in habits of poverty that will not be broken down merely by infusions of capital. Nor would such changes, in any case, be the panacea for ills that are deep-seated and manifold.

Conclusion

Egypt has the distinction of having introduced modern printing and publishing into the Middle East not once but twice, and its publishing industry is the earliest as well as the largest in the Arab world. From the last quarter of the nineteenth century onward it based its growth on both an internal market and on the relative lack of development in the rest of the Arab world, which until recently was dependent upon Egypt for the bulk of its reading matter. Since the Egyptian industry eventually sold fully 50 percent of its products abroad, the relationship may be described as symbiotic.

The symbiosis has now been broken. Shortage of capital led to stagnation in the period between 1966 and 1974, accompanied by increased competition from abroad. After 1974 the Open Door policy allowed technical updating but also brought inflation and higher costs, which reduced the competitive price edge held by Egyptian books abroad, where established selling practices were already crippled by unwieldy export regulations, and failed to bring the domestic public sufficient disposable income to stimulate book buying.

The latest blow has been the Arab boycott following the Camp David agreements of 1979, which has not only choked off the outward flow of Egyptian books and further encouraged Lebanese competition to fill the ensuing gap but has also stimulated the creation of new Arab and non-Arab publishing ventures specifically designed to serve the countries that once depended on Egypt for books.

The cumulative effect of these changes on the industry has been devastating. Given confinement to a single language bloc, no alternative export market seems possible at the moment, and even the domestic market shows increasing signs of failure: bestselling authors now publish outside Egypt, and there is stiff resistance to prices that have inflated tenfold while wages and production standards have remained low. Even interest in reading seems to have declined.

Unless the country suddenly becomes rich, the outlook for Egyptian publishing is gloomy indeed. Egypt's decline as a publishing force, however, is to some extent a measure of the new potentialities for Arab publishing—and publishing in Arabic—elsewhere, many of which are in the process of being exploited with great success.

One important and encouraging development has been the prospect of Egypt's readmission to the Islamic Conference Organization, approved by a large majority of delegates from Muslim countries after days of debate during the ICO's meeting in January 1984. Hard-line Arab countries predictably maintained their opposition; Egypt's response has been to insist that readmission be unconditional.

Political reentry into the Islamic world—the second of Gamal Abdel Nasser's three spheres—may well serve as a vehicle of reentry into the first, the Arab world, which has been so crucial to Egypt's publishing industry in the past and from which it has been excluded since 1979.

It would be foolish, however, to wait upon that event before attempting to make the changes described in the preceding pages: raising the technical standards, expanding market horizons, and shifting attitudes in government. If the appropriate opportunities are seized, these changes will be easier to make now than they have been at any time since 1979 and may at least enable Egyptian publishing to try and hold its own.

Notes

A general note on transliteration. Except where a more academic transliteration might be of some use to an Arabist, the authors have used the Roman-alphabet spellings actually favored by Egyptian individuals and organizations themselves when their names have appeared in English-language publications.

1. See Thomas Francis Carter, *The Invention of Printing in China and Its Spread Westward* (New York: Ronald Press, 1955), pp. 176–182. Carter attempted to bring Fatimid printing, long a commonplace of Central European scholarship, to the attention of a wider public with the first edition of this brilliant book in 1925, though he himself, apparently unaware of the nature and extent of Fatimid contacts with T'ang China, was skeptical of the dates arrived at by Czech, German, and Austrian epigraphers. The great authority in the field, Adolf Grohmann, reiterated his findings thirty years later, however, for the second edition; and the issue has been reopened, after decades of neglect, by Professor George T. Scanlon of the American University in Cairo, whose latest excavation has uncovered printed papers in a context that is exclusively Fatimid. Professor Scanlon's report on his discovery awaits publication and will be followed by a special study. He meanwhile cautions that none of the printed sheets thus far found appears to be a portion of a printed book.

2. The date of installation is given as 1821 or 1822 in Khalil Sabat, *Tarikh at-Tibaᶜ a fi ash-Sharq al-ᶜArabi* [History of printing in the Middle East] (Cairo: Dar al Maaref, 1966), p. 133.

3. *Ibid.*, p. 181.

4. Robert B. Escarpit, *The Book Revolution* (London: Harrap, 1966), pp. 20–86.

5. This is the judgment of a distinguished minister of culture, exceptionally aware of the potential role of publishing in Egyptian cultural life. See Tharwat ᶜUkasha (Sarwat Okasha), *Nahwu Intalaq Thaqafi* [Toward a cultural leap forward] (Cairo: Dar al-Katib a-ᶜArabi, 1969), p. 24.

6. See Tharwat ᶜUkasha, *Arbᶜa Mᶜutamarat* [Four conferences] (Cario: Dar al-Mu'ssassah al-Misriyyah al-ᶜAmah li at-Talif wa an-Nashr, 1967), pp. 214–215.

7. See Nadia A. Rizk, "The Book-Publishing Industry in Egypt," *Library Trends,* 26 (Spring 1978): 556–557.

8. See "Reports of the Industrial Chambers," *Federation of Egyptian Industries Yearbook* (Cairo: General Organization for Government Printing Offices, 1975), p. 118 and note 11 below.

9. Official figures are supplied by CAPMAS (Central Agency for Public Mobilization and Statistics) with values expressed in Egyptian pounds rather than dollars. The pound was devalued internally by 20 percent early in 1980, thus raising the accounting value of export sales. Since there continued to be a wide variation between official and free-market exchange rates, however, this move has not necessarily lowered the price of Egyptian books abroad; publishers have adjusted prices to cover the difference between the official and free-market exchange rates, thus recovering the full free-market value of the hard currency their books have earned. The price of imported books is likewise linked with free-market exchange.

10. Datus Smith, "Scholarly Publishing in the Third World," *Scholarly Publishing,* 13 (April 1981): 217.

11. Statistics supplied by UNESCO show a decline in annual title production of nearly 30 percent between 1972 and 1977 alone: see the UNESCO *Statistical Yearbook/Annuaire Statistique* for the relevant years and *Publisher's Weekly,* 218 (September 26, 1980): 97 and 220 (September 18, 1981): 123. Statistics supplied by the National Library showing title deposits are compiled on a different basis and yield different totals, despite the fact that the categories used are nearly identical. They show an even more drastic drop for the same years, however (43 percent), and indicate 1973—the year before a decline was observed by the Egyptian Federation of Industries—as a peak year. Title deposits at the National Library for each year since have been at least 60 percent lower than during this peak year.

12. Saad El Dine Gadallah, "Report on Field Survey on Newspapers, Magazines, and Books in the United Arab Republic" (Unpub. paper, The Social Research Center of the American University in Cairo and the Arab Research and Advertising Center, 1966).
13. For an assessment of the Open Door policy up to 1977, see Mark N. Cooper, *The Transformation of Egypt* (London: Croom Helm, 1982), pp. 91–125.

9. Publishing in India: Crisis and Opportunity

Tejeshwar Singh

Although it is one of the world's largest publishing nations, India shares many of the problems of other Third World nations, such as difficulties in distributing books, copyright issues, problems with new technologies, and inadequate paper supplies. Because India has been involved in book publishing for a long period and has achieved considerable success, it is an important nation to study to understand the problems and possibilities of Third World publishing. As an important Third World publishing nation, its future will affect the book industry in other developing countries and its problems are illustrative. India now stands at a crossroads. Much of its publishing industry is decades behind the industrialized nations, yet modern technologies are also available. After several years of stagnancy, Indian publishing is again growing. The future is unclear but the possibilities are exciting.

Statistical Background

The total population of India in 1981 was approximately 680 million.[1] There were 100 million school-going children in 1979–80 (in the age group six to seventeen) and 3 million students enrolled in colleges and universities. The average per capita income in 1980–81 was Rs. 128 (US$15) per month.

Literacy in 1981 was estimated at 36 percent. According to the Constitution, fifteen major languages (English not being one of them) and a very large number of dialects and subdialects are spoken in India. Of these fifteen, two languages—Sindhi and Kashmiri—are not generic to our purpose (since no books are recorded

111

as being published in these languages) and have been included with "Others" in table 9.1. Even presuming a 100 percent literacy rate for English speakers, they do not account for more than .08 percent of the estimated literate population (see table 9.1).[2] However, it is universally acknowledged that about 2 percent of the literate population use English as their first language.

Though the book industry has been in existence for many years, there has been no systematic attempt to enumerate Indian publishers.[3] The absence of reliable statistics concerning any aspect of the book business is a serious handicap. According to a directory published eleven years ago, there were over 11,000 publishers in 1972.[4] It is difficult to accept this figure. Part of the inflation in numbers is probably

Table 9.1. Languages Spoken in India.*

Language	Total Population Languagewise in 1971 (in millions)	Total Estimated Literate Population in 1981 (in millions)	Percentage
Assamese	8.96	3.75	1.53%
Bengali	44.79	18.80	7.68
English	0.19	4.90	2.00
Gujarati	25.86	10.86	4.44
Hindi	208.51	87.56	35.77
Kannada	21.71	9.13	3.73
Malayalam	21.94	19.04	7.78
Marathi	41.76	17.54	7.16
Oriya	19.86	8.33	3.40
Punjabi	14.11	5.92	2.42
Sanskrit	Nil	–	
Tamil	37.69	15.83	6.47
Telugu	44.76	18.78	7.67
Urdu	28.62	12.02	4.91
Others	29.38	12.34	5.04
Total	548.16	244.80	

* The data in this table have to be treated with caution. "What is your mother tongue?"—the question asked by census workers—is loaded with both emotional and political overtones. The reply given is not necessarily the most accurate one. The census also does not take into account those who speak more than one language, which is now a very common feature in India.
Sources: For column 1: Government of India, *Census of India—Social and Cultural Tables*, s. 1, p. II-C (i) (New Delhi: Registrar and Census Commissioner of India, 1976). For column 2: The language data collected during the 1981 census are not likely to be available until 1985. These figures have been arrived at on the following assumptions: that the population of India in 1981 was 680 million; that the percentage of the population speaking each language remained constant over the period 1971–81; that the number of literates in the country was 36 percent of the total population in 1981 or 244.80 million (see Government of India, *India 1982—A Reference Annual* [New Delhi: Ministry of Information and Broadcasting, 1983], p. 9); that 2 percent of the literate population had English as their first language; that the literacy rate among Malayalam speakers was 70 percent (see Government of India, *India 1982, Ibid.*, p. 11). After taking the literate population in English as 4.90 million, the remaining literate population of 220.91 million yielded an average literacy rate of 33.85 percent which was applied to each of the remaining twelve languages to arrive at the figures in column 2.

due to the fact that the directory enumerated publishers by the language they published in and multilingual publishers were counted more than once. In all probability, some of the firms were magazine publishers. About 1,000 publishers were government bodies or institutions. After making all allowances, it would be safe to assume that there were about 6,000 to 7,000 commercial publishers in India in 1972, not more than 3,000 of whom were active (i.e., publishing at least five books a year), and that the situation is not much different today.

There are two sets of figures in the directory that can be accepted: first, there were 1,300 author-publishers (i.e., authors who publish their own books), and second, the three major languages of publication were Hindi (24 percent), English (17 percent), and Bengali (14 percent). The remaining thirteen languages accounted for 45 percent of the publishers.[5] Today, it is likely that the number of publishers publishing in Hindi and other regional languages has increased but not at the expense of those publishing in English.

The data in table 9.2 on the number of books published are based on information supplied by the National Library, Calcutta, to the Ministry of Education in New Delhi. The National Library is the most important library in the country and is supposed to receive one copy of every book published. This requirement is ignored by many publishers and hence the figures in table 9.2 do not provide a complete picture. The actual number of titles published annually in India could be twice as great as the figures listed in table 9.2. However, the National Library data include reprints, revised editions, and the books, reports, documents, statistics, and papers (both priced and nonpriced), produced by the over 500 government publishing agencies. Since these categories account for a very substantial chunk of publishing output in India, it would be safe to assume that table 9.2 represents a reasonably accurate summary of the number of new titles published annually by nongovernment publishers.

Facts and figures concerning the printing industry are also difficult to locate and the only reliable statistics relate to the year 1979.[6] Not counting newspaper and government-owned presses, there were 43,156 commercial printers in India in that year. Of these, about 6,000 handled book work. A vast majority (37,800) were letterpress outfits, and more than 90 percent of these presses offered hand composing only. About 1,500 presses employed more than fifty people and could, therefore, be called "large." Although the number of photocomposing and offset machines has increased since the report was prepared, most books published in India continue to be composed by hand (occasionally by mono) and printed by letterpress.

Paper manufacturers have suffered severe setbacks in recent years due to infrastructural impediments such as shortage in raw materials and power. As a result, though the installed capacity has gone up to about 2 million tons per annum the actual output as a percentage of capacity has declined from 87 percent in 1978 to 58 percent in 1983.[7] Thus, the actual output in 1983 was 1.1 million tons. Faced with increased costs and lowered production and operating in a protected market (paper imports are controlled by the government), paper manufacturers have been able to increase the price of paper substantially. A fairly ordinary 80 gsm maplitho which used to cost about Rs. 4,500 (US$560) per ton in 1973 today costs Rs. 14,000 (US$1,400).

The quality of Indian paper is uneven and does not compare with international standards. Paper is frequently in short supply and publishers sometimes have to pay

Table 9.2. Output of Books by Language of Publication.

Language	1972/73	Percentage	1978/79	1979/80	1980/81	Percentage
Assamese	283	1.66%	259	142	196	1.14%
Bengali	1,055	6.20	1,039	1,025	1,046	6.10
English	7,318	43.00	7,089	7,512	7,655	44.61
Gujarati	698	4.10	979	495	757	4.41
Hindi	2,827	16.61	2,966	2,191	2,225	12.97
Kannada	286	1.68	823	919	500	2.91
Malayalam	618	3.63	819	815	757	4.41
Marathi	1,233	7.24	1,345	1,058	1,361	7.93
Oriya	489	2.87	270	402	445	2.59
Punjabi	354	2.08	273	277	308	1.80
Sanskrit	176	1.03	111	70	43	0.25
Tamil	690	4.05	1,595	900	1,135	6.61
Telugu	577	3.39	414	388	389	2.27
Urdu	324	1.90	401	198	286	1.67
Others	92	0.54	201	74	55	0.32
Total	17,020		18,584	16,466	17,158	

Source: Government of India; Ministry of Education.

a premium to obtain the paper they want. Until recently most of the paper manufactured in the country was made out of wood pulp, waste paper, and rags; efforts are now being made to find alternative raw materials. In particular, the government has been encouraging the use of bagasse. In an effort to ensure that textbooks are reasonably priced, the government has stipulated that a certain percentage of the white printing paper produced in the country will be sold at a concessional rate of around Rs. 5,000 (US$500) per ton. This paper is supplied to publishers for the printing of bona fide textbooks.

Historical Background

The 200 years of colonial rule had a profound impact on education and publishing. The British imported both their language and their educational institutions into India. Their purpose was very limited—to provide a British education for their children while they were in the subcontinent and to train a sufficient number of Indians to staff the lower echelons of the bureaucracy. At the same time, they did not particularly want to provide education to very many. Hence, they set up only a handful of schools and universities and did little to encourage mass literacy.[8]

Indigenous educational institutions stultified during this period, and by the time the British left they were completely moribund. Perhaps that is why no effort was made to revive them after independence. Instead, India embarked on a rapid expansion in the number of British-style schools and colleges.

English-speaking Indians gained an ascendancy in the social, political, and commercial spheres during the colonial period, and their position was consolidated as a result of India's educational policies. The dominance of the English-speaking elite was further encouraged by the fact that English is an international language and is also acceptable to all linguistic groups in the country. Today, English is the one language which everyone aspires to acquire.

Oxford University Press, Macmillan, Blackie's, and Longmans Green had set up offices in India by the beginning of the twentieth century. Their only activity then was to ensure that their publications were used as textbooks in the schools and colleges. Over time and with the growth of the printing industry, they began to reprint some of their books in India, but they never adapted them and did virtually nothing to encourage indigenous authorship. Some Indian schools still use reprinted British textbooks which were first published in the 1890s and 1900s.

The printing industry was also a slow starter. Printing presses were initially imported into India either by the government or by Christian missionaries and hence were not available for general use. Most Indian firms could not afford the high cost of importing presses and had to make do with treadle machines. All the paper required by the British government and by missionary establishments was imported.

When the British left in 1947, the publishing industry could not be said to be in its infancy; it was still in the womb. Aside from the four major British publishers (and a few others with a token presence in the country), there were no publishers worth mentioning. The freedom movement did spawn a few publishers, but most of them were geared to printing political tracts and pamphlets and only a tiny handful had ventured into book publishing.

Educational publishing was dominated by the four British publishers. Since they were mainly reprinters and importers, they had no need to develop a cadre of trained editors and publishing professionals. There were few printing presses and virtually no paper mills. As the main book activity was textbook oriented, retail bookshops existed only in urban centers and served the needs of the colonialists and the English-speaking Indians. In short, none of the essential conditions for a successful publishing industry existed at the time India gained independence on August 15, 1947.

The Present

Thirty-seven years after independence, Indian publishing stands at the crossroads. In this relatively brief period of time, Indian publishing has been through its infancy, gone booming through its adolescence, suffered a series of rude shocks and now, like most youngsters, is looking at its future with a mixture of uncertainty and apprehension. It is hoped that the publishing industry will arrive at maturity in the next twenty years. To understand the choices that face the industry, it is necessary to review the present situation.

School Books

The publishing of school textbooks was concentrated in the hands of the four British publishers who had a substantial presence in India. With the rapid increase in the number of schools in the country after 1947, Indian publishers began to enter this field. They faced an uphill task as most schools preferred the "Englishness" of firms like Macmillan and Oxford University Press. Gradually, enlightened teachers began to argue for an "Indianization" of education. Coupled with this, the government's policy of providing free and compulsory primary education led to the setting up of schools where one of the major Indian languages was the medium of instruction. As a result, the Indian textbook publisher began to make some headway.

In 1961 the government set up the National Council of Educational Research and Training (NCERT). It developed model textbooks for adaptation and publication by the state textbook boards. The result was the virtual nationalization of school textbooks. Commercial publishers were left to publish only supplementary readers, workbooks, and textbooks in a few subjects where enrollments were not high.

This had a very serious impact on the publishing industry. Because of the numbers involved, the ability to arrive at a precise print order, and the comparative ease of distribution, publishing school textbooks is a profitable business. If left to commercial publishers, this business would have injected a very healthy and necessary amount of finance into the industry and allowed the growth of strong and diversified publishing activity.[9] Some of the largest British and American publishers have lucrative school publishing divisions that underwrite many other areas of publishing.

The Multinationals and Foreign Texts

Besides seriously affecting the newly emergent Indian publishers of school texts, the nationalization of school textbooks had a profound impact on the multinationals. Blackie's wound up its operations in the mid-seventies and sold its interests to an Indian publisher. Longman had Indianized its operations at an early stage and the successor company, Orient Longman, can no longer be considered a multinational. Macmillan India has not yet been able to come to grips with the loss of its school textbook business. The only one of the original four that seems to have adjusted to the changed circumstances following the establishment of NCERT is Oxford University Press.

At about the time that NCERT came into existence, a number of American publishers set up companies in India. Prentice-Hall, Wiley, McGraw-Hill, and Van Nostrand have joint venture companies in India, while others—such as Addison-Wesley, CBS Books, and Academic Press—have appointed full-time representatives. A major reason for the entrance of American publishers was the PL-480 book program (also known as the Indo-American Textbook Program). Under Public Law 480, the American government provided loans to the Indian government, a portion of which were repayable in rupees in India. The American government used part of these funds to subsidize the reprinting of over 2,000 American textbooks between 1961 and 1973, covering a wide range of subjects, for Indian college students. The subsidies were very generous and, to some extent, provided the financing for the publishing industry which should have come from school textbooks. In particular, it encouraged a major expansion in the printing industry. This scheme, however, ended in 1973, and only a handful of titles are now being published.

Unlike the PL-480 scheme, the textbooks published under the British ELBS scheme are printed in England and are meant for all developing countries. Of late, the Soviet government, through an agreement with the Indian government, has started supplying English-language translations of some of their scientific and technical texts.[10]

College Texts

College textbook publishing has suffered from a number of problems. Perhaps the most serious of these has been the availability of very low-priced reprints of American, British, and now Soviet textbooks. These editions are heavily subsidized by the concerned governments and are available at prices that no Indian publisher can possibly match. For example, a 700-page physics text for the master's level was available under the PL-480 program at Rs. 23.25 (or US$2.20).

The Indian publishers' major advantage (which was only of real value in the social sciences) was that they could publish textbooks that were geared to Indian syllabi and conditions. This, however, was undermined by three factors: the increasing use of regional languages as media of instruction and the consequent fragmentation of the market, the single university textbook, and falling standards.

With the increased number of students, it has become possible to publish a textbook for use in a single university and its affiliated colleges. Some universities now publish these textbooks themselves, while others are published by author-publishers. Quite a few of the author-publishers are college or university teachers who write textbooks, have them printed (some even own treadle machines), and then require them for their courses.

The very rapid and indiscriminate increase in the number of educational institutions has led to a decline in educational standards. There were 18 universities and 1,171 colleges in the country in 1947. By 1977 the number of universities had increased to 115 and colleges to 4,158;[11] while today there are 132 universities and well over 5,000 colleges. The emphasis is not on learning but on passing examinations. To this end, most students prefer crammers, cribs, and question-answer type books. Given this environment, few publishers (except the author-publishers and the producers of bazaar notes) are able to develop a strong list of college textbooks.

Scholarly Books and Journals

The two major areas open to Indian publishers are scholarly and general books. India boasts of a very large scholarly community, many of whom are internationally renowned. Indian scientists have won Nobel Prizes and an Indian social scientist was appointed director of the London School of Economics in 1984. Similarly, there are a large number of colleges, universities, and research institutes in the country. In short, there is a substantial market for scholarly books.

The now-defunct Asia Publishing House, Vikas Publishing House, Oxford University Press, and Allied are four publishers who have (or had) substantial and, on the whole, successful publishing programs in this area. In addition, there are a number of small- to medium-size publishers who bring out between six and twenty scholarly books a year. Despite these favorable indicators, this area of publishing has not been without its problems.

Most publishing houses in India have been set up or are owned by entrepreneurs. While well-meaning and genuinely interested in the book business, they lack a proper understanding of the intricacies of book publishing. The virtual absence of trained professionals further compounds this problem as does the fact that few manuscripts are critically evaluated before acceptance. Only a small minority of scholarly publishers follow this practice, and consequently many publishing decisions are made purely on a commercial basis without considering the book's intellectual merits.

The net effect of this has been indiscriminate publishing. The better scholars became dissatisfied with Indian publishers and began increasingly to seek foreign publishers for their books.[12] Their unhappiness was heightened by certain malpractices which, though practiced by only a few publishers, gave the whole industry a bad name. Subsidies further encourage indiscriminate publishing. These range from the author who is willing to pay to get his life's opus published to august research bodies who provide publishing grants for the publication of research work of dubious value completed under their aegis.

The real test, however, is whether a publisher can profitably sell what he publishes. Until recently the sale of a thousand copies of a scholarly book posed no serious challenge to Indian publishers, but in 1979 there was a sudden and massive reduction in the grants given to libraries for the purchase of books.[13] This cutback lasted until 1983 and led to the closing of some firms and reduced production in others. Publishing output has remained virtually static since 1972, the peak having been reached in 1978–1979 (see table 9.2). Although the grants to libraries have been restored to a large extent, many academic libraries are under pressure to be more selective in their purchases. The liberal and somewhat uncritical book-buying policies pursued by these institutions prior to 1979 will be difficult to sustain. Under these circumstances, the publishers of scholarly books will have to be more careful when making a publishing decision and this, in turn, may raise the standard of authorship.

A large number of scholarly journals are published in India. Most are published either by research institutes or by university departments. The editors of these journals normally have little time or talent to devote to marketing and so the circulation of many of them is about 100 to 200 copies. Most of them are tantamount to in-house forums and this inhibits authorship. The three or four scholarly journals published by commercial houses have reasonable sales and attract contributions from a wide range of Indian and foreign academics. As a whole, the publishing of scholarly journals is in a depressed state. Few of them command any prestige, and virtually none have notable sales.

General and Children's Books

Part of India's colonial legacy is its intelligentsia's disparagement of things Indian and consequent wholesale acceptance of things Western. In English-language publishing an ideal example of the center-periphery syndrome as it exists in India is the treatment meted out to Indian creative writers. Anita Desai, for example, has been writing novels for many years, but only a handful of dedicated enthusiasts had read her books before her nomination for the Booker Prize in 1981. Her novels then became the topic of conversation in fashionable drawing rooms, and the intelligentsia invested in the Penguin editions of her novels even though Indian editions had been available for years at half the price. In short, it was only with the "center's" stamp of approval that the "periphery" was willing to accept one of its own.[14]

A few publishers—notably Oxford University Press, Hind Pocket Books, Orient Paperbacks, Writers' Workshop, Sangam Paperbacks, and a number of small one-person operations in Bombay and Calcutta—have devoted a great deal of effort to this area. But until Indians shake off their colonial hangover, it will continue to be difficult to publish profitably novels, poems, and plays. With literary critics in developed countries beginning to recognize Indian creative writing, this process may be hastened. In the regional languages, popular thrillers and books on general knowledge sell well.

In India the political quickies, the memoirs of politicians, and the scandals and exposés have always done well. Children's books, however, suffer in comparison with Western ones. American and British publishers of children's books have the advantage of a large domestic market and the likelihood of substantial export sales. This enables them to produce well-printed and designed books at prices that an Indian publisher, who has to rely primarily on a comparatively narrow domestic market, can never match without compromising quite extensively on the quality of paper, design, and print. Only one or two publishers have ventured into this area in the English language and they are generally not doing well.

The converse is true in the regional languages where there is a severe shortage of children's reading material. With the increase in literacy and gradual rise in per capita incomes, the demand for children's books in the major Indian languages has risen quite sharply in recent years. The National Book Trust (NBT) in particular has taken an active role and has an extensive multilingual program of children's books.

India and the International Environment

There are at present very few constraints on importing books into the country. Only the import of fiction and children's books requires a governmental license, the value of which is 10 percent of the importers' total book imports during the previous financial year. The other restrictions are (1) that no one company or its branches can import more than 1,000 copies of any one book during one financial year and (2) that no one can import a book which has been reprinted in India. Theoretically, it is possible to import any nonfiction book published anywhere in the world.

During the period 1979–83, when library grants had been heavily cut, Indian publishers pressed very strongly, but unsuccessfully, for a curb on the import of books. They argued that given the meager grants available, Indian books should get first priority when it came to library purchases. The only way to ensure this was to restrict imports. One proponent of this view (who has been involved with UNESCO and with the World Intellectual Property Organization (WIPO) for many years) went so far as to say that he was in favor of the free flow of information but not the free flow of books.

The inflow of remaindered books is used as an argument for import restrictions. Recently a number of Indian importers have begun making trips to the U.S. and England to purchase remaindered stocks, including old editions and written-off academic titles which are often sold to libraries. For some years now, libraries in India have been entitled to a 10 percent discount on book purchases. Because of the big difference between printed and cost price, importers of remaindered books have been offering considerably higher discounts to libraries as an incentive.

Piracy is another worrisome phenomenon. Initially pirates concentrated on the big block-busters, often inventing new titles for best-selling authors. As there is no effective law to curb piracy, they have enlarged their operations over the years and now even reprint indigenous books.

A possible way to curb piracy is for publishers in developed countries to grant reprint rights to Indian publishers at an early stage. As the resulting Indian list price is considerably lower than the original one and as royalty remitted out of India is taxed by the government, many foreign publishers and their authors feel that it does not make financial sense to grant reprint rights. In all probability, granting early reprint rights to Indian publishers would go some distance toward minimizing piracy. However, reprinting foreign books on a large scale would actually weaken the indigenous industry and its authorship by perpetuating the center-periphery relationship. Whether imported or reprinted, India has to wean itself from imported intellectual traditions and develop its own identity. Reprinting books at low prices would primarily serve to ensure that India's intellectual dependency on the West would be prolonged at the cost of local authorship.

In 1983 the Copyright Amendment Bill was passed by the Indian Parliament. This bill enshrines the main provisions of the Paris Convention concerning compulsory licensing. It is too early to assess its impact both on piracy and on the granting/taking of reprint rights, but it has considerable implications for the shape of Indian publishing to come.

Regional Cooperation

Due to political and financial constraints, there is very little cooperation between India and its immediate neighbors. The book trade between India and Pakistan has been severely restricted for many years. Bangladesh has suffered from both perennial political upheavals and a very tight foreign exchange position ever since it came into existence. Sri Lanka is a relatively small market and is wary of coming under the shadow of its big neighbor.

Most Asian countries look to America or England and not toward each other. Proposals for coeditions of children's books have been discussed between Asian countries. If the illustrations are printed at one place with each country subsequently printing its own text, considerable savings could be effected. However, except for one or two desultory gestures to this idea, nothing has come of it.

Exports

After the cuts in library grants in 1979, Indian publishers sought export markets with greater vigor. They explored mainly Africa and West Asia (particularly the Gulf countries) on the presumption that Indian tertiary-level books were both cheaper and more suitable than American and British ones. The figures in table 9.3 do not suggest that this drive has had an appreciable impact. Book exports did not rise to any great extent during the period 1977/78 to 1980/81. Taking only a 10 percent increase per annum in book prices, the real value of exports during this period has, in fact, fallen quite considerably. West Asia's share in India's export trade has declined sharply, while exports to Africa have risen only marginally.

Most likely a large chunk of the book exports to West Asia are textbooks destined for the substantial number of schools opened by expatriate Indians in the region. Most of these textbooks are published by NCERT and not commercial publishers. Exports to Africa, Southeast Asia, and increasingly to the U.K. and U.S. contain a growing number of regional-language publications for immigrant populations wishing to keep themselves, and particularly their children, in touch with the old country. These sales are not in response to a demand created by Indian publishers nor are they a quantifiable constant.

Enlarging the export market for Indian tertiary-level textbooks is an exercise of limited value. Just as India has weaned itself from British and American texts, African and Asian countries will in time develop their own books. Further, the present affluence of oil-producing nations is not destined to last forever. It would, therefore, be a shortsighted policy to develop a publishing business purely geared to the export market.

The Publishing Infrastructure

Another element of the colonial legacy is a conception of what a book should look like. Indian publishers are constantly trying (without success) to produce books that meet international standards in terms of printing, paper, and binding. The net effect of this has been higher book prices, thus creating the vicious circle of higher prices leading to lower sales resulting in reduced print runs and therefore still higher prices. In ten years, the price of an average scholarly book has more than doubled. Trying to meet international standards may be an appropriate strategy for books destined primarily for export markets. In the case of books meant for the domestic market, the focus should be on producing appropriately priced books, even if it entails compromising on production quality.

Although India's printing capacity can meet the requirements of book publishing, there are considerable bottlenecks in production. Scheduling is poor and quality control virtually nonexistent. Frequent interruptions in power supply, a scarcity of skilled and reliable machine operators, and a lack of good printing inks further hinder the printing process. Binding, which is still largely done by hand, suffers from some of the same problems but is by and large adequate for the domestic market.

Paper poses a serious infrastructural constraint on book publishing. All 500 sheets of paper in a ream are rarely the same shade, let alone being consistent from ream to ream. The better grades of paper are more expensive and are difficult to obtain. Frequent periods of scarcity cause publishers to either tie up money in paper stocks or hold up books until paper is available.

Table 9.3. Direction of Book Exports ('000 Rs).

Region/Country	1977/78	Percentage	1978/79	Percentage	1979/80	Percentage	1980/81	Percentage
East, South, and Southeast Asia	16,521.3	32.1%	17,528.8	28.6%	18,699.2	32.0%	24,615.6	42.4%
West Asia	17,886.2	34.8	25,637.0	41.9	15,607.1	26.7	8,693.0	15.0
Africa	5,308.3	10.3	4,557.0	7.4	4,745.0	8.1	7,303.2	12.6
East Europe (including U.S.S.R.)	67.2	0.1	61.6	0.1	1,413.5	2.4	303.5	0.5
West Europe (excluding U.K.)	1,331.3	2.6	1,567.7	2.6	2,978.9	5.1	1,971.1	3.4
Great Britain	4,584.4	8.9	5,949.4	9.7	6,957.4	11.9	5,969.6	10.3
Canada	324.6	0.6	275.3	0.5	614.8	1.0	885.0	1.5
United States	4,147.0	8.1	3,919.9	6.4	4,916.6	8.4	7,760.5	13.4
South America (including the Caribbean)	68.3	0.1	236.6	0.4	408.2	0.7	162.1	0.3
Australia and New Zealand	1,205.6	2.3	1,508.5	2.5	2,166.7	3.7	331.0	0.6
Total	51,444.2		61,241.8		58,507.4		57,994.6	

Source: Extrapolated from Allied Products Export Promotion Council, *Direction of Exports 1977–78 to 1980–81* (Calcutta: CAPEXIL, 1983).

Perhaps the real Achilles' heel of Indian publishing is distribution. The logistical and geographical dimensions are naturally vast in a country that is over 3,000 kilometers wide both north-south and east-west and where communications are still in a fairly rudimentary stage. However, thirty-seven years after independence retail outlets remain few and far between in urban centers and virtually nonexistent in towns. Although there are quite a few importing wholesalers with national or regional sales staff, there are only two or three distributing wholesalers with any interest in Indian books. Small- and medium-scale publishers cannot afford the enormous cost of setting up their own sales network and have to rely on the existing wholesalers, who can thus demand favorable terms for themselves.

The wholesale and retail network for trade or general books is comparatively efficient, mainly because it rides on the back of imported books, while the network for scholarly and tertiary-level books is poor. Library suppliers in India tend to be small family concerns run out of homes with minimal stock-holding, almost no staff, and a tiny capital base. Most libraries insist on books being left with them on approval but will not take responsibility for damages in handling. After the books are selected, it can take the institution up to one year to pay for its purchases. The library supplier cannot pay the wholesaler until the library payment is received, and the wholesaler, in turn, delays payment to the publisher. The publisher, who has had to pay for his paper purchases in advance and his printer's and binder's bills within thirty days, has no one to fall back on. Some of them delay royalty payments to authors, thereby earning a bad name.

Distribution complaints are a universal phenomenon and India is no exception, but the degree of inefficiency is of paramount importance. On the other hand, it is impossible to state categorically that any book has or has not realized its sale potential. Nonetheless, it would appear that Indian publishers and booksellers are not effectively reaching and servicing even 50 percent of the market for books in the country. With improving economic conditions, official efforts, and general awareness, literacy levels are beginning to rise quite rapidly, with a corresponding increase in the demand for reading material. The future of the Indian book business lies almost entirely in devising ways of reaching this market.

The Crossroads

Historical Cycles

The cliché of the bullock cart transporting a computer—or, more appositely, the hand-composing department under the same roof as the latest photocomposer—is an apt description of India's situation. Both the very old and the very new coexist, and often not happily. The contradictions that result from this time warp sometimes cause considerable upheavals.

The last ten to fifteen years have been a traumatic period for the book business; it has experienced a number of disabling developments, only a few of which have been of its own making. Due to these circumstances, the areas of profitable publishing activity open to commercial publishers have narrowed. The level of publishing output has remained static over the period 1972/73 to 1980/81, while book exports experienced a decline in real terms.

The situation is, however, not as hopeless as the foregoing may indicate. Indian publishing, in keeping with the rest of the country, is going through a particular stage in its growth. Peter Golding has detailed the following historical cycle for the publishing business:

I. (a) Small-scale individual entrepreneurs serving small markets and performing all functions from producer to seller.
   (b) Gradual specialization coupled with technological developments and increased capital inflows leading to a fully differentiated industry.
II. (a) A period of concentration leading to the emergence of large firms benefiting from economies of scale.
   (b) The separate functions reintegrating under the larger firms (vertical integration).
   (c) The horizontal integration of independent firms in the same stage.[15]

This generalized historical construct cannot be applied in its entirety to a particular country, especially a country experiencing a compressed historical cycle. Generally, however, Indian publishing could be said to have passed Golding's stage I (a) which, according to him, was the stage reached by England in the mid-nineteenth century.

According to one commentator, "South Asia is leaping over a hundred years in twenty-five years."[16] Presuming that the first thirty years or so of independence were equivalent, in terms of "caught up history," to the first one hundred years of colonial rule (c. 1750–1850), then Indian publishing has reached the appropriate stage in Golding's historical cycle. To develop this argument further, the next thirty years should see Indian publishing progress through another missed century and arrive at the equivalent of the mid-twentieth century or Golding's stage II (a).

The Twentieth Century

The major problem with this historical equation is that Indian publishing is functioning in the environment of the late twentieth century. As an industry, though, it has reached only the middle of the nineteenth century in real terms, and now it is confronted with twentieth-century pressures. Many of the difficulties the Indian book business faces today are a direct result of this incongruity in time scales.

An example of this is piracy. The British and American publishing community has made a great effort to combat piracy in India and other Asian countries. The basic assumption is that piracy is wrong and amoral. Yet up to the end of the nineteenth century, America was also a flourishing base for pirates, much to the chagrin of their British counterparts. Piracy is perhaps an inevitable stage in the evolution of the publishing industry in newly emergent countries. However, because we are in the last quarter of the twentieth century, where communications are also infinitely better and faster, the opprobrium attached to piracy is greater. The major argument against piracy is actually the deleterious effect it has on indigenous publishing—the shattered state of the Pakistani publishing industry being a case in point.

Indian publishers do not enjoy a comparatively protected domestic market. American and European publishers did not have to compete with a wide range of imported books in the early stages of their development. Thus their book industries could evolve gradually and according to their own national genius. Indian publishers do not have this advantage. Their books have to compete with imported ones, with the money spent on books by both individuals and institutions being spread over the bulk of the world's publishing output.

From another perspective, the import and sale of foreign books is almost a necessity for the growth of Indian publishing. The novels of major fiction writers, such as Harold Robbins, James Hadley Chase, and James Clavell, have a large market in India. Even though sold only in small quantities, imported scholarly books also provide a substantial amount of turnover because of their high prices. Imported books, therefore, form an important financial resource base for the Indian book industry.[17]

This can be illustrated by the experience of Asia Publishing House. Founded in 1943, Asia was the first purely Indian publishing house and was publishing 250 titles a year at its zenith. It also represented twenty-three of the larger American and British publishers. In 1960, Asia decided to terminate all agency contracts and concentrate exclusively on publishing and selling Indian-authored books. Within ten years, Asia was bankrupt. Although imported books have a negative impact on Indian publishing, they also play a positive role. The solution does not lie in banning or restricting their importation but in devising creative alternatives to the situation.

Signposts for the Future

The most positive indicator for the future of Indian publishing is India's large population and the rising levels of both literacy and incomes. The literate population (245 million in 1981) is equivalent to the entire population of the United States. Even allowing for language fragmentation and the fact that a large percentage of literates are only functionally so, this is a very solid base on which to build a publishing business.

The newspaper and magazine industry has already begun to capitalize on this large readership. The last decade has witnessed a phenomenal growth in this business. The number of newspapers and magazines published in the country has increased from 14,531 in 1977 to 18,140 in 1980 and, according to preliminary reports, to 19,144 in 1981 (see table 9.4). The combined circulation in 1980 was about 51 million. What is particularly instructive is that there were more publications in Hindi than in English, whereas the converse is true of books.

There is no doubt that the number of languages has watered down the advantage that such a vast literate population would otherwise confer. The figures in tables 9.2 and 9.4 suggest that the regional languages are gathering strength. The number of books published in Kannada, Malayalam, Marathi, and Tamil increased over the period 1972/73 to 1980/81 as did the number of newspapers and magazines in these languages (over the period 1977 to 1980). Linguistic fragmentation can be turned to advantage if Indian publishers accept multilingual publishing as a future area of development. Indian publishing has so far worked in airtight language compartments with almost no publisher active in more than one language. This division extends to the bookselling business as well. These barriers will have to be broken down and a process of cross-fertilization begun.

Distribution is another major area of concern. The growth of the Indian publishing industry in the 1970s was based almost entirely on sales to libraries. The ephemerality of this sales base was more than amply demonstrated by the effect of the cut in library grants. Indian publishers and booksellers need to increase market penetration and create "book-mindedness."

Both publishers and booksellers have concentrated their efforts in the four metropolitan areas and in two or three large cities. These urban centers account for

Table 9.4. Number of Books and Periodicals Published by Language.

Language	Percentage of Population Speaking, 1981	Percentage of Books Published, 1980–81	Periodicals Published*		
			1977	1980	Percentage
Assamese	1.53%	1.14%	50	64	0.35%
Bengali	7.68	6.10	1,003	1,376	7.58
English	2.00	44.61	2,892	3,440	18.96
Gujarati	4.44	4.41	618	688	3.79
Hindi	35.77	12.97	3,736	4,946	27.26
Kannada	3.73	2.91	432	592	3.26
Malayalam	7.78	4.41	567	719	3.96
Marathi	7.16	7.93	861	1,047	5.77
Oriya	3.40	2.59	151	240	1.32
Punjabi	2.42	1.80	312	384	2.12
Sanskrit	–	0.25	27	29	0.16
Tamil	6.47	6.61	653	771	4.25
Telugu	7.67	2.27	463	520	2.87
Urdu	4.91	1.67	1,047	1,234	6.80
Others	5.04	0.32	1,719†	2,090†	11.52
Totals			14,531	18,140	

* Of the 18,140 periodicals published in 1980, 6.5 percent were dailies, 0.5 percent were tri- or bi-weeklies, 29.1 percent were weeklies, and the remaining 63.9 percent were described as "other periodicals."
† Includes bilingual and multilingual publications. Bilingual publications numbered 1,194 in 1977 and 1,428 in 1980. Multilingual publications numbered 279 in 1977 and 339 in 1980. Thus, the number of publications in languages other than the fourteen main ones were 246 and 323 respectively. Since no data were available on what languages the bilingual and multilingual publications are in, they have been included with "others."
Sources: For column 1, see table 9.1. For column 2, see table 9.2. For column 3, 1977, Government of India, *India 1980—A Reference Annual* (New Delhi: Ministry of Information and Broadcasting, 1980), p. 145. For column 3, 1980, Government of India, *India 1982—A Reference Annual* (New Delhi: Ministry of Information and Broadcasting, 1983), pp. 145–147.

about 15–20 percent of the institutions and book-buying public. The remaining 80 percent are scattered across the country, and their book needs are hardly catered to at all. There is, as yet, no book club in the country and only one or two very small and desultory mail order operations. Hence, a very large portion of the potential book-buying audience has virtually no access to books.

A readership survey conducted among visitors to the Third World Book Fair (1978) in New Delhi revealed that book buyers normally hear about books from "book reviews and advertisements and friends (word of mouth)," while only 8 percent "got information about books from bookshops."[18] There are few book reviewing forums. The national dailies devote very little space to book reviews in their Sunday editions. There are two journals, one a quarterly and the other a fortnightly, exclusively devoted to book reviews. Their circulations are very low and their coverage limited. The cost of advertising in the mass media is extremely high and is only suitable for a block-buster type book; most publishers cannot afford to advertise.

These factors, coupled with the poor spread of retail outlets, reinforce the argument in favor of some form of direct approach. The 1978 readership survey cited above covered 9,079 respondents of whom 46 percent earned less than Rs. 500 (US$50) per month and only 25 percent had monthly incomes in excess of Rs. 1,000. Among its findings were that "about 9.0 Indian fiction, 8.5 Indian non-fiction, 7.8 foreign fiction and 7.2 foreign non-fiction" were purchased by respondents annually and that on an average "about Rs. 142 and Rs. 176 were spent on fiction and non-fiction respectively a year."[19] These figures are encouraging as they indicate a broad range of interest and a willingness to spend at least some money on books even among people from low-income groups. The trouble is that they have very limited access to bookshops and to information on books.

Perhaps the only systematic attempt made in India to reach book buyers directly was the Home Library Plan launched from Hyderabad in May 1960. This scheme was restricted to books in Telugu. In twenty years it has enlisted more than 46,000 subscribers (most of them living in rural areas) and sold over 800,000 books.[20] Another example of creative marketing is the activities of the Lok Milap Trust which operates from Bhavnagar in Gujarat. Since 1973 this organization has been annually producing sets of three to five books in Gujarati ranging from children's books to serious literature and "making them available at very little above cost . . . [to those] who subscribe in advance."[21] It is surprising that, with the exception of Hind Pocket Books, no other publisher or bookseller has tried to emulate these examples. "The developed countries have evolved a complicated system of book distribution. . . . It would be absurd for developing countries to copy such a system."[22]

Equally important is the need to publish books at appropriate prices. If markets can be expanded, print runs can be increased realistically and prices brought down. But if the costs of printing and, especially, paper continue to increase, a larger circulation may not lead to a substantial reduction in prices. The only alternative is to reexamine book production standards which have been uncritically imported from the West. Indian publishers should be willing to produce books composed by hand or on typewriters, printed on inexpensive paper with adequate binding instead of trying (unsuccessfully) to emulate British and American standards of production.[23] The average buyer is mainly interested in a book's contents and not its appearance.

This change in attitude on the part of Indian publishers could well be one of the major keys to a healthy future for them.

The Government

In keeping with many excolonial countries, India has adopted planned economic development within a socialist framework. As a result the government has a very major role in the industrial development of the country with many areas of economic activity under its direct control. Publishing has been affected directly or indirectly by many measures introduced by the government, and any discussion on the future of Indian publishing has to take cognizance of this. There are a number of ways that the Indian government can assist the growth of the book business without necessarily interfering with it.

One of the main reasons prompting the government's control of the large and lucrative textbook publishing business was its belief that commercial publishers would price books very high, ignore subjects where enrollments were low, and pay scant attention to national aspirations and needs. Without questioning these assumptions, the government could involve commercial publishers in textbook production while still retaining editorial control. This would ensure quality in production and relatively better distribution without affecting the government's objectives. It would also inject some much-needed finance into the industry.

The government (and its many agencies) is by far the single largest consumer of paper in the country. A great deal of this usage is wasteful and if properly monitored and controlled could significantly effect the price and availability of paper. If it is not possible to reduce the price of paper, publishing firms could be subsidized based on their paper consumption so as to mitigate the crippling effect of the soaring price of paper.

Current book distribution methods are woefully inadequate and new approaches, such as direct mail, need to be explored. However, the postage rates for books, especially those sent by Value Payable Parcel, have gone up considerably in the last two or three years making it very expensive to send books by this method. The government can assist the growth of the business by reducing postal rates for book parcels.

Libraries, other than institutional ones, are few in number and extremely inadequate. While the government has actively promoted literacy, it has done little to ensure that literacy skills once acquired are retained. A network of libraries in rural areas would support these efforts and, simultaneously, create new markets for Indian publishers.

There are other ways the government can assist the Indian book business, but the first step is to recognize that "an independent publishing enterprise is crucial for developing countries. . . . Without an indigenous publishing enterprise, a nation is doomed to 'provincial' status and will continue to be dependent on outside elements for its intellectual sustenance."[24]

Conclusion

The chairman of a large multinational company producing a wide range of consumer goods declared recently: "The rural market offers opportunities which are vast and relatively untapped. . . . There has been a real and absolute increase in the standard of living of the rural populations. . . . New techniques have to be continuously developed and tested in order to service this varied market."[25] A successful transition for the Indian book business from the nineteenth to the twentieth century can be ensured primarily by recognizing this growing market and by developing appropriate books and distribution techniques.

In the Indian publishing industry's favor is the fact that the book-reading and -buying public is growing and will continue to expand for many years. This is in contrast to developed nations where literacy rates and population growth have leveled off and book sales have not increased in real terms for some years now. To take advantage of this potential growth, Indian publishers will need to adopt positive and constructive approaches and to develop a publishing idiom suited to the people. "India is too big for outside help, and will have to draw the remedies from its own resources."[26]

Notes

1. The only reliable statistics available at the time this essay was written related to the year 1981 (or the financial year April 1, 1980 to March 31, 1981). The figures in this paragraph are taken primarily from Government of India, *India 1982—A Reference Annual* (New Delhi: Ministry of Information and Broadcasting, 1982), pp. 10, 11, 46, and 165.
2. Very few of those for whom English is a first language are likely to record that fact while answering census questions. Most of them would indicate the language they ought to be speaking and which, quite literally and most probably, is their "mother's tongue." Only tribals and those educated by Christian missionaries would declare that English is their first language.
3. *Survey of Indian Book Industry* (New Delhi: National Council of Applied Economic Research, 1976), pt. 1, p. 10.
4. Dinkar Trivedi, ed., *Directory of Indian Publishers* (New Delhi: Federation of Booksellers and Publishers Associations in India, 1973).
5. The base figure for these calculations is 10,273 publishers as the directory does not provide language of publication for the 993 governmental and institutional publishers.
6. These figures have been culled from Government of India, *Report on Survey of Printing Industry in India* (New Delhi: Directorate General of Technical Development, Ministry of Industry, 1980).
7. *Economic Times,* January 14, 1984.
8. There is a succinct discussion of the impact of the colonial legacy on Indian publishing in Philip G. Altbach, "Literary Colonialism: Books in the Third World," *Harvard Educational Review* 45 (May 1975): 226–236; also see Philip G. Altbach, "Scholarly Publishing in the Third World," *Library Trends* 26 (Spring 1978): 490–503.
9. One estimate puts the current value of the school textbook business at one billion rupees ($10 million) per year. Narendra Kumar, "Publication of Textbooks by Public Sector," *Indian Book Industry,* June 1983, pp. 7–8.
10. For a fuller discussion of the impact of subsidized foreign textbooks, see Ella Datta, "College Books from Abroad," *Times of India Sunday Magazine,* June 23, 1974; and U.S. Mohan Rao, *Books on Science and Technology, A Report on Publishing, Printing and Demand* (New Delhi: National Book Trust).
11. J. L. Sardana, "Development of College Libraries in India," *College Librarian* 1 (April 1978): 24.
12. For an elaboration of these points, see Amrik Singh, *Times of India Sunday Magazine,* January 2, 1977.

13. For full details of the cuts, see Usha Rai, "Book Famine Hits Libraries," *Times of India,* November 22, 1979.
14. For the author's reasons for not wanting to be published in India see Anita Desai, "Excuse Me, But India Is Not for Me," *Statesman—Fourth World Book Fair Supplement,* March 2, 1980.
15. Peter Golding, "The International Media and the Political Economy of Publishing," *Library Trends* 26 (Spring 1978): 454.
16. Romesh Thapar, *Book Development in National Communications and Development* (Karachi: UNESCO Regional Centre for Book Development in Asia, 1975), p. 4.
17. According to one report, "Of the industry's total annual turnover of Rs. 25 crores (Rs. 250 million), approximately Rs. 15 and 16 crores are accounted for by sales of foreign . . . books." "Publishing: Getting Ready for the Boom," *Business India,* July 24, 1978, pp. 21–33.
18. *Reading and Book Buying Habits* (New Delhi: National Book Trust, 1982), p. 8.
19. *Ibid.,* pp. 4 and 6.
20. K. S. Duggal, "Remembering a Publisher with Vision," *Indian Book Industry,* October 1979, pp. 9–10.
21. Samuel Israel, "The Colonial Heritage in Indian Publishing," *Library Trends* 26 (Spring 1978): 550.
22. Robert Escarpit, "Trends in Worldwide Book Development, 1970–1978," Studies on Books and Reading, no. 6 (Paris: UNESCO, 1982), p. 37.
23. For an elaboration of this point see Philip G. Altbach and Eva Maria Rathgeber, *Publishing in the Third World: A Trend Report* (New York: Praeger, 1980).
24. Philip G. Altbach, *Publishing in India. An Analysis* (New Delhi: Oxford University Press, 1975), p. 3.
25. A. S. Ganguly, Speech delivered at the Annual General Meeting of Hindustan Lever Limited, Bombay, June 24, 1983.
26. Robert Escarpit, "Trends in Book Development," p. 19.

10. A Brief Account of Book Publishing in China

Fang Houshu

China is an ancient civilization with a long history of book publication, which began more than 2,000 years ago. Among China's contributions to publishing were the invention of paper in the first century and the technique of engraved woodblock printing in the ninth century.[1] The technique of moveable type printing came about in the eleventh century. With the invention and development of paper and printing techniques, the publication and dissemination of books flourished. From the tenth to the twelfth century, Kaifeng in Henan Province, Meishan in Sechuan Province, Hangzhou in Zhejiant Province, and Jianyang in Fujian Province became the centers of engraved woodblock printing.[2]

A great number of the books published in China were on history. There is also a long tradition of publishing large volumes and series, for example, the four sets of related works compiled during the northern Sung Dynasty toward the end of the tenth century, namely, the *Wen Yuan Ying Hua, Tai Ping Yu Lan, Ce Fu Yuan Gui* (each of which ran into some 1,000 volumes), and *Tai Ping Guang Ji* (500 volumes). The *Yong Le Da Dian,* the world's first encyclopedia, was compiled in the Ming Dynasty in the early fifteenth century and consists of 22,900 volumes with a total of 37 million Chinese characters. Later efforts were the *Si Ku Quan Shu* [Imperial library of Chien Lung], consisting of more than 79,000 volumes, and the *Library of Ancient and Modern Books,* numbering 10,000 volumes with 100 million characters, both of which were compiled in the Qing Dynasty around the nineteenth century.

Under the yoke of prolonged feudal society, however, publishing grew at a snail's pace. In particular, as China was reduced to a semicolonial and semifeudal society after the Opium War in 1840, publishing in China lagged behind that in the developed countries of Europe and the United States. During the Kuomintang's rule in old China, publishing reached a precarious state; many of the already few privately owned publishing houses and bookstores were on the verge of extinction. After the founding of the People's Republic of China in 1949, broad vistas opened for the development of publishing.

Publishing was divided into the three specialized fields of publishing, printing, and distribution in the new China. In the collectively owned publishing, printing, and distribution establishments there is a total of 217,000 workers and staff members, of whom 21,000 are publishers, 76,000 are distributors, and 120,000 are printing technicians and workers. Publishers and distributors have formed the Publishers' Association of China, and printing technicians and workers the Chinese Association of Printing Technique. The administrative organ in charge of publishing throughout the country was formerly the State Publication Administration under the State Council. Following the structural reform of May 1982, the State Publication Administration was merged into the Ministry of Culture of the People's Republic of China and became the Publication Administration under the Ministry of Culture. Under the new leadership, it supervises the implementation of state policies, guidelines, regulations, laws, and decrees regarding publication; coordinates the working relationship among publishing, printing, and distribution; and promotes the publication and distribution of outstanding reading materials on various topics. The Ministry of Culture also invited fifteen well-known publishers and writers to form a State Publication Commission as a governmental advisory organ on publication. The main tasks of this commission are to make surveys of publishing policy, to formulate plans for book publishing, to initiate transformation of the publishing system, to formulate publishing regulations, and to train publishing personnel. It also advises governmental publishing institutions in maintaining the country's publishing orientation and carrying forward publishing undertakings.

The Current Publishing Situation

There are presently 243 publishing houses in China (excluding Taiwan Province). In the capital, Beijing, the national center of publication, there are 129. The largest is the Ministry of Culture itself followed by other State Council departments and nongovernmental organizations around the country. Shanghai, the largest city in China, has always been an important base for publishing, and 16 publishing houses are located there. Publishing houses are located in all the other provinces, autonomous regions, and municipalities, with three or four in some places and a minimum of one, directly under the central government, in other places.

In the Beijing publishing houses labor is divided according to the different branches of learning or different categories of books to be published. For instance, the People's Publishing House publishes classical works of Marxism, collections of important Party and government documents, and works on philosophy, history, and economics. The People's Literature Publishing House mainly publishes ancient and contemporary literary works, both Chinese and foreign, and works on the history of literature and literary critiques. These publishing enterprises exert a fairly significant influence on the art and literary circles of the country.

The Zhong Hua Book Company specializes in collating and publishing ancient Chinese works, and the Science Publishing House and Popular Science Publishing House publish, respectively, works by noted scientists and popular reading materials for disseminating scientific knowledge. In addition, specialized publishing houses produce works on agriculture, forestry, water conservation, geology, oceanography, railway technology, communications, metallurgy, machine building, atomic energy, the lighting industry, the chemical industry, physical culture, medical science, and so on. There are also publishing houses devoted to specific groups of readers, such as the China Youth Publishing House and the Workers' Press. The country also shows great interest in children as exhibited in its publishing operations for children and juveniles. Nine juveniles' and children's publishing houses have been established throughout the country. Four years ago, the Encylopedia of China Publishing House was established in Beijing.

As a multi-ethnic, socialist country, China has always attached great importance to the cultural development of the different nationalities and the publication of books in minority languages. There are fifty-five nationalities in China in addition to Han (the largest national group accounting for 94 percent of the total population), the main ones being the Mongolians, Tibetans, Uigurs, Miaos, Yis, and Zhuangs. The Zhuang nationality has a population of over 10 million; thirteen nationalities have populations of over one million; twenty-eight nationalities have populations of over 100,000; and the populations of the remaining nationalities are very small. A Translation Bureau for minority languages and a Nationalities Publishing House are located in the capital, and there are twenty-two publishing houses in areas inhabited by minority nationalities. The publication and distribution of reading materials in these languages is subsidized by the state.

With the development of education in China, textbooks have come to occupy an important place in the publishing business. In 1982 more than 4,000 textbooks were published for over 200 million students. Textbooks for primary and high school students are written by noted experts at the invitation of the Ministry of Education. They are then published by the People's Education Publishing Houses under a unified plan, printed, and distributed throughout the country. University and college textbooks are published by publishing houses specializing in specific subjects. Twelve university presses have been established to meet the needs of teaching and scientific research.

Large publishing houses in China have staffs of 300, 400, or even more, while smaller houses have less than 100 staff members. All publishing houses are divided into editing, publishing, and administrative departments. In recent years, distribution departments have been established to handle mail orders and wholesale purchases. Many influential writers and scholars are affiliated with publishing houses as part-time leading members or editors, thus furthering the close working relations between publishers and experts in their publishing fields. Authors have permanent occupations and fixed salaries of their own, and, in addition, they are remunerated for their writings. Publishing houses determine their publishing program without interference by the government. They attach great importance to the social effects of publications and serve the people and socialism by encouraging the publication of fine reading materials. Publishers advocate debate among different academic views and encourage the development of different schools of thought.

Development of Publishing

Between the founding of the People's Republic of China in October 1949 to the end of 1982, some 400,000 books were published, and 77.8 billion copies were distributed. After 1979 when the country began to stress socialist modernization, fairly rapid progress was achieved in various fields. This is particularly true of publishing. In 1982, the People's Republic published a total of 31,784 books, an increase of 110 percent over the figure for 1978. Printed materials reached 5.879 billion copies, an increase of 55 percent from 1978. As the number of voluminous works has increased, so has the average unit price of books. The total value of books sold in 1982 reached RMB 1.84 billion yuan (roughly US$920 million)—double the figure for 1978.

With the increased development of the national economy as well as the growth of scientific, educational, and cultural undertakings, readers feel an increasingly urgent need for books. The Xinhua bookstores, which are located throughout the country, are often packed with prospective book buyers. The average number of readers at the Wangfujing Bookstore, the largest bookstore in Beijing, exceeds 20,000 on weekdays and 40,000 on Sundays. Many bestsellers sell out, although print runs frequently reach one million copies. Sometimes 10 million copies are printed; for instance, 7 million copies of the *Collected Works of Zhou Enlai* have been printed, 6 million copies of the *Collected Works of Liu Shaoqi*, 3 million copies of *Peng Dehuai's Self-Account*, and over 5 million each of the classical Chinese literary works *Dream of the Red Mansion, Pilgrimage to the West, The Three Kingdoms*, and *Water Margin*. Over 100 million copies of the *Xinhua Dictionary* have been printed, and 120 million copies of the documents of the Twelfth Congress of the Chinese Communist Party, published in September 1983, were sold within two months. Outstanding children's books, picture books, popular science and literary works are also distributed on a large scale. The annual issue of New Year pictures runs to as many as 600 to 700 million copies.

Economics of Publishing

Because publishing in China is not based on profit making, a policy of low profits usually prevails. In the early days of the People's Republic, the government established a unified standard for fixing book prices. The standard for primary and high school textbooks is the lowest. Also fairly low is the standard of fixed prices for children's books, readers of popular knowledge, art and literary works, political documents, and books on ordinary social sciences, which are in large circulation. The state has reduced the fixed prices of books several times in order to alleviate the burden on readers and facilitate the wider dissemination of knowledge. The fixed price for each printed page is now RMB 0.045 to 0.15 yuan (US$0.023 to 0.008). In 1950 the government established uniform retail prices for books throughout the country. Book prices are determined by the number of printed sheets (one printed sheet = 787mm × 1,092mm/2) in a book in accordance with the government's price standard. The price of a book includes the publishing house's direct costs (cost for paper, printing, and author's remuneration), administration expenses, and profit, accounting for 70 percent of the total. The remaining 30 percent of the cost is the bookshops' distribution expenses. Newly published books are delivered to the first-grade wholesale departments of Xinhua Bookstores at a discount of 30 percent. The wholesale departments are billed upon receipt of the books and have to pay the publishing houses within five days. They cannot return unsold books. The wholesale departments of Xinhua Bookstores give retail shops (municipal and country bookshops) a discount of 22 percent of the list price. Books are sent by the distribution centers to bookshops throughout the country; the packing and transportation fees are all borne by the distribution departments. In addition to direct retail sales, the country and municipal bookshops also resell books to collective or privately owned bookshops and cooperatives at a discount of 13 to 15 percent of the list price. The book distribution fee is fairly low in China. Bookshops must sell books according to the unified list prices; they are not allowed to raise the book prices. This helps alleviate the economic burden of the readers. The average person bought 5.4 books in 1982.

Books are sold at the price fixed by local Xinhua Bookstores, even when they are shipped to such remote areas as Tibet or Xinjiang and the distribution fees exceed the book prices because of the cost of long-distance transportation. The excess distribution fees will be subsidized by the head office of the Xinhua Bookstores at the end of each year.

Recent Progress

There are 176 specialized book presses in the country, 77 of which have staffs of over 500 and 34 with staffs of over 1,000. The largest, the Beijing Xinhua Press, has a staff of 3,700. More than 8,000 commercial presses print ordinary materials, and some of these are partly responsible for printing books.

There has been rapid progress in the manufacture of printing machines. In 1980, 256 different machines were available, double the number available in 1970. The annual production output of machines reached 12,700 in 1980, more than twice the 1970 figure. The complete-set equipment needed for building new book presses and printing equipment for updating old factories are locally made, with a few exceptions. Printing machines are exported by China.

Most of the books published in China are distributed by the government-owned Xinhua Bookstores, established in 1937 in Yenan, capital of the Chinese liberation areas. On the eve of the liberation, it had over 700 branch shops. After the founding of new China the head office was set up in the capital. The store now has 6,722 retail branches throughout the country. The rural marketing and supply cooperatives handle book sales in the vast countryside. There are more than 64,000 book-sale centers attached to rural cooperatives throughout the country. In the past two or three years, over 6,000 collective or privately owned bookstores, book stalls, or book dealers have been set up in the cities and rural towns. There are also a number of bookshops run by colleges or factories and book-sale centers run by specialized shops. According to statistics available at the end of 1982, there are over 86,000 book-sale centers in the country, including the retail centers of Xinhua Bookstores. In addition, more than a hundred publishing houses sell books directly to the readers, accounting for 2 percent of the total book sales in the country.

Copyright and Foreign Collaboration

The state protects the rights and interests of writers and translators. For first-edition books, the publishing house pays the writers or translators percentage royalties, as well as the basic remuneration fee. Additional royalties are paid when the book is reprinted. The basic remuneration for manuscripts is RMB 3 to 10 yuan per thousand words, the highest being 20 yuan per thousand for scientific works of great academic value. Percentage royalty is paid at a certain percentage of the total amount of basic remuneration. The percentage royalty is approximately 50 percent of the basic remuneration for books with less than half a million printed copies and approximately 70 percent of the basic remuneration for books with less than one million printed copies.

China started its cooperation with foreign countries in publishing in 1979. More than forty Chinese publishing houses have concluded over 120 contracts for joint publication with more than seventy publishing establishments in twelve countries, including Japan, the U.S., and the U.K., as well as Hong Kong and Macao. More than 400 books and journals have been planned for joint publication, and over 20 of them have already been published. Jointly published books cover a wide variety of subjects, emphasizing tourism, architecture, historical relics, arts and handicrafts, zoology and botany, as well as works on literature, history, science and technology and multivolume reference books.

Many of the jointly published books are very popular. For instance, 300,000 to 400,000 copies of the pictorial *Travel in China,* jointly published by China and Japan, have been published; 110,000 copies of the large-size pictorial *China,* jointly published by China and Yugoslavia, have been published; and *China Tourist Guide,* jointly published by China and Italy, will come off the press soon.

Based on the principle of equality and mutual benefit, the two parties of joint publications adopt diversified forms of cooperation. For instance, some books are edited by a Chinese publishing house and printed by a foreign one, bearing the names of both publishers. In some cases, a Chinese publishing house accepts a book manuscript edited by a foreign publishing establishment for joint publication. The head office of the China National Publishing Industry Trading Corporation in Beijing (with branch offices in Tianjin, Shanghai, and Guangzhou) deals with the export of books and printing materials and undertakes joint publication with foreign countries. The import and export of books are also undertaken by Guoji Shudian (International Bookstore) and China National Corporation for Import and Export of Books.

Conclusion

As China continues to modernize and to interact with the international publishing system, its publishing industry will continue to grow. Recent progress has been impressive. Given the size of China's population and the increasing levels of literacy, the publishing industry has a considerable responsibility to provide reading material for a large and literate population. The economic problems that remain are considerable, but it is possible to look toward the future with optimism.

Notes

1. "The Chinese records are very precise about the date of the invention of paper as well as the person responsible. The Han dynastic chronicle firmly attributes its invention to one Ts'ai Lun in A.D. 105. Ts'ai Lun was a eunuch who seems to have been charged by the court with the responsibility of collecting information and reporting on various experiments in paper making that were taking place in China. Unlikely as it is that Ts'ai Lun himself set out to invent paper, which was essentially an evolutionary process, it is more probable that he was credited with the invention in his official capacity as supervisor of the experiments. The word used for paper (*chih* in Chinese, *shi* or *kami* in Japanese) is found in records of events preceding Ts'ai Lun's time, but since no true paper has been discovered predating A.D. 105, it is now generally assumed that what is referred to in earlier times was 'quasi-paper,' made from silk fibers. The paper 'discovered' by Ts'ai Lun was different from this 'quasi-paper' in its composition of, according to contemporary records, tree bark (which tree is unspecified), old rags, and fish nets. In succeeding centuries the manufacture of paper was refined and spread throughout the Chinese empire, but it was not until about A.D. 400 that paper can be truly said to have supplanted bamboo and silk as the principal writing surface." From David Chibbett, *The History of Japanese Printing and Book Illustration* (Tokyo: Kodansha International, 1977), p. 18.

2. Although there is still no conclusive evidence to confirm that printing originated in China rather than Korea or Japan, "One of the most significant discoveries made by Stein at Tunhuang was a printed copy of the Diamond Sutra of Chinese origin, which bears a date equivalent to 868. The technique employed to produce this work was clearly very sophisticated, because it contains as a frontispiece an elaborate and intricate illustration of a type not seen in Japan until the twelfth century. Such sophistication must have developed over a long period, and consequently this is one more piece of circumstantial evidence which leads to the belief that in time the single missing link of an item of Chinese printing predating 751 will be discovered." From Chibbett, *The History of Japanese Printing and Book Illustration*, p. 33.

11. Publishing in the Philippines

Alfredo Navarro Salanga

Historical Overview

Book publishing in the Philippines is said to have started in 1593, in the seventy-second year of Spanish rule, nearly half a century before the *Bay Psalm Book*, the earliest book published in America. In that year, the *Doctrina Christiana*,[1] a religious handbook in Spanish and Tagalog (one of the major native languages of the Philippines) was printed by Juan de Vera, a Chinese Christian convert who used the ancient Chinese method of xylography or block printing.

This method used wooden blocks planed and squared to the size of two pages. The surface was rubbed with paste, probably made from boiled rice, to smooth and prepare it for receiving the characters. The text was finely drawn on thin transparent paper and then rubbed off on the block, leaving the writing in reverse. With a sharp tool, the engraver cut all the uninked portion off the wooden surface, leaving the characters in high relief. The face of the block was then inked, a thin sheet of paper was laid on the block, and a dry brush was run gently over it to take on the impression. Using this method, an experienced craftsman could produce two thousand copies a day.[2]

In 1602 the same Juan de Vera set up the first printing press in the Philippines under the guidance of Francisco Blancas, a Dominican friar.[3] First located in de Vera's residence in Binondo, Manila, the press was transferred in 1616 to the College of Santo Tomas in Intramuros and moved thereafter to its present site at the University of Santo Tomas along España Street. It is now known as the UST Press.

The Spanish missionaries published the first books, writing on a common theme: teaching the *Indios* to accept the blessings of the friar's authority along with the basic tenets of Catholicism. These books were considered grammar books as well as doctrinal tracts and for the most part were published in Spanish.

Filipino writers, however, were not long in following their *conquistadores* in the field of book publishing and printing. Tomas Pinpin, a native of Bataan, learned printing techniques from the Spanish missionaries. Now considered the father of Philippine printing, he managed the Dominican Press (formerly de Vera's) from 1610 to 1639. Within this period he printed fourteen books, the first of which, *Librong Pag-aaralan Nang Manga Tagalog Nang Uicang Castila* [A textbook to be used by the Tagalogs in the study of the Castilian language], he also authored. It was a bilingual book (Spanish-Tagalog) containing 119 pages in five sections.[4]

When the city of Manila was officially opened to foreign trade in 1785, scientific missions were sent to the archipelago. The most significant of these was that of Antonio Pineda who arrived on July 30, 1789. Pineda drew the expansion plans for Manila Bay and conducted studies on Philippine flora but died before these could be completed. A group of Augustinians became interested in Pineda's unfinished study and in 1837 published a monumental book entitled *Flora de Filipinas Según el Sistema Sexual de Linneo* [The flora of the Philippines according to the Linnean system]. It took Candido López of the Santo Tomas Press twelve years to print the book without assistance. The plates illustrating the various types of Philippine flora were done by lithography.[5]

By 1800 some 541 books had been published in the Philippines. They were mostly dictionaries, grammars, and catechisms for teaching the Catholic faith. By this time the missionaries had learned Tagalog, and most books were printed in this dialect.[6] Authorship, however, still remained Spanish. According to Encarnación Alzona it was the "age of obscurantism," when ecclesiastic censorship and domination prevented the publication of Filipino writings and limited publishing to books on the lives of saints, tales of miracles, novenas, and devotions.

This did not prevent the Filipinos, however, from criticizing Spanish rule. In 1833 Francisco Baltazar wrote and published *Florante at Laura,* a satire on Spanish rule. The book evoked feelings of nationalism among Filipinos, and toward the close of the nineteenth century the Reform Movement was born. Filipino students and expatriates in Europe finally gave vent to their long pent-up dissatisfaction with Spanish colonial rule. Foremost among these reformists was José Rizal, the Philippines' national hero, who authored the anticolonial novels *Noli Me Tangere* and *El Filibusterismo.* The former was published in Berlin in 1887 and the latter in Ghent in 1891.

In 1889 a newspaper, named *La Solidaridad,* was founded by Filipino reformists in Spain. During its six years of existence, *La Solidaridad* carried on its pages the impassioned writings of the Philippines' best journalists and writers—Rizal, Marcelo H. del Pilar, Antonio and Juan Luna, José Panganiban, Pedro Paterno and other Filipino heroes.

With the advent of American rule at the turn of the century, Filipino writers hurdled the initial difficulties of learning a new language and soon wrote and published works in English. Textbooks published by Americans for Americans in the

United States were the tool of instruction in Philippine schools. Later, Ginn & Company, an American publisher, encouraged Filipinos to write school textbooks. In 1918 Camilo Osias wrote the first readers in English for Filipino elementary students. In 1926 Serafin E. Macaraig established a regular educational publishing firm and encouraged Filipinos to write school books from the elementary to college level. In 1932 Delfin R. Manlapaz published his own laboratory manual in physics and handbooks in college mathematics.

More Filipinos went into textbook publishing after World War II.[7] Foreign competition prompted the organization of the Philippine Educational Publishers' Association (PEPA) in 1958 to meet the challenges of educational book publishing in the Philippines and to provide more books written by Filipinos for Filipino audiences. The creation of the PEPA was considered a giant step for Filipino publishing.

Toward the end of the 1970s, some sectors of the publishing and printing industry decided to create the Book Development Association of the Philippines (BDAP). The association was patterned after book development councils in other countries and sought to unify, under one organization, publishers, printers, booksellers, book distributors, book designers, and writers. The BDAP has, since its establishment in 1979, sought to promote Philippine books in particular and book consciousness in general. Since 1980 it has been sponsoring the annual Gintong Aklat (Golden Book) Awards for the best books published within the calendar year. It also organized the Manila International Book Fair in 1981 and 1982 and, in a bid to strengthen publishing in the region, spearheaded the organization of the Association of Southeast Asian Publishers (ASEAP) in 1981. To seriously promote Philippine books abroad, BDAP has participated in book fairs in Canton, Singapore, and Frankfurt and has set up a Filipiniana library in the Philippine Embassy in Washington.

Problems and Perspectives

One of the problems confronting the book publishing industry in the Philippines is the lack of accurate information on book publishing statistics. There is no office, either in the private or in the government sector, with information on the exact number of titles locally published every year, much less a complete list of these titles.

When President Ferdinand Marcos issued Decree No. 812 (Decree on Legal and Cultural Deposit) on October 18, 1975, it was regarded as a step forward in, at the very least, rationalizing book publishing statistics. The decree requires private publishers and heads of various government offices to furnish the National Library and four state university libraries with two copies each (in the case of private publishers) and fifty copies each (in the case of government publications) of new publications within one month from the time a book is off the press. Many, however, have not bothered to comply with this requirement because there is no effective penalty for noncompliance. Much of the data on book publishing statistics, therefore, are generally unreliable. These are available by collation from articles published in the newspapers, seminar papers, and a handful of books dealing on the subject.

The mainstay of the book industry is textbook publishing. With less than thirty full-time publishers, a total of about 700 titles a year is produced with an average print run of 3,000 copies. About 70 percent of this output is composed of school textbooks and general reference books; monographs, tracts, and miscellaneous publications such as indices, atlases, and almanacs account for a further 23 percent.

Literary works comprise about 4 percent of the total, and the rest, about 3 percent, are scholarly books published by universities and research institutions.[8]

Only about a dozen publishers are organized to handle all aspects of book publishing—from the writing of the manuscript, editing and production, to distribution. These are mainly the textbook publishers who also own and operate their typesetting, printing, and binding facilities and have chains of outlets in Metropolitan Manila and some of the major cities in the country. Almost all are family corporations. Ironically, however, the larger and more successful of these publishers appear to depend a great deal more on their bookstore business.[9]

Only a few nontextbooks are published because the population has a low level of reading consciousness. Print runs are small and per-copy costs are high, resulting in correspondingly high list prices. Readers of creative writing are few. Filipino writers complain that publishers are reluctant to print their work. Publishers, on the other hand, complain that readers buy imported books over books by native writers unless they are published in Boston, New York, or London. Locally published literature books are often more expensive than equivalent imports since print runs seldom exceed 1,000 copies and even then the items sleep on the shelves.[10]

Few scholarly manuscripts see print in the Philippines. By definition, a scholarly work has a strictly limited readership even in the developed countries of the West. They are mostly published by university presses, and, more often than not, authors are not paid for their manuscripts; they are expected to be grateful that they have been published at all. In contrast, the lifting of martial law in January 1981 paved the way for a proliferation of newspapers, comics, and gossip magazines and these popular reading materials sell millions of copies.

The publishing industry in the Philippines needs to pursue long-range plans and projections. By the year 2000, it has to serve an estimated population of 73.4 million. The industry, moreover, is expected by the government to help educate people about family planning and other development programs and projects. Andres Cristobal Cruz, deploring the kind of materials published in the print media sector, had this to say:

We find in the mass media publishing sector editorial content that are irrelevant to the culturing of values conducive to civic and collective virtues. Instead of enhancing respect and acquaintance with ideas, our publications promote the cult of personality and personalism and the society page; instead of inculcating the virtues of productivity, our newspapers and radio-TV instill imprudent consumerism; instead of maintaining and enriching the dialogue and discussion of worthwhile entertainment, the arts and the humanities, mass media is mostly sexist and scandal mongering as could be seen in its treatment of materials from movie publicists.[11]

There are only four major daily newspapers published in the country, and they suffer from lack of credibility as they are controlled by the government. After martial law was declared on September 21, 1972, these newspapers flourished because they were the only ones allowed to publish. These are the *Bulletin Today,* the *Daily Express, Times Journal,* and the *Metro Manila Times.* When martial law was lifted, a new type of newspaper came to the fore: the weekly tabloid. Foremost of these was the crusading *We Forum,* which, however, was closed down on December 7, 1982, when its publishers, columnists, and writers were arrested and charged with "subversion and inciting to rebellion."[12] A sister publication, *Malaya,* was allowed to continue publication and is today considered the leading opposition paper.

The assassination of former Senator Benigno Aquino, Jr., on August 21, 1983, opened a new chapter in Philippine political consciousness and in the publishing industry. The major dailies became the subject of an opposition-led boycott and more alternative newspapers (mostly tabloids) were published. To date, these are the *Malaya*, the *People's Voice*, the *Guardian*, *Philippine Signs*, *Metro Kabayan*, and *Veritas*.

Comics, gossip magazines, and pornography are still the most saleable items, however. On a typical newsstand, the ratio of these magazines to newspapers is easily nine to one. One of the unfortunate contributions of these magazines is the proliferation of "Taglish" (a corrupted combination of Tagalog and English) and "swardspeak" (the lingua franca of the local gay community). While the print media publishing sector definitely enjoys public patronage, the book industry sector, according to the Book Development Association of the Philippines, is in a relatively pathetic stage.

Textbook Publishing

The mainstay of the book industry is textbook publishing and the single predominant influence is undoubtedly the government's eight-year Textbook Development Program. Funded by the World Bank, the program is aimed at correcting the chronic shortage of textbooks in public schools, reflected in a 1976 study which showed that there was one textbook for every ten students. The program hopes to reduce this ratio to one copy for every two students.

The textbook project, set up in the 1970s, has ushered in major changes in the book publishing industry. The textbook market in the Philippines accounts for nearly 90 percent of the total market for books, while nontextbook materials comprise only 10 percent of the book market. Private publishing firms formerly had a monopoly of this market, but, under the new scheme, textbooks and accompanying teachers' manuals are now developed by government-designated curriculum centers. Editing and production are undertaken through the project implementing unit, the Textbook Board Secretariat, which also supervises the printing and binding of the books by international competitive bidding in accordance with the procurement procedures of the World Bank. The largest publishing activity ever undertaken in the Philippines, this textbook program calls for the development of all the basic textbooks for the elementary and secondary public school level—109 titles in all—and their distribution on a loan-free basis. To date, close to 45 million copies have been released to the 40,000 public schools throughout the country.[13]

While this project was welcomed by the government, the private publishers reacted strongly and negatively. The general feeling is that they have been relegated to footnotes in the textbook publishing industry. Jesus Ernesto R. Sibal, president of the Philippine Educational Publishers' Association (PEPA) says:

In the Philippines, which Malacañang [the Presidential Palace] assures us is a free enterprise system, a backward step was recently taken with the writing and production of books for the government elementary and secondary schools by the so-called Curriculum Development Centers. The officials directly concerned with the project say that the books are intended to be later sold at cost to the nongovernment schools as well, and the private schools are today the only remaining textbook market for private publishers. We think this is a retrogression because it abridges the healthy expression of a desirable variety of views. The schools have been limited to choose from what the government allows and the government only buys books which it commissions. And besides, it is well known that governments are inefficient entrepreneurs. Their products range from mediocre to inferior, are expensively produced, and are seldom delivered when and as needed. When there is only one publisher—the government—its publications are in danger of being no more than the mouthpiece of the government and the public grows skeptical about the integrity of the books used in the schools. Competition on the other hand, encourages the participation of a multiplicity of authors, publishing firms, and all the sectors of society, and only the best entries win. The public is thus assured that the textbooks are products of qualified writers with a diversity of information and opinions and of publishers with professionalism and publishing expertise.[14]

According to Sibal, prior to the decree establishing the Textbook Development Program, a multiple adoption of textbooks existed, and the Ministry of Education and Culture ordered each approved book for each course in equal quantities. Since 1975, however, the loan funds released by the World Bank for textbooks have been, for all practical purposes, cornered by the Educational Program Implementation Task Force (EDPITAF) which has set up barriers against the availability of funds for the purchase of privately published, Textbook Board-approved books.[15]

Literary and Scholarly Publishing

Though less important as a commercial venture than the textbook industry, the publishing of Filipino literature in English has had a spectacular record. Only twenty years after English was introduced the first novel written in English, *A Child of Sorrow* by Zoilo M. Galang, was published in Manila (1921). By 1966, some sixty-four Filipino novels in English had been published. Abdul Majid, a scholar from the University of Malaya found this remarkable, saying that of the former British colonies in Asia, Africa, and the West Indies, no English novel was produced so shortly after the arrival of the English language. Even India, the first of the British colonies to issue a novel, did so only after some two centuries of British rule.[16]

A number of scholarly journals are published by schools and universities. Scientific and professional associations as well as research establishments add to the proliferation of learned publications. The variety and number of learned journals, however, are not matched by those of scholarly books. A survey of serious books published in the country from 1900 to 1935 in the University of the Philippines Library revealed barely a dozen titles that could be considered scholarly works. This number nevertheless increased from barely one book a year before World War II to about fifteen annually. From 1970 to 1974 some seventy-three scholarly books were registered at the Copyright Office. These figures show that more scholarly books are now being produced each year than were produced during the first thirty years of the American occupation. The University of the Philippines Press, the first university press established in the country (in 1965), was organized to provide "a concrete and deliberately conceived facility for the encouragement, publication, and dissemination of scholarly, creative, and scientific volumes, monographs, and tracts which commercial publishers would not ordinarily undertake to publish."[17] A faculty committee, known as the Board of Management, formulates policies, makes major decisions, and approves manuscripts for publication. The board is composed of a chairman and five members representing the humanities, the social and the natural sciences, and other professional fields.

The press has three major sections: the editorial section, which oversees the publication of accepted manuscripts, designs the book, copyedits and prepares the manuscript for the press, and sees the book through its various stages of production up to binding; the promotion and distribution section, charged with promoting and undertaking the sale of university press publications; and the printery, which has both offset and letter press facilities. The main job of the printery, however, has been to meet the printing needs of the various units of the university. Because of this demand on its facilities, it is actually able to print only a few of the books approved by the press management, which is forced to send out most of its books, through public bidding, to private printers.

The Ateneo de Manila University Press was organized in June 1972 as part of that university's effort "to disseminate the fruits of Philippine scholarship beyond the confines of the classroom by publishing books of enduring importance for the professional scholar and the serious general reader."[18] The Ateneo University Press is also committed to developing and producing textbooks and hopes to provide effective textbooks at all levels of the educational system by pooling its resources and the efforts of writers, editors, and artists.

Economics of the Industry

Book publishing in the Philippines is generally conceded to be a high-risk, low-return business venture. While other industries can avail themselves of loans with low interest rates, the publishing industry does not enjoy this benefit. Publishing is considered a no-priority investment and books are not "bankable."[19] With the prevailing bank interest rate of 24 percent per annum on loans, publishers are further discouraged because of the low return on investment on books. It normally takes at least two years to sell out the print run of most titles.

Foreign books also pose a threat to the local book industry. A local book publishers' association recently deplored the fact that the ratio of imported books to locally published titles in the country sometimes reaches one hundred to one. While these foreign books can be imported by paying 12½ percent advance sales tax, practically all the raw materials or components of locally published and printed books, not to mention machinery and equipment, are subjected to average duties and taxes of 50 percent. The necessary materials are expensive to buy, and, worse, at times is not available.

On November 29, 1982, for instance, the Board of Investments (BOI) and the Central Bank of the Philippines tightened the controls on importation of book paper and coated paper board allegedly to protect local producers from competition with underpriced imports. The regulation called for prior evaluation and approval by the BOI and the CB of all import applications before an importer of these items could even open a letter of credit with a bank. It is not uncommon for printers and publishers to complain of delays in the processing of import applications at the BOI and the CB. These controls have resulted in an artificial shortage of book paper and paperboard and as much as a 47 percent increase in prices.[20]

On February 19, 1983, the BOI recommended to the Central Bank a liberalization of these controls, noting that local producers of pulp and paper were not in a position to supply the needs of printers and publishers at a competitive price and in comparable quality with imports. The BOI recommended that the regulation be relaxed provided that importers reflect the true current market prices and correct "home consumption values" (the values of the products in their countries of origin) and that importers pay all taxes and duties.[21]

Because of the high cost of materials, locally published and printed books are expensive despite their generally poor quality. This also accounts for the country's publishing fewer books than any other Asian country.

An example of the expense involved in book production is the case of medical books. Some ₱200,000 to ₱600,000 is spent per medical book and it takes two to four years to have it released. Often by the time the book is ready for publication, much of the information is already obsolete. Medical book publishing's only saving grace is an informal consortium for different medical colleges where doctors who teach a certain subject are asked to pool resources to write a book on a particular subject. They will then encourage their students to buy their books. The publisher finds out how many students there are in that field and bases his print run on the findings.

Publishers of coffee-table books and literary works, on the other hand, do not survive through publishing alone. Louie Reyes of Vera-Reyes, Inc., briefly summed up the kind of publishers who go into this publishing sector: "I think there are better businesses to go into; in New York, only crazy people go into the publishing game. You have to have a strong love for what you are doing. You need a Quixotic attitude—you want to do something for the country, you want to do something for literature. But you shouldn't go into it for money. Well, it is not my bread and butter. I have my printing press. As of now, I don't think that the business is that profitable locally."[22]

High printing costs and the constricting book market also result in publishing companies' avoiding Filipino authors. In turn, the number of Filipino authors diminishes. At present few publications accept poems and short stories. Filipino creative writers are complaining, and with reason, of the miserably low fees they are paid. A poem published in a book or magazine is valued anywhere from ₱35 to ₱50. In 1975 poets were receiving ₱35 per poem, and after eight years, there has been only a slight increase. In the 1960s, for example, the highest fee ever paid for poems was the ₱50 minimum standard set by the now-defunct Philippines Free Press. That amount was considered "intoxicating" at the time; it is still the minimum standard. Poet José Lacaba contends that poets whose works are anthologized in a textbook should be receiving higher fees, considering the captive market for textbooks. In 1981 the price was still pegged at ₱50 per poem while, in some instances, the poets were not even informed that their works had been published. They only learned about it, Lacaba said, when they chanced upon the book, and, besides "no one likes to waste energy in following up a ₱50 fee."

For the short story published in a textbook, the payment is a bit higher at ₱100. In most cases, this is the only payment the author will receive even if the book is reprinted. Some writers have been prompted to publish their own works although the difficulty is that they work within a very limited budget. Marra Pl. Lanot, fictionist and poet, claims that the authors come up with thin volumes because that is all they can afford. The authors also have to market and promote the book themselves. This so-called vanity publishing dates back to the 1950s when writers decided to shun publishing firms because of the length of time it took for a book to be approved and published. Writers sometimes had to wait two years before finally being published.

Another prevailing practice that has discouraged creative writers is that the authors do not usually receive any fee for their manuscripts when these are published by a publishing outfit. They are paid royalties ranging from 10 percent to 15 percent of the book's retail price. Name writers like Nick Joaquin who carries the government honorific National Artist for Literature, however, gets 50 percent or full advance payment for the manuscript and the full 15 percent royalty. This favoritism has proved disastrous in that publishers hardly encourage Filipino writers to write for book publication. Added to writers' problems is the fact that royalties are seldom paid; in many cases authors receive additional complimentary copies of their books instead.[23]

Coffee-table book writers get relatively higher fees. Gilda Cordero-Fernando of GCF Books pays ₱10,000 and up to each author. Coffee-table book production is, however, very minimal. Louie Reyes opts for a different payment scheme. Instead of paying royalties to the author, he pays a lump sum of as much as ₱80,000 because he buys the manuscript outright.

Textbook writers also get relatively better fees. Manuscripts are bought for ₱2,000 to ₱5,000, in addition to the 10 percent to 20 percent royalty on net income. The practice among publishing houses is to maintain a pool of writers who can be commissioned to write textbooks. Editors hired to polish textbook manuscripts are given monthly stipends ranging from ₱500 to ₱2,000. Virgilio Almario, a publisher of children's books, notes that this monthly honorarium may seem high but considering the profits earned, the fee is still low.

Government Policy on Publishing

There is a lack of clear and direct government support and incentives for book publishers in terms of low-interest loans, expeditious government book purchases, or even clear government policy on book development by the private sector.[24] The burdens of taxation and other governmental regulations add to the problems of publishers.

Some authors are not aware of copyright laws. The usual arrangement is for the author to co-copyright the book with the publisher. For commissioned works, publishers own the copyright.[25] Under the old law, copyright was acquired only upon registration and deposit of the work and upon compliance with official requirements and formalities. Publishing without compliance often resulted in the author's loss of exclusive right, granted by the Philippine Civil Code, over the work, which would then become part of the public domain.

The New Intellectual Property Law (Presidential Decree No. 49, issued on November 14, 1972) has eliminated these technical requirements. Copyright and the other rights conferred by it are acquired and protected from the moment of creation. Even without prior registration and deposit of a work, the author may restrain by court injunction any infringement of his rights and, in addition, have the infringing copies and devices impounded. What he cannot demand without such registration and deposit, however, is the payment of damages arising from such infringement. Hence, deposit and registration are retained under the decree not as conditions for the acquisition of copyright but as prerequisites to a suit for damages.[26]

Authors who do not register their works tend to lose a lot when publishers print their works without their permission. Some publishers use an author's work for an anthology or a collection of poems without the author's knowledge. Without registration of the work, however, no suit for damages will prosper.

For the past several years, the government has provided protection to various industries, including paper and ink, to give them a chance to develop. Unfortunately this has proved detrimental to the growth of indigenous publishing because the high cost of production discourages publishers. In Philippine government circles, moreover, publishing is regarded as a no-priority investment area. The PEPA notes that while the nation has a detailed development plan up to the year 2000, publishing is not in the plan.

The government's policy of allowing cheap book importation while local publishers have to pay heavy duties on practically all their imported raw materials stifles the local publishing industry, which is placed in an uncompetitive and unproductive position. A ratio of one hundred imported books to one locally produced book certainly does not augur well for the industry.

There are no tax incentives or discounts whatsoever from the government. Louie Reyes, who was president of the Book Development Association in 1981, said: "If you ask me, I'll even say that there is a grand conspiracy to keep the Filipino people ignorant." Publishers tend to patronize the printing processes of Hong Kong and other neighboring countries because production costs are cheaper; it is cheaper to have Philippine books published, printed, and bound in Hong Kong. Reyes also points out that several American, Australian, and British publishers who want to have their books published and printed in Manila turn to neighboring countries instead because of their lower production costs. Sometimes publishers evade paying high raw materials importation duties by publishing half of the work in the Philippines and the other half in Hong Kong.

Although some Philippine publishers have tapped foreign book markets, there still is a need for the Philippine government to cooperate with publishers in exporting books. Books cannot be sent out of the country unless the publisher has an export license and a letter of credit from the foreign buyer. Some of these buyers want the books on consignment or on a deferred payment basis. To ship the books, a publisher must obtain some thirteen signatures at the Central Bank. To avoid this red tape, the publishers just have their books printed in Hong Kong and Singapore and ship them from there.

Other complaints aired by publishers include confusion as to which category of industry applies to publishing. "I read somewhere that beer bottles are more vital than books," Reyes says. In addition, publishers do not know with which government ministry to coordinate. The Ministry of Education, Culture and Sports has claimed that it only concerns itself with textbook publishing; general trade books are not in its domain.

In December 1977, Presidential Decree No. 1203 was promulgated, authorizing the reprinting, under certain restricted conditions, of any duly prescribed textbook or reference book, domestic or foreign, whose price may have become so exorbitant as to be detrimental to the national interest. This reprinting scheme has further discouraged local publishers because the imported textbook or reference book reprinted here turns out to be cheaper.

Summary: Problems and Opportunities

That the Philippines has lagged behind in the production of books may seem incongruous inasmuch as the country boasts a highly literate population (90 percent literacy) and an over-educated population largely concentrated in Metropolitan Manila, Southern Tagalog, and Central Luzon. Also, more than 25 percent of the population are enrolled in schools, colleges, and universities. Still, the development of the book industry has remained in the doldrums if not actually moribund.[27]

A number of features of Philippine publishing which contribute to this state of affairs have been discussed in this chapter. In this section some additional problems will be discussed briefly.

Cultural Dependency

Three and a half centuries of colonial rule, first by Spain and then by the U.S., have left the legacy of a popular interest in American and European books. These imports flood the market and drive out books of local origin. Moreover, new knowledge, particularly in science and technology, is produced at a very much faster rate in Europe and America. For this reason, books from these parts of the world appeal to Filipinos who have studied abroad or who were taught by foreign-trained professors.

Lack of Encouragement for Reading

Despite a high national rate of literacy, Filipinos are not a reading people. The proliferation of comics, the advent of television, and the popularity of radio coupled with the difficult economic conditions have contributed to the demise of the reading habit.[28] Other factors include the absence of book reviews and book news, the low priority given to libraries, and issues of language.

Very few publications publish book reviews and book news. While book reviews are part and parcel of most foreign newspapers, they are rarely found in local publications. The Philippines has no bestseller list, either for local or foreign books. A Filipino walks into a bookstore completely unaware of the latest books or the latest bestsellers. More often than not, a book is judged by its cover. Few schools recommend local books, particularly in the field of literature; the study of Philippine literature has not been encouraged. Many students study the literature of other nations but not their own.

More libraries and reading centers are needed in rural areas as well as in most urban areas. In government housing projects little attention is given to establishing libraries or reading centers. Likewise, although a subdivision developer is required by law to provide open space for recreation, facilities for developing the mind are wanting. The largest subdivisions, housing projects, and exclusive villages may boast of complex sports facilities, but few of them have reading centers. The "Read Today Lead Tomorrow" campaign of the Publishers Association of the Philippines, Inc., may have gained some ground in promoting reading, but other influential sectors need to join the campaign.

Comic books and movie fan magazines are sold by the millions every month, an indication that Filipinos do read. These are the fastest selling printed commodity, and their publishers get higher priority in the procurement of newsprint than publishers of other printed matter. While these comics and movie magazines are one of the cheapest forms of reading entertainment available, they offer the lowest form of cultural and intellectual growth.

Literacy and Language Issues

The quality of literacy in English, in the national language, and in other native languages leaves much to be desired. There is no single language common to the whole country. Three languages enjoy status in varying degrees: Pilipino, English, and Spanish. The number of native languages varies from eight to three hundred depending on which definition is applied. About 54 percent of the population know Pilipino, although that figure is controversial; estimates range between 44.4 percent and 75 percent.[29]

Bilingualism and multilingualism are a natural offshoot of the language situation in the Philippines. As a linguistic phenomenon, multilingualism—an individual's alternate use of two or more languages in a day's time, an hour's time, or at any one time—is considered a disruptive force, weakening command of either language. More English than Philipino is, however, being used in school and in some social situations, while Philipino is used more at home, with servants, in casual conversations, to give command, and for purposes of persuasion. The primary medium of instruction in the schools and universities is still English. In every stage of education, from the elementary to the secondary level, students take one Pilipino subject each grade with all other subjects taught in English. The majority of textbooks used, therefore, are in English.

The language situation affects the publishing of books and even magazines in the country. Movie fan magazines, for instance, discourage the correct use of English or Tagalog, opting for "Taglish" and "swardspeak" because they are more popularly used.

Underdevelopment of the Book Market

The country's book market is far from developed; the small distribution system accounts for the limited numbers of books printed, and, therefore, the high unit cost of production. In addition, there is a gross imbalance between urban and rural availability of reading materials. Roughly 95 percent of all books other than text-books are sold in Metro Manila and in a few key cities. Many cities and large towns are without any real bookstores to speak of, and even those with bookstores are never exposed to any substantial number of books.

The country's geographical situation compounds the distribution and marketing problem. Books in cities other than Manila cost at least 5 percent more, exclusive of postal charges. Besides being expensive, transportation and postal facilities are inadequate and often unreliable.

One glimmer of hope in this bleak picture may be the UNESCO-initiated course in publishing offered by the Institute of Mass Communication of the University of the Philippines in June 1984. A consultative meeting of experts from all over Asia met in Manila from August 1 to 6, 1983, to formulate the proposed book publishing curriculum. The participants fully endorsed the aims and objectives of the proposed curriculum. Some thirty participants from Asia and the Pacific will enroll in the course annually, for a period of not less than three months. The UNESCO Regional Office for Book Development in Asia and the Pacific will provide financial assistance to at least ten participants annually. Both the government and the private sector will be invited to sponsor the course and also to evaluate it regularly to make it more responsive to book development needs and problems.

To develop indigenous publishing in the country, the Book Development Association of the Philippines recently made the following recommendations to the government: (1) to reduce the taxes on components or raw materials of locally published and printed books in order to encourage more publishers to venture into local publication and thereby stimulate Filipino creative talent; (2) to remove as much as possible the red tape that surrounds the exportation of books, so as to encourage foreign booksellers to market Philippine books abroad; (3) to give private publishers a share in the elementary and high school textbook market and to work for the elimination of venalities surrounding the purchase of textbooks; (4) to make available to Filipino publishers preferred loans at low interest rates to encourage them to publish more books; (5) to implement immediately the International Standard Book Number (ISBN) coding system and to require all publishers to join it, thereby discouraging and eliminating fly-by-night publishers;[30] (6) to ensure that the Decree on Legal and Cultural Deposit is strictly complied with by all publishers and to penalize those who fail to submit a copy of their books to the National Library; and (7) to adopt policies and implement procedures that will take into careful consideration the opinion and advice of the publishers and to draw from their experience and expertise by making them real partners of government.

Notes

1. John A. Lent, "Book Publishing in the Philippines," *Unitas* 41, no. 2 (1968): 4.
2. Carlos Quirino, "The First Philippine Imprints," *Journal of History* 8 (September 1960): 219–228.
3. Pablo Hernandez, O.P., "History of the Church in the Philippines," *Boletin Eclesiastico de Filipinas,* 48 (April 1974): 629.
4. Lent, "Book Publishing," p. 21.
5. Rod Paras-Perez, "The Graphic Landscape: A Critical Perspective," in Imelda Pilapil, ed., *Filipino Engraving—17th to 19th Century* (Metro Manila: Ylang-Ylang Graphic Group, 1980), p. 8.
6. Lent, "Book Publishing," p. 4.
7. Notable among them were Dr. Ernesto Y. Sibal, who established the Alemar-Phoenix Publishing House in 1958 and who constantly championed the Filipinization of Philippine textbooks; Ceferino M. Picache, who organized Bookman Incorporated in 1947 and became one of the biggest school book publishers in the country; Pablo I. Bustamante, who published his first reference books and teaching guides for the elementary and intermediate schools in 1948; José N. Francisco, who with his wife organized Jonef Publications in 1948 "in the firm belief that the Filipinos, better than the foreigners, can write their own school books"; Olimpio L. Villacorta, who put up the Modern Book Company, which initially specialized in the distribution of medical publications but became a full-time publisher in 1947.
8. Edgardo J. Angara (president of the University of the Philippines) (Keynote speech delivered at the Consultative Meeting of Experts on Book Publishing in Asia and the Pacific, Asian Institute of Tourism, Quezon City, August 1, 1983).
9. Pacifico N. Aprieto, "Book Publishing in the Philippines" (Paper presented at the Consultative Meeting of Experts on Book Publishing in Asia and the Pacific, Quezon City, August 1–7, 1983).

10. Jesus Ernesto R. Sibal, "Textbook Publishing in the Philippines," (Paper delivered at National Training Course on Book Production and Distribution, National Library, May 10, 1978).
11. Andres Cristobal Cruz, "The Role of Publishing in National Development," (Paper delivered at National Book Week Celebration, National Library, Manila, 1978).
12. *Bulletin Today,* December 8, 1982.
13. Alan C. Robles, "Textbook Project Enters 5th Year," *Business Day,* June 18, 1981, p. 8.
14. Sibal, "Textbook Publishing in the Philippines."
15. Robles, "Textbook Project Enters 5th Year."
16. Abdul Majid, "The Filipino Novel in English," *Philippine Social Sciences and Humanities Review* 35 (March–June 1970): 1.
17. From the UP Board of Regents resolution creating the University Press, March 31, 1965.
18. Ateneo de Manila University Press Catalog.
19. Book Development Association of the Philippines, Status Report on the Philippine Book Industry, October 1981.
20. "Printers Fear Rise in Cost, Shortage of Paper, Paperboard," *Business Day,* February 7, 1983, p. 3.
21. "Paper Import Rules May Be Eased," *Business Day,* February 23, 1983, p. 2.
22. "Publishers Discuss Problems," *Business Day,* June 18, 1981, p. 10.
23. "Local Writers Hardly Treated as Royalty," *Business Day,* June 18, 1981, p. 8.
24. Sibal, "Textbook Publishing in the Philippines."
25. "Local Writers Hardly Treated as Royalty."
26. Esteban R. Bautista, "The New Intellectual Property Law," *Philippine Law and Jurisprudence* 1 (June 1975): 495–515.
27. Narciso Albarracin, "Production and Distribution of Books," *Book Council Bulletin* 1 (May 1978): 6.
28. Book Development Association of the Philippines, Status Report.
29. Carmen Guerrero Nakpil, "The Way We Speak, The Way We Are," *The Pilipino Chronicle,* April 30, 1983.
30. The Book Development Association of the Philippines has pointed out that some unprofessional publishers are demeaning the book industry with their disregard for generally accepted trade practices. These publishers do not contribute to the growth of the industry, save for the one or two titles they add to the country's overall book production effort, according to the BDAP's status report.

12. Publishing in Latin America:
An Overview*
Alberto E. Augsberger

Publishing cannot be separated from other aspects of what can be called the "book market." Copyright, paper production, the distribution machinery for books and textbooks are all part of the book market. This chapter deals with the publishing industry as a key part of the book market in Latin America. Publishing in Latin America has made significant progress in the past several decades but still has a long way to go. There are regional disparities and unmet book needs in many Latin American nations. Distribution remains a key problem. Paper supplies vary, and the economics of the book industry is a complicated issue. Yet Latin America does have a viable and growing publishing industry.

General Considerations

The underlying structure of publishing is made up of various activities, which are all centered around the production of works of a literary, scientific, educational, artistic, or informational nature, generally printed on paper. The publishing process is also called the "publishing industry," a term that denotes the manufacturing and

*This essay is an abridged version of Alberto E. Augsberger, *The Latin American Book Market: Problems and Prospects* (Paris: UNESCO, 1981). We are indebted to CERLAL (Regional Center for Book Development in Latin America and the Caribbean, Bogotá, Colombia) and to the Book Promotion Division of UNESCO, Paris, for their permission to include this essay.

commercial aspects of publishing. This applies to anything produced as a result of such activities, whether it be a book, a magazine, a newspaper or anything else that is reproduced in print. This study is concerned with books and related areas of publishing.

Some controversy has arisen about the nature of publishing. It can be seen as a commercial enterprise or as an industrial activity. Correct classification is important since the publisher's status as a trader or an industrialist will determine the way he is treated for credit and tax purposes and his entitlement to benefit from various promotional schemes. The correct classification of publishing will also determine the appropriate legal framework for firms and the scope of other normative provisions.

Originally, publishing was not distinguished from printing and bookselling. Although the activity of the publisher subsequently diverged from that of the printer and the bookseller, it was not always possible to demarcate the province of each, since some publishers were also printers or booksellers, while some booksellers turned their hand to publishing.

Because of such combinations of functions it has been difficult to get a clear idea of the role of the publisher. The craft phase of publishing, when everything was improvised and uncertain, gradually gave way to a full-fledged industry. Printing introduced important technological changes, which called for specialization. Printing from movable type led to an increase in production, so that booksellers began to play an independent role, concerned exclusively with the distribution of books. The process of producing books on a larger scale grew more complex, until book production eventually became an industrial operation.

Industrialization is not an inherent aspect of publishing; it is the necessary outcome of a combination of creative activity and transformation. The publishing process, which takes place in technically programmed sequences, is an industrial operation aimed at making a product—a book—by transforming the constitutive elements of all the stages involved (original material, paper, printing services, and so on) and distinguished from all of these elements to the extent that such a transformation occurs. A publishing company has to be more industrial than commercial; publishing may be described as a decentralized industrial activity.[1]

The publisher must know and understand the market. He must also have enough capital to acquire the materials needed for the different stages of the process, all of which he coordinates and which are entirely his responsibility. A definition of the publisher's role which reflects this view accurately is contained in a study produced jointly by a number of Brazilian publishers' organizations. It states that a publisher is a "natural or artificial person" who, on his own account or with due authorization, transforms into books original material chosen or commissioned by him and coordinates the creative work of authors with that of editors, illustrators, and others engaged in book production and also with the industrial processes required for the reproduction of the original material, with a view to subsequently promoting the sale of the work.[2] The apparent lack of specialization means that the publisher has to build up a broad range of knowledge which will enable him to deal with both the intellectual demands of publishing and the production and marketing side of the business.

The publishing industry has a slow turnover and relies on a complex process of capital investment with an uncertain return. It takes years for the publishing industry to recoup an investment. If it is to thrive, or even survive, it needs large-scale international markets and a measure of linguistic uniformity. Publishing activities must therefore be planned methodically, and a strategy based on such planning must be worked out.

The decision to publish a work entails more than a mere appraisal of manuscripts. It calls for knowledge of the wishes and motivations of the intended readership and of their socio-occupational categories and ages. The publisher also needs a detailed knowledge of the different distribution channels; he must make a careful study of commercial information about sales in the past and of the relevant population statistics and arrange for surveys to be carried out.

Publishers must compare the planned publication with similar works published by their competitors, in terms of content, quality, and price. They must investigate the potential market and study the consumer and his habits. They must find out who their potential buyers are, where they live and how many of them there are, how great their need of the new book is, how they satisfy their need for such material at present, what rival books are available and how they sell, whether they will have to make a special effort to convince the public to buy the book, what the buying power of the target readership is, and what persons are likely to influence the buyer—wife, husband, children, teacher.

Publishing calls for sound editorial skills (a knowledge of authors), a good grasp of book design (aesthetics, the combination of text and image), and a knowledge of book production (manufacturing costs) and of the best distribution channels for the work. This presupposes an understanding of the problems involved in publishing, what can be done, and what it will cost. In other words, it presupposes a knowledge of communication rather than a subjective approach to publishing (publishers who have a "nose" for a good book or who work by intuition). A modern publishing company must apply the principles of sound management; it must plan so as to actually make the sales that are forecast, and its budget must show investments and results. In present-day circumstances, there is no other way of deciding what to publish, how much of it to publish, and how to go about publishing it.[3]

Regional Characteristics

Generally speaking, only some Latin American countries can be said to possess a publishing industry, and then only on a small scale; there are differences in the level of development throughout the region and within each country, in publishing and in other spheres. Countries such as Argentina, Brazil, and Mexico have highly developed book industries whose output is, comparatively speaking, satisfactory in quantitative and qualitative terms. A larger group of countries, such as Colombia, Chile, Cuba, Peru, Uruguay, and Venezuela, make a small contribution to the region's overall publishing output. Other countries do very little publishing.

Notwithstanding such dissimilarities, there are certain recurring traits that characterize publishing throughout the region. In general, the multifaceted nature of this industry rules out any kind of airtight classification, particularly in terms of exact specialization. In Latin America, the roles of publisher and bookseller are usually combined and are frequently linked to those of printer and distributor. While this is by no means the universal practice, it is common, particularly in countries where publishing has been largely neglected. This lack of specialization indicates the poor state of development of the book trade in the area.

This situation is reflected, for instance, in Argentine legislation, which recognizes the multifaceted nature of the book trade in an explicit provision of Law No. 20.380, known as the Argentine Book Law. Article 22 of this law states that:

The benefits established under the terms of this law may be enjoyed by the following types of firm:
(a) single-activity firms: those engaged in a single activity (printing, bookbinding, publishing or bookselling);
(b) semi-integrated firms: those engaged simultaneously in activities listed in paragraph (a) and others not listed in that paragraph;
(c) integrated firms: those engaged simultaneously in two or more of the activities listed in paragraph (a).

In the case of semi-integrated or integrated firms, only the particular activity corresponding to each heading will be taken into account, the benefits granted being allocated solely for that activity.

This provision recognizes that publishing, printing, and bookselling may be combined, complementary, or separate activities. At the same time, it seeks to give each branch of the trade a separate identity, which is most desirable, for it helps to raise the level of professional specialization and to ensure the observance of the legal provisions governing the activities of printers, publishers, and booksellers as defined in Article 21 of the above-mentioned law.

In many cases firms in each category engage in two or three main activities. This makes it extremely difficult to determine the number of publishers who are also operating as distributors and agents—importers—or to distinguish the latter from the former and from booksellers. Functions are sometimes combined, and categorization is difficult because of the lack of professional specialization. This region is unlike highly developed countries in that production is not concentrated in a handful of publishing companies or through coordinated production, integration of firms (mergers, shares, and so on), or copublishing projects. A Latin American publishing house is a highly individualistic enterprise; most publishing firms are family businesses or closed corporations.

Other characteristics of the publishing business in the region are reflected in the findings of the seminar, "The Role of the Book in Change Processes in Latin America," held in Costa Rica in 1974.

The principal findings were:

- There is a lack of communication among Latin American publishers, who do not know what books are being produced in the region, and the demand for books is decreasing accordingly.
- Because publishing companies are extremely scattered and often small, the publishing trade with few exceptions has failed to achieve the large-scale productivity that would make books affordable by the Latin American masses.
- Publishing is affected by numerous customs and tariff barriers, the inefficiency of the postal services, and, in several countries, censorship and restrictions on the entry of certain publications.
- There is no marketing infrastructure to provide a basis for advertising and publicizing new books and for distributing them through an efficient network of branch offices, distributors, and sales agents.

- The book industry is affected by monetary problems which increase the price of books and in some cases actually prevent free trade between the different countries.
- Editions are small because of the limited trade opportunities. This increases costs and leads to higher book prices.
- Publishing costs have increased in recent years—by approximately 300 percent between 1970 and 1974—but no short-term or long-term measures have been taken to deal with the situation.
- The public sector has generally failed to grasp the strategic importance of the publishing industry in manpower training and has failed to adopt policies and introduce legal provisions designed to encourage, promote, assist, and develop the book industry.
- The inadequate bargaining power of the scattered and disunited publishers and their consequent inability to deal with this situation calls for cooperative measures to overcome these basic problems, forge closer links, and improve cultural relations between the various countries.

There are a number of additional points whose importance is not always realized. The indigenous publishing industry in Latin America began as a typical substitution industry. It was first established in the years following the Spanish Civil War and expanded considerably immediately after World War II. It has all the good and bad characteristics of substitution industries. With a view to meeting the needs of an existing market, previously supplied from outside the region, local publishers and printers generally followed the patterns of production, taste, and prestige of the European countries whose production they sought to replace. Like many other businesses during and after these wars, publishing did not expand in response to internal demand, it adapted to external events.

With a few exceptions, the first step was to form companies whose capital was largely owned by foreign interests or to establish companies as veritable enclaves, which determined the future expansion of the trade and exercised a powerful, if not decisive, influence on the market. In this field, as in so many others, the deep-rooted practice of uncritically embracing every new idea from abroad frequently led to accepting schemes without any thought as to how well they met the requirements of the real situation.

Another related point is that most publishing houses began as craft enterprises. They never became large companies in the economic sense of the term, or, if they did so, they very soon became associated with foreign interests. Some of them simply sold out to these interests; in such cases, the adoption of foreign patterns was almost inevitable.

Other publishing activities, however, are a tribute to the abilities and inventiveness of the Latin American peoples. One example is the Fondo de Cultura in Mexico, which successfully implemented an idealistic cultural project. The Fondo de Cultura began by producing numerous translations of works on economics, a subject on which very little had been published in Spanish. However, its catalogue was gradually enlarged, and it has increased the number of Spanish-speaking authors as well as broadened the range of disciplines covered.

Nonetheless, existing commercial criteria and managerial structures impeded the establishment of a genuinely Latin American publishing industry. Individual interests, foreign patterns, and criteria that were often detrimental determined the situation in the publishing trade. Other contributing factors were the lack of modern printing facilities and a shortage of production personnel—technicians and artists working in book production. The last and principal factor, however, was the lack of a regional and national publishing policy. The problems of the book industry are indicative of weaknesses in the whole Latin American business sector and illustrate the lack of national cultural policies which would provide a well-defined framework for a book policy.[4]

Publishing Output

Book production is a commonly used indicator for evaluating a country's cultural development. According to the statistics published by UNESCO, 591,000 titles were published in 1976, approximately 70 percent of them in developed countries. The imbalance between book production in developed and developing countries has remained more or less constant since 1955. In that year developing countries produced 22 percent of the published works in the world; this figure reached only 30 percent over a period of twenty years. By contrast, Third World countries account for 68 percent of the total world population.

The number of titles published per million inhabitants reflects a similar situation. There has been a gradual advance in most regions in this respect, but with a marked difference between the ratio recorded in developed countries and that found in the rest of the world. In 1976, 565 titles per million inhabitants were published in Europe, as against 92 in Latin America, 27 in Africa and 70 in Asia.

Compared with world book production, Latin American output is not large. Although it has not decreased, it accounted for only 5.2 percent of the titles published in 1976, compared to 1.9 percent for Africa and 45.6 percent for Europe. However, the number of titles published in 1960 (17,000) had increased fifteen years later, on a proportionately similar scale to the trend recorded in world production. The increase was more marked during the last six years of the period under review.

This increase in the number of titles published still fell short of the regional requirements, where a marked demand for expansion reflects the gradual increase in demographic ratios and the upsurge in school enrollments. The figures in table 12.1, estimating Latin American book production by countries, reveal some of the fluctuations that have taken place.

During the mid-seventies the publishing industry in the region did not expand production sufficiently to keep pace with the potential market. The increase that occurred in Brazil and Mexico in previous periods did not continue at the same pace. Brazil, for example, which produced an average of 4,972 titles per year over the 1963–66 period, doubled this figure over the following five years. During the next five years, however, expansion continued at a slower rate. The same thing happened in Mexico, although more reliable data might show that progress was made as a result of the modernization of printing plants (which has also occurred in Brazil).

Argentina, the other major Latin American book producer, is regaining its traditional level of production. Despite the increases in production shown in table 12.1, data collected since 1976 indicate that the production level achieved in that year has not been matched. Although a slight cyclical swing is to be expected, there can be no sustained development in the publishing industry until a clearly defined book

Table 12.1. Book Production in Latin America Compared to Other Countries.

	Number of Titles					
	1974	1975	1976	Children's Books	Textbooks	Translations
LATIN AMERICAN COUNTRIES						
Argentina	4,795	5,141	6,674	367 (1976)	360 (1976)	1,361 (1976)
Bolivia	248	339		5 (1974)	11 (1974)	
Brazil	9,948	12,296			1,597 (1975)	1,684 (1973)
Colombia	848	1,272	1,320*	506 (1975)	158 (1975)	15 (1973)
Costa Rica	180	186	60	16 (1975)		
Cuba	869	851	726	54 (1976)		15 (1975)
Chile	796	628	529		90 (1976)	24 (1973)
Ecuador	31					1 (1973)
El Salvador		14				
Guatemala	84					6 (1971)
Haiti						
Honduras	26					
Mexico	5,733	5,882	4,851	351 (1976)	213 (1971)	218 (1973)
Nicaragua	171	226	106			
Panama				2 (1975)		
Paraguay						
Peru	1,322	1,090	925			32 (1973)
Dominican Republic	32	20	48	3 (1976)	32 (1976)	32 (1973)
Uruguay	601	481*			42 (1976)	
Venezuela				7 (1975)		77 (1971)
Barbados	113	87	199			
Guyana			33	1 (1976)	3 (1976)	1 (1976)
Jamaica			1			
Trinidad and Tobago		7	18	4 (1975)		
OTHER PRODUCER COUNTRIES						
Federal Republic of Germany	48,034	40,616	44,477	2,056 (1976)	1,863 (1976)	6,458 (1973)
Spain	24,085	23,527	24,584	825 (1976)	3,476 (1976)	4,489 (1973)
United States	81,023	85,287	84,542	2,210 (1976)		1,968 (1973)
France	26,247	28,425	29,371	604 (1974)	568 (1974)	1,934 (1973)
United Kingdom		35,526	34,340	2,269 (1976)	1,260 (1976)	682 (1973)
USSR	32,133	78,697	84,304	1,783 (1976)	2,283 (1976)	4,402 (1973)

Source: UNESCO, *Statistical Yearbook*, 1977.
* Estimated.

policy is formulated which frees the industry from the vagaries of general economic policies.

Of the other producers in the region, Colombia showed a steady increase, which brought it into fourth place in the table of book producers. The number of titles published in Colombia has risen at an average annual rate of around 20 percent from 848 in 1974 to just under 2,000 in 1978, if recent unofficial figures prove to be correct. The opposite has occurred in Peru and Chile, where publishing output has been declining for a number of years. Cuba and Uruguay are in a similar situation to Peru and Chile. Bolivia achieved a modest yet promising increase in 1974–75.

Production in the other countries of the region is mostly insignificant. However, the Venezuelan publishing industry, for which only estimated figures for 1975 are available, has developed sufficiently for it to be ranked in the second group of Latin American book producers. Regional production continues to be concentrated among a few countries (Brazil, Argentina, and Mexico) which, with slight annual variations, jointly account for around 70 percent of the total output.

Between 1960 and 1976 world and regional book production increased at a similar rate, with a rise of just under 80 percent in world book production and slightly over 80 percent in regional book production. However, in the sixties world production rose by 57 percent, while regional production increased by only 29 percent. These figures indicate that in recent years Latin American production was far higher than world production as a whole.

The statistics in table 12.1 show little or no production of textbooks and inadequate production of children's books, whereas in developed areas of the world titles devoted to education in general and to children's education in particular have made up a very high proportion of the total number of published titles, especially in recent years.

There is a serious shortage of regional statistics and considerable gaps in those that are available, particularly in regard to the size of an edition. Statistics are sometimes fragmentary, as in the case of the number of translations used in each country. In general, the categories of available data are not identical. For example, the category "titles" includes books and pamphlets in some cases (Brazil, Colombia, Peru, and Barbados) and only first editions in others (Chile).

It would obviously be risky to draw definite conclusions from the data provided. Most of the information is incomplete or inaccurate, provisional, and, depending on the sources, even inconsistent. Nevertheless, it may perhaps be argued that the major problem in Latin America is not so much low production as inefficient distribution and circulation of books. Excessive emphasis on increasing the number of titles should be avoided; the aim should be, rather, to print larger editions of each title. Although there is a need for sustained growth in book production, policies regarding access to books, stock turnover, handling, availability, legal formalities, functionality and book reading habits should also be strengthened and ratified.

Progress and Problems in Latin America's Publishing Industry

Various factors determine the overall situation in Latin America and in turn effect the form and potential of its book market. In economic terms, the region's gross domestic product is growing steadily, if slowly. There are national dissimilarities, but the overall prospects are encouraging.

Increased demographic growth, producing a wider band of young people in the age pyramid, an increase in life expectancy, and a decrease in the death rate also effect the book market. Although illiteracy rates are still alarmingly high, they are gradually falling, both in absolute and relative terms. School enrollments at all levels are rising, and the demand for skilled workers is increasing.

All the countries are making greater efforts in education, which is seen as a lifelong process of spiritual and intellectual enrichment, designed to improve people's material circumstances and also the quality of their lives. Hence, the individual is subject, for a longer period of his life, to the influence of educational activities, those implemented by the system as well as other, noninstitutionalized activities. Interest and investment in cultural affairs is also increasing. These are encouraging signs, which auger well for the expansion of the Latin American book market. The number of readers with better economic and educational prospects is growing, and will continue to do so.

The state is involved in publishing because of the role of books in education and development and their importance as a medium of communication. Its involvement extends beyond accession to the international copyright conventions (Geneva, Berne, and the regional conventions). In addition to international agreements the state is responsible for legislation designed to foster and develop the local publishing industry in an international perspective and within a regional context. The recently introduced "book laws" are an example of such legislation. Several nations have adopted these laws, in the form best suited to their own needs, and other nations are preparing to do so.

Two book laws have been adopted since 1973 (although their implementation is still at an early stage), indicating a growing awareness of some of the industry's problems. The publishing industry has failed to expand production in the region, a fact borne out by the high proportion of books imported from outside the region. North American and European firms are setting up subsidiaries or branch offices, a sign that publishers and booksellers in the developed countries believe there is a market for books in Latin America. In some countries, the state finances certain educational books, with a view to either providing them free of charge or meeting educational needs at reasonable prices, and, in this way, supports publishers in the private sector.

With the exception of these book laws, no state has adopted clearly defined book policies. There is a serious shortage of the reliable, up-to-date information needed to ascertain annual production—titles and print size, original works and translations, first editions and reprints or new editions, and so on. Although most countries have made it legally obligatory to deposit works to secure copyright protection, they do not maintain the copyright registers in a manner conducive to compiling statistics and classifying available information.

With a few exceptions, there is no definition establishing, even if only for statistical purposes, that publications which are claimed to be books really are books. Statistics on imports and exports, the production and consumption of printing paper, library purchases, publishing houses, bookshops, the printing industry, and so on also suffer from the lack of definitions and general imprecision. There is no way of finding out how efficient distribution is or assessing the gravity of the illiteracy problem by applying the criterion of "functional literacy," let alone ascertaining how many persons relapse into illiteracy. There are few studies showing how competition from the other mass media affects the book trade and the use of leisure time. There is a similar lack of information on authors and translators (in terms of their numbers and the status of their professional organizations) and on reading trends, skills, and habits. Current local bibliographies are either out-of-date or nonexistent.

The most recent statistics, although they are not entirely up-to-date, show that the media, particularly radio and television, reach a very wide audience. Studies suggest that people devote more leisure time to the audio-visual media than to reading. The material transmitted by these media must be studied in order to discover whether it encourages the reading habit or not. This will be important in determining the future needs of potential readers. In recent years, the readership of newspapers and magazines has not increased at the expense of that of books, but this may be explained by the fact that books are reviewed in the literary sections of newspapers and magazines.

Latin American countries have copyright laws, some of which are more up-to-date than others. Their effectiveness in everyday practice varies. Some authors belong to professional organizations which, in some cases, represent their interests by collecting royalties or handling other matters relating to their rights. Local laws are not always in line with the provisions of the international conventions, and they differ in regard to the periods of copyright protection after the death of the author. The "domaine public payant" system has been introduced in various forms, and there is a wide variety of forms of licensing. Generally speaking copyright laws do not develop authors' and translators' skills or encourage them to continue writing. Most of them receive no social insurance protection, unless they also have some other form of employment.

Only four countries in the region are paper producers, and they produce newsprint. The shortfall in newsprint is expected to be reduced over the next five years, but it is unlikely that regional producers will be able to supply the paper needed by the book publishing industry. Therefore the paper used in book production (whose consumption is not distinguished from that of other paper in statistics) will probably continue to be supplied primarily by the traditional paper-producing areas.

This will undoubtedly lead to further friction between publishers and paper manufacturers. Each state will have to decide, in accordance with the degree of importance it attaches to book publishing, how to supply sufficient quantities and varieties of printing paper at internationally competitive prices and in consignments suited to the changing requirements of book publishers. These decisions must be consonant with overall policies on economic and social development, education, communication, and so on.

At present, only three countries have printing and bookbinding equipment suitable for book manufacturing, and it is not always of a high standard. Some is out-of-date, and there are also differences in the variety and capacity of the plants. Except for these countries, the region does not possess the printing facilities needed to sustain a modern publishing industry. Research into local printing capacity (whether used or not) is needed to assess the number of books and other publications that can be produced. Such research, which will provide basic data, should also cover typesetting methods, the preparation of the photolith plate, the different printing processes, the quality of color printing, traditional bookbinding methods and the "cut-flush" method, and the availability of accessories such as inks, films, adhesive cloth, cardboard, Bristol board and other bookbinding materials.

Information on the scale of the book trade in each country would help define what is meant by the "circulation of books." Although we cannot say exactly how extensive the book trade is, we can estimate its size and the different factors that affect circulation. Many local regulations affect circulation; the situation is so uncertain that almost every year changes are made in some countries. The available information is not comparable because it is compiled on the basis of different criteria (weight, postal packets, internationally acceptable currency, local currency).

The customs treatment of books varies from country to country. Recently an unsuccessful attempt was made to introduce a single document covering all consignments, thus standardizing trade formalities in the LAFTA (Latin American Free Trade Association) countries. The document was designed in accordance with national requirements and could have been used for imports and exports alike, thus simplifying procedures and formalities. Currently each country has different invoice requirements, some countries levy duties that are not applied in other countries, and in one country import and export formalities have to be carried out through a customs agent, regardless of the value of the consignment. Import licenses, foreign exchange permits, trading licenses, the requirement to obtain consular visas on invoices, statistical control fees, and other forms of restriction and domestic taxation hamper and disrupt the activities of the book trade. There is no information on these problems apart from that provided by LAFTA in 1974, and that applies only to the LAFTA countries.

As a rule, publishing houses, regardless of their legal status, also operate as representatives of foreign publishers and sometimes they distribute the books for other local or regional publishers. Some firms operate as booksellers as well as publishing their own books, while others engage solely in book publishing. It is therefore extremely difficult to say exactly what is meant by a "publishing house," and it is equally difficult to say how many publishing houses there are in operation.

With the exception of Mexico and Colombia and, to some extent, Argentina and Brazil, which have introduced tax concessions for publishers, no Latin American country has established a system capable of assisting the publishing industry in meeting its immediate needs. This applies not only to taxation but also to special credit facilities. The development of publishing houses with a significant level of book production depends on solving local economic problems, including high rates of inflation.

Compounding this problem is the relative isolation of many publishers and the shortage of trained personnel. In theory, publishers' access to copyrighted works is governed by local legislation or, in the case of some countries, by the system established under the 1971 Protocols. In practice, very little information is available due to the shortage of bibliographies, the limited number of national copyright information centers, the distance from developed countries and lack of communication with them, and so on. In addition, throughout Latin America there is a shortage of specialized personnel and a lack of training programs, even in countries like Brazil which have reached a significant level of book production.

Book production ranges from books for the basic market, which are produced on an alarmingly small scale in a number of countries, to the publication of large-scale works such as encyclopedias and dictionaries. More than 30,000 titles are produced in the region. By contrast, the region's consumption amounts to more than 50,000 titles, the difference being made up of Spanish imports.

There are two ways books are distributed from publisher to reader: the latter can either buy a copy of the work or consult it through the library system. The publisher's aim is to sell the book, whoever buys it. He may do this through the traditional network of traders (distributors, representatives, and booksellers) whose business is buying and selling books, or he may sell them to libraries, either directly or through the above-mentioned traders, or he may use the new channels of distribution.

Distribution involves some form of book promotion, informing the public that the book has come out. This is undertaken either by the publisher or by a firm specializing in book promotion. However, existing book laws make state participation essential, and such state support is frequently lacking.

Information on the number of titles that circulate through the distributor-bookshop channel and on the total value of the books sold through this channel is not available in Latin America, nor is it possible to determine the relationship between the distribution cost, the number of books sold, and the percentage of titles produced in one year that are on sale in bookshops. Despite the lack of information, it appears that bookshops are now places where books are sold in response to reader demand rather than as a result of promotional activity. Nevertheless, a handful of excellent booksellers, who advise readers and provide a useful service, are still to be found.

The efficiency of the library systems varies considerably from country to country. Some library structures are weak and services inadequate, with a shortage of specialized personnel and training resources. Other countries have better structures but inefficient services, yet they have no difficulty recruiting personnel. Others are in an intermediate position. The allocation of public funds for libraries in these countries does not reflect the importance of library services in the life of the community.

Regional statistics on libraries are very scarce, but library stocks are clearly far below the books-per-inhabitant figure recommended by the experts. Chile is the only country with tax legislation favoring investment in libraries. There are very few factory libraries. Library purchases are insignificant compared with library purchases in other regions, where they account for up to 13 percent of the book production.

In the past libraries were not regarded as links in the information system. Today they are seen as part of the transfer of technology, within the framework of a more general communication policy. Yet few Latin American countries use modern computerized systems, the ISBN, or similar systems. The essential part played by libraries in the educational system has also been disregarded.

Suggestions for a Regional Book Policy

At the present time, no country can claim a monopoly on the book trade; each produces more or less the books its readers want to read. This implies that each country's participation in the international market is limited. Just as books cross borders by virtue of the universal message they convey, so too the publishing industry should operate at a level beyond localistic exclusivism. In the immediate future, cost considerations and the demand for more books and greater variety will increasingly necessitate cooperation among publishers in different countries. The contractual relations that derive from these circumstances have led to new legal procedures and operational systems—for example, copublishing in its various forms.

Copublishing originated some decades ago, as a necessary and useful way of pooling financial resources, reducing risks, and, at the same time, taking advantage of the savings made possible by printing the color pages at one press and then adding the texts in each language. This practice, which is so common in Europe, is comparatively rare in Latin America.

Two meetings of publishers were organized by CERLAL and convened within the framework of LAFTA in 1973 and 1974. These meetings made a detailed study of trade between the contracting parties and the obstacles that hampered it; a total of twenty-three recommendations were unanimously approved. The recommendations concern three main points: preparations for a common market for books; elimination of all duties and charges on the transit of books, magazines, and publications; and the development of uniform bases for legislation on copyright, the transit of persons, and a common system governing capital originating in countries of the region. A meeting in Buenos Aires in April 1977 put the final touches on the preliminary draft of an agreement on free circulation, which was then submitted to the different countries for their consideration.

Furthermore, an analysis of book publishing in Spanish and Portuguese shows that the failure lies mainly not in production but in distribution. Corrective measures should therefore be concerned primarily with distribution. The common market project advocated by CERLAL, on the basis of the agreement on free circulation, is directed toward making better use of the region's publishing capacity; it is designed to put into effect recommendations made within the framework of LAFTA and to remove obstacles to trade.

Any single model for a uniform book policy within Latin America would be premature or ineffectual. Furthermore, any attempt to promote or support the publishing industry must be preceded by decision making at the national level, including input from local sectors, for the objectives must be consistent with national policies. Overall regional systems should first be set up, with specific policies which consider the situation of each country. The initial step involves gathering information with two short-term objectives: to determine each country's stage of development, its growth possibilities, and the size of its potential market; and to carry out research on reading habits and interests, on the media that influence the book market, and on other relevant aspects.

Notes

1. E. A. García, *Desarrollo de la Indústria Editorial Argentina* (Buenos Aires: Fundación Interamericana de Bibliografía Franklin, 1965).

2. *Uma Política Integrada do Livro* (Rio de Janeiro: Sindicato Nacional dos Escritores de Livros, 1976), vol. 1.

3. R. P. Robles, *La Decisión Editorial* (Bogotá: CERLAL, 1971).

4. Heriberto Schiro, *Políticas Oficales para el Fomento de la Producción Editorial, Tercer curso Latinoamericano de Producción y Distribucion de Libros* (Bogotá: CERLAL, 1973).

13. Book Publishing in Brazil
Laurence Hallewell

Historical Overview

The failure of European belief in a benevolent Providence has been supposed to have begun on the morning of All Saints' Day 1755, when the great baroque churches of Lisbon collapsed upon the most devout population in Christendom as it knelt in prayer. Had the *philosophes* been aware how that population was sustained—and had built those very churches—on the profits of a colonial exploitation unprecedented in ruthlessness by even the standards of eighteenth-century mercantilism, perhaps they might rather have seen in the earthquake the righteous vengeance of a long-suffering Jehovah.

Of all the New World colonies, none was as oppressed as Brazil, nor kept as backward and dependent—politically, economically, technologically, or culturally. It is all the more remarkable, therefore, that modern Brazil should have come to share with the United States the peculiar distinction of having developed from a colony into the culturally dominant constituent of her linguistic area and politically its most important member.

In size Brazil vastly exceeded the mother country. She achieved parity of population with it in 1810, something that the United States would not achieve vis à vis the United Kingdom for another fifty years and that no Spanish-speaking country would do vis à vis Spain for a hundred. But Brazil's escape from Portuguese tutelage was a long, drawn-out affair. Political independence was delayed until 1822, later than anywhere else in mainland Latin America save viceregal Peru, and even then the Braganza dynasty reigned in Rio for another sixty-seven years. In 1910 Portugal itself became a republic, and that revived dreams of a Luso-Brazilian federation among the Brazilian establishment. As late as 1937 the new constitution imitated the contemporary Portuguese model, down to its very name of *Estado Novo*.

For higher education Brazil remained totally dependent on Portugal's solitary University of Coimbra until the 1810s, in contrast to Spanish America where the Universities of Mexico and Lima had been created at the onset of colonial rule. Small schools of law, medicine, and engineering were set up in early nineteenth-century Brazil, but the country had no university in the accepted sense of the word until the mid-1930s, and real growth in higher education did not begin until twenty years after that. Linguistic emancipation was also tardy. Transatlantic differences of language, both spoken and written, are now much greater in Portuguese than they are in either English or Spanish, but this is a development of the last fifty years. The nationalist call for a Brazilian Portuguese was not widely heard before the 1920s, nor generally heeded before the mid-1920s. Until then the usage of Lisbon was the norm for every educated Brazilian. Now the wheel has come full circle; European Portuguese, among the younger generation at least, is being steadily Brazilianized through television and its steady diet of carioca *telenovelas* (imported soap operas from Rio).

Publishing has developed in a similar way. In colonial times almost every country in the Western Hemisphere acquired a printing industry before Brazil, even Danish Greenland (in 1793). When a press was finally established, it was only because the Portuguese had to transfer their entire administrative apparatus to Rio de Janeiro to escape Napoleon's 1807 occupation of Portugal. During the rest of the nineteenth century the Brazilian book trade continued to depend on imports from Portugal and France—there was a sizable Portuguese-language publishing industry in Paris. Although Brazilian printers, like their contemporaries in the United States, could pirate foreign copyrights with impunity, Brazil produced only one-fourth as many books as she imported. Due to the high costs of printing in Rio, even Brazilian imprints were often manufactured abroad, especially after 1912 when Brazil adhered to the international copyright conventions.

Twentieth-Century Developments

The 1918 establishment of the first important Brazilian firm dedicated exclusively to book publishing marked a change. By 1920, the last year of the postwar boom, São Paulo publishing reached 209 titles in 901,000 copies. The real takeoff of the industry dates from the 1930s, when the country's shortage of foreign exchange (due to the world depression) reduced book imports by two-thirds. The World War II reading boom gave a further boost to the new industry, pushing output up to about 3,000 titles a year in 15 million copies. It also created a market large enough to permit the emergence of technical and other specialized publishing houses. The immediate postwar period was, in contrast, one of stagnation, thanks to an exchange-rate policy that subsidized foreign books (as "essential imports"), making them cheaper in Brazil than in their country of origin. Economic nationalism returned in 1956 with the accession of Kubitschek, who initiated a deliberate fostering of the book industry, with concessions on taxes, postal rates, and paper costs and the granting of import licenses for modernizing the printing industry.

Since then the book trade has had to contend with Brazil's recurrent bouts of high inflation, which reached 10 percent a month in 1963–64 and again in 1980–83. The period 1964–79 witnessed censorship of varying intensity and arbitrariness, with frequent wholesale police seizures of unwelcome publications. The oil crisis of 1973–74 and a simultaneous (but unrelated) sudden rise in paper costs produced a spate of bankruptcies, whose victims included some of the trade's best-known names. More recently, the August 1982 balance-of-payments crisis has led to severe restrictions on commercial credit, difficulties in paying for foreign rights and imported film, and, even more seriously, to a squeeze on the real incomes of the middle (i.e., book-buying) classes. Despite all this, publishing in Brazil has gone from strength to strength. In 1967 output reached 190 million copies of 5,618 titles; in 1978 it went to 211 million copies of 12,717 titles, and in 1980 to 242,900,000 copies of 13,267 titles, to make Brazil almost the largest producer of books in the Third World.[1]

The Portuguese-language book market is now almost the inverse of the Spanish. In the former the American component dominates, in the latter it is still the European. Brazil's output rivals that of Spain (225 million copies of 24,569 titles in 1979); Portugal, with 6,274 titles in 1978 and 5,726 in 1979, is on the level of Argentina (4,698 titles in 1980) or Mexico (around 5,000). Spain exports as much as the other Spanish-speaking countries together and four times as much as her nearest rival, Mexico. Brazilian book exporting, which was nonexistent in the early 1950s, is not yet so successful, partly from lack of the Spanish product's price advantage, but it gives every promise of becoming so. Compared with their Portuguese rivals, Brazilian books offer greater variety, have a more attractive appearance, and benefit from more aggressive marketing. For the African reader they are also free of the taint of colonialism. Apparent parity in direct exchange between the two countries (in 1980 $2,422,944 worth of Brazilian books sold to Portugal, $2,511,621 worth of Portuguese books sold to Brazil) overlooks the very considerable quantity of books by Brazilian authors that are reprinted in Portugal. The translation rights of European and North American works used to be sold exclusively to houses in Lisbon or Oporto; before Kubitschek Brazilian publishers were often denied the foreign currency needed to meet their overseas royalty obligations. Now the Portuguese translation rights are divided, or sold exclusively to Brazil. Often the Brazilian purchaser will sell the Portugal-only rights. For a typical U.S. bestseller a major Brazilian house such as Record or Nova Fronteira might pay $3,000 or so, and then sell the Portugal rights (which would be unlikely to account for more than one-tenth of all sales in Portuguese) for about $500. This allows for different translations for the two markets, a matter of considerable reader sensitivity, particularly where modern colloquial language is involved, in a novel such as Salinger's *Catcher in the Rye*, for instance.

Brazil further resembles Spain in the almost equal division of its publishing industry between two centers, the nation's traditional administrative capital and its more go-ahead commercial one; 385 miles separate Madrid from Barcelona, Rio de Janeiro is 251 miles from São Paulo. In Brazil, these two centers produce 97 percent of the country's book production, with São Paulo more concerned with educational publishing and Rio more committed to trade books, especially belles lettres. Not long ago the two conurbations (the world's third and ninth biggest, respectively) took up almost as large a slice of the country's retail sales, but the growth of the provincial book market is changing this. Rio/São Paulo purchased 75 percent of Brazilian books ten years back; they are now down to barely 50 percent.

This bifurcation of the industry is reflected in book trade organization. The Brazilian Book Chamber, primarily a booksellers' organization, is located in São Paulo; the National Syndicate of Book Publishers is in Rio. Cataloguing-in-publication, which in many countries is a function of the national library, is performed by the Book Chamber (CBL) for books published in São Paulo and all the more southerly states, and by the Syndicate (SNEL) for books published in Rio and all the states to the north. Curiously, the allocation of International Standard Book Numbers, which is usually the responsibility of trade organizations, has been left to the chronically under-funded National Library, which, no doubt, accounts for the fact that it has yet to be generally accepted and adopted. C.I.P., in contrast, is now well established and has been almost universal among the major commercial publishers for about a decade.

The industry's output figures for 1980 (the latest available) break down as follows:

Textbooks: 102,287,000 copies of 4,595 titles
Trade books: 65,347,000 copies of c.5,200 titles
Partworks: 60,704,000 copies of c.50 titles
Pocketbooks: 24,656,000 copies of c.2,500 titles
Doorstep credit sales: 11,101,000 copies of c.600 titles
Bookclub editions: 3,474,000 copies of c.300 titles.

Although there are almost 300 trade book publishers, more than half the books in this category come from the dozen or so houses that average a title a week or more. The market leader is Distribuidora Record, with 394 titles in 1980 and 502 in 1981, three-quarters being fiction, much of it North American, although their list does include several important Brazilian names, such as the best-selling Jorge Amado. Next, with about a hundred fewer in both years, come Vozes (church owned and witness to the social commitment of modern Brazilian progressive Catholicism) and left-leaning Brasiliense, publisher of Brazil's best-known children's author, the late Monteiro Lobato. Close behind the three leaders come Companhia Melhoramentos, a huge paper-making and paper-products conglomerate, also important for its juvenile publishing, and Nova Fronteira, founded by the right-wing journalist-politician Carlos Lacerda, whose forte is quality modern fiction in translation. Fiction makes up nearly half of Brazilian trade publishing: 30 million copies of about 3,500 titles, split almost equally between national and foreign authored books. Children's books amount to around 1,000 titles each year, in 11 million copies, about 60 percent Brazilian and 40 percent translated works.

Partwork publishing, sold through Brazil's ubiquitous street corner newsstands, was pioneered in 1965 by Editora Abril, the very successful magazine publishing house owned by Victor Città, an American-trained Italian immigrant who has family connections with similar firms in Argentina and Mexico. Sales of 60 million copies were attained in 1968, but then fell off, reaching a low of 8.7 million in 1977. This has been attributed to poor market research, editorial mismanagement, and the arrival of several rival firms on the scene. These problems, it seems, have been overcome, and sales of 300,000 copies of an individual issue are now commonplace. The first issue of a new work is often given away free as a "come-on," and the subsequent fifty or one-hundred weekly or fortnightly parts cost about the same as a weekly mass circulation illustrated magazine. Most titles continue to be adaptations of foreign, especially Italian, ventures, but there have been several successful Brazilian originals with profitable export sales. Spanish American rights have sold particularly well. The success of partwork publishing has encouraged Abril and its chief rival Rio Gráfica (a branch of Brazil's major television network, Rede Globo) to use newsstand distribution for other publishing ventures, from books on slimming to meretriciously cased reprints of Dostoevsky, and these have reached sales of 50,000 to 100,000 or higher.

Abril has also been a partner with Distribuidora Record, Difusão Europeia do Livro, and Bantam Books of New York in Edibolso, producing pocketbooks, the equivalent of the Anglo-American paperback. This form of marketing has been far less successful in Brazil, with average print runs of only 10,000, no more than twice those of traditional trade books. Maybe the price differential is insufficient; *livros de bolso* sell for about one-third the cost of a "hardcover" book. Or perhaps the conservative Brazilian consumer has yet to be won over to the concept of the cheap, disposable product.

Much more profitable has been Abril's 51-percent-to-49-percent venture with the West German giant, Bertelsmann A.G., into book club publishing. Brazilian book clubs date to 1943, but until 1973 when Abril's Círculo do livro was started, annual sales hovered around the 30,000 mark. The Círculo aimed at a market far larger than this, and the subsequent economies of scale permitted it to offer a physically superior product—superior even to the normal trade book in that it invariably appears cased in an attractive hard cover. But Círculo's main advantage was its use of door-to-door canvassing for the initial recruitment of members. The result has been a remarkable, and still continuing, growth. The 3.5 million sales for 1980 quoted above are now ancient history: 1982 saw 5 million in sales spread over 500 titles.

Door-to-door sales are not new in Brazil, having been introduced for the installment sales of encyclopedias and collections of literary classics by the Rio branch of the W. M. Jackson Company of New York in 1911. Jackson had the field to themselves until the late 1930s; a large influx of other firms began in the early 1950s, when the impulse seems to have been the depressed state of the Brazilian book market. By the 1960s installment selling was attractive for its remarkably high rate of profit. This resulted in far too rapid growth, and early in the 1970s the market became saturated. This unfortunately occurred just when the oil crisis was creating other problems for the book trade, and it was a significant factor in the bankruptcy of several long-established houses. Installment sales which had reached 7,989,500 in 1966, or 16.9 percent of all book sales, crashed to 1,552,800 in 1974, a mere 0.8 percent. Recovery has been slow. The 1966 total was not matched until 1978, and, although it has now been comfortably exceeded (12.6 million sales were made in 1981), the market share is only 4.57 percent, well below that of 1966. Unfortunately the boom years attracted a number of profit-grabbing firms whose inferior quality books built up consumer resistance. The best of Brazil's subscription publications, however, are excellent in both form and content, even if not all of them are original; this form of merchandising is an important way of recycling material designed initially for partwork presentation.

Educational Publishing

As the figures for 1980 show, slightly less than half the books Brazil produces are for classroom use. A century ago the market for textbooks hardly existed in Brazil. The entire school population was only 150,000 or so, and many rural schools managed without any printed books at all. The rise of the first Brazilian bookseller-publisher to concentrate on the textbook market occurred in the first thirty years of the Republic (1889–1919), just as Brazil's rapidly increasing wealth from coffee growing was at last making possible some reasonable provision for primary education, at least in the more southerly states. During the rise of the Livraria Francisco Alves (still an important name in Brazilian publishing), school attendance grew from 260,000 to 1,250,000. The decade following the Revolution of 1930 saw some badly needed improvement in secondary education, and the corresponding rise of the Companhia Editora Nacional, which controlled two-thirds of Brazilian textbook publishing from 1930 to the early 1970s.

The great growth period in Brazilian education began in the late 1950s. In twenty years primary school attendance grew from 8.8 million to 22 million. Secondary school attendance went from 260,000 to 2,500,000. The number of undergraduates climbed from 93,000 to 1,300,000 and that of graduate students from 2,500 to 34,000. The educational book publishing industry expanded and diversified accordingly.

United States aid was important to Brazilian sci-tech and higher education publishing in the immediate postwar years, paying author royalties, translation fees, and some of the direct production costs for Portuguese versions of American texts. In the late 1960s this involvement was greatly extended by the USAID-sponsored COLTED program, whose goal was the free distribution of textbooks to secondary and elementary school pupils, regardless of parental means. The Brazilian book trade benefited from the injection of several million dollars in orders, and the number of textbook titles in print climbed from 2,500 in 1968 to almost 6,000 a year later. The government of the next president, Medici, terminated the program, however, being unsympathetic to indiscriminate free distribution of school books. A return to the earlier system safeguarded the right of individual schools (and, at secondary level, of individual masters) to choose their own books, but the conformism of schools gave the industry the benefit of enormous print runs: 300,000 for primary-level texts, 200,000 for secondary-level, with sales of individual titles reaching a million copies or more. Such figures have probably never been equalled outside those countries—such as Salazar's Portugal or the popular democracies of Eastern Europe—where textbooks are decided upon centrally.

The textbook market was not seriously affected by the 1973–74 crisis, and its very healthy profits encouraged the entry of many new firms. This increased competition tended, however, to reduce the sales potential of individual titles. Modernization of teaching methods has ended the traditional reliance on one textbook for each unit of the curriculum, and the education departments of the various states have begun to require that texts adopted be those best suited to local conditions. As a result, average print runs are now considerably below the levels of five years ago; around 50,000 is now normal for primary school texts, about half that for secondary school titles.

In 1980, 102 million textbooks were published, in the following categories:

Primary school texts: 71,777,000 copies of 1,900 titles
Secondary school texts: 17,292,000 copies of 680 titles
Undergraduate texts: 6,697,000 copies of 1,862 titles
Postgraduate texts: 242,000 copies of 79 titles
Adult education texts: 6,290,000 copies of 74 titles

The last category includes 4.3 million copies of one text printed for the federal government's adult literacy campaign (MOBRAL). The 1980 output averages out to a little over three books for each primary school child, double that for each secondary pupil and undergraduate, and ten books for each graduate student. However, the two higher education categories are underestimates, due to the exclusion of many sci-tech titles that must have been intended, in part at least, for the education market. There were, for instance, 7.8 million copies of 273 medical titles published in Brazil in 1980, and 4.4 million copies of 716 titles in law.

Textbook publishing at the secondary and primary levels is extremely competitive and very well organized, and standards of physical presentation are high. Extensive promotion will often involve selling a pilot edition of 10,000 or more at a calculated loss. A few giant firms, wholly Brazilian owned, dominate the market and, according to a British observer, have editorial, promotional, and distribution systems that "can only be described in superlatives."[2]

The authors are overwhelmingly (c.90 percent) Brazilian too, and although royalty rates, at 7 to 9 percent, are below those for trade books (10 to 15 percent), quite a few are able to live comfortably from their writing. A recent article in the news magazine *Veja* publicized the high incomes (by Brazilian standards) of the more successful, most of whom are former teachers enabled by their earnings to retire from the classroom.[3] *Veja* was, nevertheless, not entirely happy with their work; too many were guilty of writing down to their readers and some committed gross factual errors (one author referred to "Michel" Proust and described the windmill as an invention of Leonardo da Vinci). Unnecessary and irrelevant detail was often included. And whereas the books of ten years ago had been "drugged full of right-wing propaganda," there was now too much distortion in the contrary direction. For this foreign observer there is also too much sentimentality and a willful refusal to admit to Brazilian realities that must be transparent to even a schoolchild.

The dominance of Brazilian authors in school textbook writing and in a few other fields (e.g., law books) brings the proportion of foreign works on the Brazilian market down to the fairly satisfactory level of around 40 percent: 2,472 of the 6,115 new editions appearing in 1980. This conceals the relative importance of the foreign text in higher education, where the market is still not large and profitable enough to entice qualified Brazilians to write for it in adequate numbers. For the same reason it is difficult to recruit translators and adapters to prepare Brazilian editions of suitable foreign texts.

The initial growth of Brazil's higher education in the 1930s took place under French tutelage, but the great post-World War II expansion has involved a steadily increasing adoption of North American models, in the style and content of textbooks as in everything else. Brazilian-owned publishers are important all the same. Companhia Editora Nacional has had some of its texts adopted by universities in Spanish American countries; Guanabara Koogan, mainly a medical publisher, has, by linking with the social science house Zahar, become the largest academic publishing group in all South America, and the *abertura* (post-1978 political liberalization) has stimulated the growth of firms committed to a progressive viewpoint, with Cortez e Moraes the outstanding example in the educational field. But the multinationals, and particularly the North American multinationals, have gained a firm foothold.

The Role of Multinationals

Apart from the Jackson Company's venture into door-to-door credit selling, the first multinationals in Brazilian publishing were almost all European. Editorial Labor Brasil SA was set up by the Argentine branch of the Barcelona medical and academic house in 1937. Swiss- and Portuguese-owned DIFEL (Difusão Europeia do Livro) came in 1951, primarily to publish translations from the French, but since 1960 it has increasing sponsored works of Brazilian authorship and has accordingly changed the interpretation of its acronym to Difusão Editorial do Livro. The German Herder arrived in 1952; after being sold to another German firm, its Brazilian subsidiary started trading as EPU (Editora Pedagógica Universitária). Hachette do Brasil followed in 1953, Spanish-Mexican Grijalbo in 1958, and Bruguera in 1960; this last named began as a subsidiary of the Buenos Aires firm, but it was later sold to Robert Maxwell's British Publishing Corporation (connected with Pergamon Press) and changed its name to CEDIBRA. Another Argentine firm, El Ateneo, came to Brazil in 1962. More recently, in 1976, the Dutch multinational Elsevier-Noord Holland has created Editora Campos.

Although the Encyclopaedia Britannica Company formed a Brazilian subsidiary in 1951 to market its English-language products, it was several years before it began publishing in Portuguese. There were no other American arrivals till the late 1960s. While it lasted the book import subsidy was a strong disincentive to direct participation in the Brazilian market, and even when it was abolished most firms preferred to sell their English-language international editions made in Hong Kong, India, or other low-cost economies. The *Reader's Digest* at this time actually closed its Brazilian operation and centered all its Portuguese-language activities on its Lisbon branch (but taking care to use the Brazilian rather than the European form of the language). In 1968, however, John Wiley acquired a 49.4 percent share in the sci-tech publisher LTC (Livros Técnicos e Científicos). McGraw-Hill made an unsuccessful offer to buy Companhia Editora Nacional about this time and then established McGraw-Hill do Brasil in 1970. Interamericana do Brasil, a subsidiary of Holt-Saunders (and through them of CBS) came in 1972, and were followed by Harper & Row do Brasil (HABBRA) in 1976 and by Addison-Wesley, who trade as FEB—Fundação do Educativo Brasileiro. Prentice-Hall's negotiations to buy into a Brazilian firm were quite protracted and Prentice-Hall do Brasil was not formed until late in 1982.

These U.S. firms realized that American texts were not always readily adaptable for use in Brazil, and as most of them had already established branches in Mexico to cater to the Spanish-language market, they began translating works that had been prepared for the latter. The extent of this practice may be gauged by comparing the annual totals for translations from Spanish with those from English according to the Statistical Service of the Education Ministry. Before the advent of the American multinationals some two to three hundred English-language books appeared in translation in Brazil each year: 358 in 1963, 244 in 1964, 278 in 1965. This shot up to 656 in 1970, 991 in 1972, and 1,079 in 1976, although part of the increase was due to the growth of the general book market and the consequently greater number of novels and other nonacademic titles being translated. Translation from English also benefits from subsidies from USICA and the World Bank. Traditionally Spanish was far less important as a source language: only 13 translations from it in 1963, 9 in 1964, and 16 in 1965. In 1972, however, 167 titles were translated, in 1973 some 280, and in 1974 the total jumped to 1,784. Since then the number of publications from the Spanish has averaged 1,350 a year, exceeding those from any other language, including English.[4]

The Role of Government

Free enterprise, protection for home-grown capital, a receptivity to foreign investment, and direct governmental participation in the economy coexist in a mix that is peculiarly Brazilian and affects the book trade as much as any other industrial activity. Publishing is frequently subsidized by the *co-edição* mechanism, whereby an official body underwrites production costs by guaranteeing to purchase an agreed portion of the edition. The National Book Institute (an organ of the federal Education Ministry) has been coediting titles it requires for distribution to public libraries since about 1968. The coedition of university-level texts was pioneered by São Paulo State University Press (which found it so cost-effective that it gave up its own publishing program entirely), and the system has since been adopted by a number of other state and federal universities, although not on the same scale.

Direct publishing by the thirty-seven major branches of the federal government amounts to around a thousand titles a year (books and pamphlets) in some ten million copies. This includes the output of neither the federal university presses nor the publishing departments of federally created *fundações* (foundations), government entities with a high degree of financial autonomy. Two of these that have important publishing programs are the Fundação Getúlio Vargas (a teaching and research institute for administration and the social sciences) and the Fundação Instituto Brasileiro de Geografia e Estatística (whose responsibilities include the nation's decennial population and production census). The University of Brasília in the federal capital is also a *fundação,* and its press is now the nation's fifteenth largest publishing house. In the early years of military rule the University's difficulties with authority severely affected its publishing program, which dropped to two titles in 1968. Its present performance (101 titles in 1981) is witness to the recent transformation of the political climate in Brazil. Indeed its success, built on vigorous nationwide promotion, has provoked an outcry in the trade press as unfairly competing with private enterprise.

Distribution Problems

The main problem, however, of the Brazilian book trade lies not in publishing but in retailing. The number of bookshops in Brazil has been variously computed, according to definition or conception, at from 75 to 600. Even including any retailer selling trade books there are no more than 1,200—in a country larger than the continental U.S. and more populous than Japan. Many retailers are just supplying school textbooks, and many traditional bookshops depend on their school book sales for economic viability. Cities like Recife and Fortaleza with populations well over a million have less than half a dozen halfway decent bookshops each. The problem is not new, and a decline (usually attributed to insufficient profitability and the ever-rising city rents) has been noted since the mid-1950s. As the publishers, in self-defense, turn to alternative distribution methods (door-to-door, mail order, book club, newsstand selling) the situation will only deteriorate. Even school books are increasingly sold through schools (which, having no overhead and a captive market, can make do with discounts of 20 percent instead of 40).

Distribution difficulties are also threatening another, completely distinct, form of publishing: that of chapbooks, or popular poetry in pamphlet form. This quaint survival of an industry that vanished from England in the 1830s and from North America in the 1850s is popular in the conservative outback of northeastern Brazil and among homesick *nordestino* migrants in the big cities of the south, but it can barely pay its way in its traditional form: the rent of a stall at the country fairs, where it has always been sold, is now an impossibly high burden. The technology of Brazil's up-to-date printing industry may have an answer. A São Paulo firm is mass producing by offset lithography with polychrome covers what had been hand-composed by letterpress in tiny editions from backstreet jobbing printers.

Notes

1. Figures are from the Sindicato Nacional dos Editores de Livros. Adding pamphlets, which SNEL does not record, would make a total of 20,000 titles in 300 million copies. The figures published by the Statistical Section of the Education and Culture Ministry (SEEC/MEC) which do include pamphlets (and also the production of some government publishers and small local presses overlooked by SNEL) are slightly lower than this, almost certainly because they monitor the output of commercial publishers less effectively than SNEL.
2. [T. Maugham], *Brazil: Translation Rights Market: Report SPA/264/2* (São Paulo: British Council, [1981?]). The same author, who was then the Council's books adviser in Brazil, also wrote a *Directory of Publishing and Bookselling in Brazil* (Rio de Janeiro: British Council, 1980) which has an informative introduction.
3. "Lições milionárias," *Veja* 756 (March 2, 1983):42–49.
4. L. Hallewell, "A participação das empresas multinacionais na indústria livreira do Brasil," *Revista brasileira de bibliografia e documentação* 14 (July/December 1981):188–203. Hallewell has also written *Books in Brazil: a History of the Publishing Trade* (Metuchen, N.J.: Scarecrow Press, 1982) which includes a bibliographical essay.

14. United States Publishers and Textbooks in Latin America*

Sherry Keith

Schoolchildren are probably the largest captive reading audience in the world today. Over the past two decades the rapid expansion of all educational levels, primary, secondary, and post-secondary, has created millions of potential readers throughout Latin America (see table 14.1). The educational textbook market has mushroomed as a consequence of this boom. In Brazil during 1977 the educational materials publishing industry produced some 211 million copies of 12,717 book titles, of which 2,647 were university-level texts.[1] In today's era of the mass media the tendency is to disregard the cultural and ideological influences of the printed word in shaping information, attitudes, values, and opinions. However, school textbooks account for a significant proportion of the total printed materials that appear in any country. Educational materials frequently reach a more massive audience than newspapers or magazines. Even in Latin America a single book can reach millions of students over a three- to five-year period.

Latin Americans are not unaware of the influence school materials have on shaping the minds of the coming generation. In his study, "New Multinational Educators," Armand Mattelart details the trend toward creeping penetration by U.S. and Western European transnational publishing and media forms of Third World educational

*This essay is excerpted from a study commissioned by the Latin American Institute for the Study of Transnationalism (ILET) in 1979.

175

media.[2] This trend has accelerated specifically in the area of instructional materials publishing in Latin America during the past decade, especially in the past five years.

Expansion of U.S. Publishers in Latin America

The growth of American textbook publishing firms in the Caribbean and Latin American region is the story of changing production and marketing strategies. Latin America's demand for all levels of school textbooks has been increasing rapidly and steadily over the past two decades. A brief glance at the change in educational enrollment figures for the primary, secondary, and post-secondary levels from 1960 through 1980 gives a clear indication of a dramatic increase in the need for educational materials. The boom in tertiary-level enrollments since 1960, more than 800 percent, is illustrated by table 14.1. There were also dramatic leaps in secondary and primary school enrollment, with changes of more than 400 percent and 300 percent, respectively, between 1960 and 1980. With such sharply increasing enrollments there has been a concomitant growth in the demand for school materials, especially textbooks.

U.S. publishing firms are well aware of the school population trend within the region. At the Frankfurt Book Fair in October 1979 Edgard Blucher noted the dramatic growth in the demand for educational materials within Brazil:

During the 1950s . . . Brazil moved from 93,202 students (and 21,064 faculty members) to 342,886 students (and 49,310 faculty members) in 1960 to 1,117,000 students in 1977; an increase of 1,002 percent in 17 years. These may seem staggering figures. The fact is that the demand for university education grew at 190 percent between 1972 and 1977 in all fields . . . the impact of these factors on the production of educational materials has, of course, been considerable. These figures are not mere statistics. They represent a goal, a target, or perhaps, simply, the dream of a unified market.[3]

The presence of North American-based firms in Latin America has been growing slowly during the past two and one-half decades. U.S. publishers first appeared in Latin America during the late 1950s and early 1960s. They did not make their presence felt, however, as publishing houses per se. Rather, it was through the push for exports that many North American companies had their first and continuing contacts with the region. Textbooks and workbooks accounted for approximately 20 percent of annual U.S. book exports during the 1970s, greater than any other specific category of book exports.

Table 14.1 Growth in School Enrollments in Latin America.

Year	Primary Enrollment	Secondary Enrollment	Tertiary Enrollment
1960	26,628,000	4,088,000	572,000
1970	43,983,000	10,662,000	1,640,000
1980	87,032,000	17,510,000	4,811,000

Source: UNESCO, *Statistical Yearbook*, 1983.

The Decision to Export

There are several market entry strategies available for publishing firms entering foreign markets. The most commonly used is to test the local market response to the product through export. This strategy has the advantage of low risk because no capital is invested locally.[4] For the publishing industry, as well as the educational materials segment of that industry, exporting has been the dominant, if not exclusive, form of entry into the Latin American market.

The educational export market to Latin America began with the straightforward selling of college textbooks, published in English, to university audiences throughout the region. Larger textbook companies or school book divisions of big publishing houses hired their own representatives to canvass the market prospects and make contacts throughout Latin America. These companies were represented locally by Latin Americans, who were responsible for promoting and selling their books. Often a representative worked several countries together: for example, it is common to deal with the Andean countries—Bolivia, Colombia, Chile, Peru, Ecuador. Larger countries like Mexico, Venezuela, and Brazil (also due to linguistic differences) sometimes warranted a single sales representative for the domestic market.

Many smaller companies that wanted to export to the region but did not anticipate sufficient sales to warrant hiring local sales representatives, exported through another publisher or one of the large international distributors for U.S. companies. Generally firms with less than $100,000 of business annually in the region chose to work through a larger firm or distributor that had a well-established marketing structure already in place. Due to the highly decentralized system of promotion and marketing in Latin American countries, the cost of maintaining one's own sales representative(s) are too great for a small volume of exports.

From Exporting to Publishing

Most of the major U.S. educational publishers who established export operations in Latin America during the 1950s and 1960s made the transition to local publishing (that is, actually undertaking various steps of production in Latin America itself) through developing translation programs. The strategy used to develop local translation programs and the rationale behind them is well expressed by the notes from a North American publisher making a seminar presentation at the Frankfurt Book Fair in 1979. His theme was developing a book for the local market—the approach from outside.

In the same language. Although there is a large potential market for books in English there are also great national differences in syllabuses and therefore needs for textbooks. Publishers in other major languages also find regional variations in their markets. An extreme example is the underdeveloped world where, although outside languages are widely used in teaching, imported books are rarely appropriate to more basic courses and to local requirements. The practice of medicine or agriculture may be very different and technology is generally less advanced.

Through translation. The situation in Latin America will be outlined. Over the last 10 years English and French language texts have dropped from students' reading lists, largely replaced by Spanish and Portuguese translations of North American and European texts. How well do translations published from Spain and Portugal fare in Latin America? Do Latin American publishers find it necessary to get the book revised by local academics to fit local needs more closely? Are publishers of translations meeting increased competition from books written by Latin American authors? It is worth noting that North American publishers responded to the change from English language texts by starting their own companies in Latin America or buying existing imprints. This change has largely come about through there now being a large enough market for Spanish or Portuguese texts. Brazil, for example, is now training nearly 10,000 doctors a year which represents a major market for medical texts. An outline of the history and performance of some of these imprints specializing in translations should be interesting.[5]

The translation programs focused on, and continue to focus on, university text-book materials. They tended to be highly concentrated subject matter-wise, principally in mathematics and science. Because books were translated into Spanish and Portuguese they could penetrate a much wider market than exported English titles. Many translations are made by Latin American university professors who specialize in the particular book's field. This helps with promotional aspects. By using local university faculty as translators, the book is more likely to be adopted as a course text, frequently by the translators themselves and among their colleagues. All of the major educational publishers currently operating in Latin America have fairly extensive translation programs, including McGraw-Hill with more than 400 titles in translation and Addison-Wesley with 100 titles in Spanish.

Market Strategies

U.S. publishers are careful to investigate potential markets before expanding their exports or establishing a regional office or foreign subsidiary to engage in actual book production. Their first and most important target is the university textbook. At this level the North American publishers have a foregone monopoly on the actual materials. Particularly in scientific and technical subjects such as chemistry, physics, engineering, and medicine, U.S. publishers already hold the rights to the most up-to-date, sought-after books at the advanced educational levels. Before establishing a new line of books or pursuing the translation of a title which already exists in the United States, the sales representative will survey likely professors in the universities for their interest and commitment to using the textbook in their courses. Often the company will offer the professors translation privileges to secure their commitment to the text once it is published.

One of the most common complaints among North American publishers within Latin America is distribution problems. The distribution network at the college/university level is organized differently than in the United States. There are few university bookstores, and professors rarely communicate with the major booksellers about their choices regarding required or supplementary textbooks for their courses. The publisher's representative typically has to canvass professors, to try to convince them to use a particular textbook, and then contact the local booksellers and convince them that they should stock the text or series of books. In some instances, North American publishers have joined forces with major booksellers in the country where they are operating. This is the case, for example, with Wiley & Sons—known as Limousa in Mexico—who has a joint venture with Noriega, one of the largest book-sellers in Mexico City.

In spite of distribution difficulties, the Latin American market is attractive and profitable. Publishing companies use all the strategies of other large transnational companies in their overseas financial transactions. On the North American side, two of these mechanisms are double selling and the establishment of DISC corporations. Transfer pricing in the book industry occurs through the selling of books or rights to publish by the parent company to its subsidiary. The subsidiary then sells the books on the Latin American market. This procedure of double selling amounts to a double profit. The parent company makes a profit on the sale of materials to the subsidiary, and the subsidiary makes a profit on the sale of the book on the local market. Double selling can be extremely advantageous. In countries where there are strict currency and foreign exchange regulations, the company can make a relatively large profit margin by selling high to its subsidiary.

A second strategy, particularly beneficial for book exporters, is known as the DISC corporation, the domestic/international sales corporations. DISC corporations pay a lower tax rate than regular corporations within the United States, 35 percent rate as opposed to 48 percent rate on profits. Moreover, DISC corporations do not pay taxes on profits generated from expanding export sales from one year to the next. The possibility of the DISC corporation means that the transnational publishers can afford higher profit taxes to be paid in the U.S.

Establishing Subsidiaries

Generally speaking, a translation program is the first step toward establishing overseas subsidiaries. Occasionally a company will begin a translation program in the United States and keep all production strictly on an export basis. However, the five large dynamic publishers (Addison-Wesley, Holt-Saunders, Harper & Row, McGraw-Hill and John Wiley & Sons), that dominate the Latin American market all established local subsidiaries to carry on their production as well as marketing activities. There are some decisive advantages to producing educational materials within Latin America instead of exporting them from the United States. Translations with minor adaptations to the local market can be made more easily from within Latin America, editorially speaking. It is also cheaper to translate and adapt books within the region than it is from abroad.

The major educational publishers established subsidiaries throughout Latin America largely during the 1940s. U.S. publishers moved into select countries of the region—Brazil, Mexico, and Venezuela—which had large domestic markets, a local tradition of publishing, and an already established printing industry. Their subsidiaries were staffed largely by Latin Americans, although their business activities were carefully monitored by the international division of the parent company.

The growth of these subsidiaries has led to a division of labor within the region itself. For example, Panama is the choice of several publishers for warehousing and serves as a trans-shipment center for Central and South America. The regional sales manager for one small-scale publisher just breaking into the Latin American market wrote of the Free Zone of Panama to the vice president of the internation group:

Printing here will not be productive. Labor costs are high and quality is not impressive. McGraw uses Colombia and Mexico for printing. Warehousing in the Zone is cheap and the available services make it attractive. Provided _____ did not sell within the Republic of Panama, no tax would be paid, only warehousing and distribution costs. I doubt the treaty will adversely influence business in Panama or the Zone.[6]

There are several criteria for choosing a site for production or marketing. Economic considerations are clearly the most important. Publishers try to cut production costs and maximize profits. Thus they print in Colombia and Mexico where quality is fairly high and labor is fairly cheap. Typesetting, however, is not necessarily done within Latin America itself. It may in fact be done in Singapore, where costs are considerably lower. One editor explained that the savings on overseas typesetting is approximately 50 percent per page. In fact, some of the largest publishers have their own typesetting subsidiaries in other parts of the world.

Although market size may influence the choice of where to locate, it is secondary to other considerations, such as cost, laws governing foreign companies operating within the country, foreign exchange regulations, taxation policies, and the like. This is why Mexico is especially attractive to most publishers. The country has a large potential market, no foreign exchange regulations,[7] cheap labor, well-established technology in the field of printing, and, of course, is very close to the United States. One drawback is the laws governing the establishment of foreign companies which require 51 percent Mexican capital. Publishers have responded to this restriction in a variety of ways. Wiley & Sons, for example, has had a long-standing partnership with Carlos Noriega, a large Mexican bookdealer. Addison-Wesley established a subsidiary in Mexico and in Colombia before the restrictions came about. Other companies have branch offices as opposed to subsidiaries, and some companies are negotiating partnerships. Some publishers interviewed acknowledged the necessity of moving toward joint ventures, while others expressed hesitation stating that it was difficult to find a "good" local partner.

Publishers who entered the Latin American market early—and these are by and large the biggest U.S. firms—may prefer to use the wholly owned subsidiary bases they have already established for exporting to the region. New firms may find the only way that they can break into the market is to establish a joint venture with local capital.

Countries with currency restrictions are not considered favorable sites for locating subsidiaries, and they are regarded as difficult customers for exports. One publisher mentioned the Andean countries—Bolivia, Peru, Chile, and Ecuador—as especially problematic. It is not uncommon to wait eight to twelve months before receiving payment for a shipment of books exported to these nations and due to currency fluctuations it is difficult to predict a profit margin on sales.[8]

Political factors were never mentioned directly as either deterrents or incentives to locating a subsidiary, but upon questioning one publisher as to why there are virtually no U.S. publishers operating in Argentina, one of the centers—or perhaps former centers—of publishing in the region, he stated that publishing there was not attractive due to economic, social, and political conditions.[9] More directly, political considerations were mentioned in a representative's letter to his boss during a field exploration of the publishing potentials in Latin America: "The Canal Zone College is the only market of size and the enrollment numbers only 1500. However, because of the uncertainty of the Canal Treaty, the college may not be a market for long."[10]

Finally, no publisher identified local competition as a factor influencing the choice of investment. There is no way to tell to what extent the expansion of U.S. publishing is squeezing out local publishers or simply preempting local business opportunities. One publisher's notes on a symposium on international publishing held at the 1979 Frankfurt Book Fair, read:

The progression from using an agent to setting up one's own organization: For this progression to take place a marketing presence is needed first, and if an outside agent is used no development will occur. This might be fine for most areas where it is judged there is little potential, but in others only your own staff will feed back useful marketing information and eventually editorial suggestions. A locally based editorial office is the desired goal should it be decided that the market will support one; *if an international company does not move in, a local imprint will probably emerge to meet the particular requirements of that area* [emphasis added].[11]

Educational Materials Sold in Latin America

Educational materials form the most important market for U.S. publishers within the region. A wide range of these materials are currently being sold in Latin America. They include textbooks at the primary and secondary school levels as well as college/ university textbooks and reference materials. Reference books such as specialized catalogues, directories, dictionaries, encyclopedias, and the like are almost exclusively institutional sales and are sold to libraries—public and private—governments, and schools. Finally, there are a wide range of technical and professional books which, especially in science, medicine, and business administration, are directed toward university markets, although they are not sold exclusively for use in education institutions.

Clearly a greater number of post-secondary/college/university-level titles are produced, but the sales picture is not as clear-cut.[12] One publisher said that sales of elementary and secondary books and college books split about fifty-fifty.[13] This is related to several factors. The more obvious is, of course, that college/university texts are far more specialized and, therefore, used by a much smaller audience than elementary/secondary materials. Another reason is related to the importance of the English as a Second Language (ESL) textbook series in the overseas sales programs of many North American companies. These series have enjoyed notable sales at all levels of the educational system. However, the overall sales trend tips toward college/ university books because most companies' operations amount to little more than the straightforward export and translation of North American titles.

The six dominant North American publishing companies in Latin America reveal a slightly different trend. These companies have established what they call "indigenous" publishing programs and have large-scale local translation programs. They have penetrated the private school clientele at the primary and secondary levels and in some cases have been successful in introducing the ESL text series into public secondary schools. Due to a large volume of sales and the use of entire math or science series in private schools, the sales trend among these firms is more equally balanced between the upper and lower educational levels.

Despite the growth in U.S. educational publishing throughout the region, there are important structural obstacles to both U.S. and indigenous publishers expanding their sales at the primary level where the market potential is vast. In spite of the growth of primary school enrollments during the past two decades, the demand for textbooks has not grown commensurately. With a few exceptions, most countries do not provide textbooks and related instructional materials free of charge.[14] Students are generally required to purchase their own books. Most students cannot afford primary school textbooks. A study in Brazil estimated that purchasing textbooks for students attending the first four grades of primary school would absorb about 8 percent of a family's annual income if three children were enrolled in school.

The financial limitations of the primary student clientele coupled with government policy have severely restricted the demand for primary school books. Until changes in either government policy regarding the provision of textbooks or the standard of living and income levels of the majority population take place, the potential market will remain latent. U.S. publishers will continue to tailor their products to the middle- and upper-income groups, who by and large send their children to private schools.

Subject Area Specialization

U.S. publishers specialize in certain product lines and specific markets in Latin America. There is a significant concentration in science, mathematics, engineering, and business administration. The social sciences, history, art, and literature are secondary to these fields. A survey of the Latin American sales catalogues distributed by U.S. publishers shows that subject area titles are heavily weighted at each level in the educational system toward science and mathematics. There are virtually no social sciences publications at the elementary and secondary levels, and most titles at the post-secondary level are in psychology. To some extent this may reflect the specialized book lines of the particular publishers surveyed. However, there are clear ideological reasons which were mentioned by nearly every publisher interviewed in this study. One publisher stated the criteria quite succinctly: "We choose titles that travel well, like science and mathematics."[15]

Publishers seem to consciously avoid more culturally specific or controversial subject areas like sociology, economics, political science, and history. "Latin Americans are very nationalistic," stated another publisher. Obviously books in these areas would be more difficult to sell. However, the ideological sensitivity of the social sciences and humanities is not the only reason for staying away from this line of books: there are economic costs associated with adapting these books to Latin American social, economic, and cultural realities. One of the largest U.S. publishers in Latin America, Addison-Wesley, estimated that about 70 percent of all educational books sold in Latin America were direct translations, 20 percent were indigenously developed, and only 10 percent were adaptations. Adaptations are titles, previously published in English, that have been not only translated but also altered substantially for the local market conditions and cultural context. Adaptations are more costly to produce than direct translations and presumably only marginally less trouble and expense than original titles produced by a local writer. Social science and humanities titles would require the maximum in adaptations to be usable in the Latin American context. Likewise, there is little competition from local Latin American publishers in the areas of math and science titles; North American firms have a clear monopoly on the dissemination of scientific research information. In the social sciences, however, Latin Americans have not been nearly so handicapped by international and local political economic conditions. There is a substantial body of Latin American social scientific research and literature which has been locally generated and locally published. Cost-wise and profit-wise, North American companies are much better with quick, straightforward translations of their own science, math, and business titles than they are in trying to translate, adapt, and market social scientific texts.

Latin Americans, however, would like to persuade North American companies to change their practice of selling predominantly translations. At the Latin American Symposium of the 1979 Frankfurt Book Fair, Edgard Blucher of Brazil told publishers that:

There seems to be no future in Brazil for publishers not engaged in developing local authorship and insisting on concentrating on translations. Among the several governmental sources which we could quote in support of this assertion is the Second Basic Plan for Scientific and Technological Development. . . . Developing local textbook authorship is a sensible policy for publishers on many counts, not the least of which is the need of the industry to stay ahead of state initiative and its eagerness to interfere in the private sphere, the publishing business included. Lastly, it should be emphasized that the economic and political survival of a publishing house in Brazil is bound to be a function of the growth of its back list by means of national authors.

While Mr. Blucher puts forth several logical arguments for developing local authorship through foreign publishers' sponsorship, his comments also belie the profitability and dominance of translation programs in contemporary publishing in Latin America.

The one exception to the predominance of science, math, and engineering is the English as a Second Language text series which are found everywhere in Latin America. In fact, the true bestsellers in terms of educational materials are ESL textbook/workbook series. The largest ESL program is Regents Publishing Company of New York, which is a subsidiary of the giant French publisher Hachette. All major U.S. publishers, however, have ESL programs designed for the secondary school level as well as the post-secondary level. ESL programs are the only precollegiate text series that have been sold to the public sector as well as private secondary and even primary schools. ESL programs are developed editorially in the United States for international marketing purposes. They may be translated and adapted to suit the Latin American market in some cases. Because of North American publishers' command of the English language and the unlikely possibility that local publishers will produce such materials, some series are purchased for use in government schools.

Competition with Indigenous Publishers

An important question connected with the growing presence of U.S. publishers in Latin America is the degree to which they are competing with local publishers and preempting local capital in the publishing industry. This theme can only be explored fully through a field study within Latin America, but some preliminary remarks based on evidence collected for this study are in order. Because of the expanding Spanish and Portuguese translation programs, U.S. publishers are reluctant to sell translation rights to Latin American publishers. A Harcourt Brace Jovanovich executive said his firm used to sell translation rights in Spanish, but they have ceased this practice. With the development of marketing structures and distribution channels, it is more profitable for U.S. publishers to translate and market their own materials than to sell the rights to a local publisher. Thus they no longer sell all or part of their titles to local colleagues, or, alternatively, they would impose unacceptable terms.

It would appear from the limited data available that North American publishers are not, as yet, directly competing with Latin American publishers. The overwhelming majority of university-level titles sold by North American publishers are direct translations of books they already publish within the United States. The technical and scientific nature of these books makes it unlikely that they would be produced within Latin America under the present political and economic conditions. At the secondary and elementary levels the case is different. American publishers have been excluded from the largest market, the public educational sector. They have, none-theless, managed to penetrate the educational materials market in the private school sector. Although this is a much smaller market, it is more flexible and better endowed financially. This market could easily be served by the local publishing industry, and the extent to which North American texts are replacing local texts is still unclear. A survey of private school materials, both present and past, needs to be undertaken to determine what has been happening with respect to textbook sources over the past decade.

These large-scale North American multinational publishers have greater financial resources than local publishing houses and, consequently, better developed market-ing/distribution possibilities. The scale of the international operations of large pub-lishing companies is impressive. Although individual publishers will not reveal what proportion of their sales come from Latin America, international sales account for up to 20 percent of the larger publishers' sales. International sales are always growing as a proportion of total sales. Also, eight companies account for more than the 80 percent of all international sales of educational materials by United States publishers. These are the largest firms within the U.S. domestic market and their hegemony over the international market is even greater than what they command internally.[16] From a survey of publishing houses listed in the 1979/80 *International Literary Market Place*, it is evident that although relatively few U.S. companies have publish-ing subsidiaries in Latin America, practically no Latin American houses have subsid-iaries in other nations. The major Latin American-based company was Grijabo, of Mexico, which is also a Spanish-based firm, with a local subsidiary in every country of Latin America.[17] This publisher, however, does not deal in textbooks.

U.S. companies have approached publishing in Latin America as a transnational enterprise. All of Latin America is their potential, if not actual, market. They ap-proach business from the perspective of an international division of labor, splitting up their activities among several countries to get the best price for each stage of the publishing process. Operating from a global vantage point the transnational pub-lishers may lack grassroots contacts, but they make up for this in the flexibility and strength of capital. These companies find it easy to attract local intellectuals as em-ployees; a cadre of these intellectuals is almost essential for successfully marketing North American textbooks. One Colombian who represents a large U.S. firm said he did not know of a single case where a Latin American who worked for an Amer-ican publishing house had left to work for a local publisher. Why not? Well, salary is one reason, and the scope of the work is wider and the possibility of travel within the region and to the United States much greater.

Political and Economic Impact of U.S. Textbook Publishers

The publishing industry exercises power and influence in the political-economic sphere, the actual economic and political influence generated by the publishing industry's entrepreneurial activities. Without a complete market study it is difficult to measure the exact economic impact of U.S. textbook publishing firms in the region. How-ever, certain generalizations can be made from the information at hand. First, the data indicate that U.S. transnational publishers are dominant in certain segments of the textbook market throughout Latin America and not, as yet, in other segments. Their market control is greatest at the collegiate level in the fields of science, mathematics, and engineering. They also have an important position in the private secondary school market in the same subject areas and in English as a Second Language materials. The firms, however, have not been able to penetrate the public-sector primary and secondary school textbook markets. Thus, their greatest influence is over the smallest but most elite segment of the educational system. This has crucial ideological significance.

The presence of transnational firms has other relevant consequences. It reinforces the integration of the domestic publishing market with the international capitalist market. Participating in and enforcing international copyright regulations so that developing nations are tied to the market system of disseminating ideas and information is very important. The existence of transnational firms in the Third World serves as a monitoring device on alternative forms of disseminating information. Transnationals are quick to jump on pirating activities and maneuver to prohibit them.

Another economic influence is the degree to which transnational publishers preempt the economic opportunities of indigenous publishers. They do this through their monopoly on knowledge and information within the developed countries. This operates, of course, through the privatization of knowledge and ideas by virtue of copyrighting. Transnational publishers own the copyrights to much crucial information, preventing local publishers from translating and disseminating it without purchasing copyrights, translation rights, and paying royalties.

Large-scale international firms have superior financial and marketing structures which place indigenous publishers at a disadvantage in several respects. One is in recruiting local expertise. International firms pay better salaries and provide perks which few local publishers can afford. Once a transnational publisher has become established within a country, it can command the best local talent for translations and, perhaps more important, win contracts with local authors to publish their indigenously produced work. The Addison-Wesley International Publishing Group's flyer advertises some of the advantages of publishing with a transnational:

What does all this mean to an Addison-Wesley Author?: . . . effective worldwide . . . distribution; local representatives in most parts of the world; consideration for translation in eight languages; sale of translation rights to foreign publishers; worldwide advertising and promotion; exhibition at major book fairs and conventions; possible adaptation to suit foreign market; international professional academic exposure; penetration of international adoption markets; a share in the profitability of Addison-Wesley's worldwide marketing network.[18]

The fact that the limited materials produced indigenously are not published by local houses is an important deterrent to the healthy growth of a national publishing industry.

The worldwide marketing, production, distribution networks of U.S. textbook publishers give them a competitive advantage over local publishers. Due to economies of scale and the internationalization of production and marketing, multinational companies can frequently price their books under the locally produced materials. They can also avoid the limitations of specific local conditions that the indigenous publisher has to face, such as the high cost of imported paper and ink, expensive warehousing, and other factors affecting cost. These circumstances can put the local publisher one step behind his international competitor and do not stimulate the growth of a national publishing industry.

The future trend may be the growth of joint ventures between U.S. transnational publishers and local publishers. What will this mean for transnationals? Probably great advantages. Joint ventures may open new markets to U.S. publishers. In particular, they may provide entry into the public sector textbook market at the primary and secondary school levels. In terms of profits, joint ventures are not a bad prospect. As one publisher explained, an initial investment of $1 million which grows to the size of $5 million with 51/49 percent division of ownership, is still a very good deal for the international partner because the company's net worth has increased from $1 million to $2.4 million with growth in profits divided accordingly.[19] Joint ventures may well accelerate a trend toward concentration within the Latin American publishing industry similar to what has been experienced within the United States. One could foresee a handful of joint venture corporations gobbling up a larger and larger proportion of the local markets through the acquisition of smaller, indigenous companies that cannot afford to compete with the international giants. This, however, is merely a hypothesis, which needs to be explored within Latin America itself in the coming years.

Cultural and Ideological Influence of U.S. Textbook Publishers

The publishing industry also exercises power and influence in the cultural-ideological sphere, the ways books and information mold the ideas, attitudes, and actions of those who consume them, in this case students. Publishing is the major mechanism for disseminating U.S. scientific and technological information. Through the ever-increasing spread of science and technology textbooks to Latin American intellectuals, the growing hegemony of U.S. ideas and technology is assured within the region. The extensive use of U.S. text and source materials in the universities and technical schools of Latin America also helps to develop a cadre of intellectuals and technocrats favorable to and trained in the application of U.S. technology. These texts play a key role in establishing the authoritative position of the United States in these fields.

The importation of scientific and technological models to Latin America through educational publishing is particularly forceful in view of the social class structure of most Latin American nations. While U.S. books—or their direct translation—may not be extensively used within the public sector, they are extremely pervasive among the elite, private educational institutions which train the techno-professional classes. These people, individually and collectively, exert tremendous influence over the economic, social, and political directions of their nations. They increasingly look to the U.S. for scientific and technological leadership, despite the evident cultural, economic, and social differences between their own countries and the United States. In some cases the authority of the printed word may outweigh the relevance of the methods and techniques it extols.

The ideological strength of the transnational U.S. publishing industry lies in its integral post within the international capitalist world. It is an important gatekeeper to the ideas and information needed by the developing world. Although U.S. textbook publishers may not be the strongest economic force within Latin American publishing, they are certainly potent ideological forerunners who bear watching.

Notes

1. Edgard Blucher, "An Indigenous Publishing Programme: An Approach from Inside Latin America" (Paper presented at the Frankfurt Book Fair, October 1979).
2. Armand Mattelart, "New Multinational Educators" (Paper presented at IAMCD Conference, Paris, 1976).
3. Blucher, October 1979.
4. Dymsza, William A., *Multinational Business Strategy* (New York: McGraw-Hill, 1972), p. 108.
5. Blucher, October 1979.
6. Confidential memo of regional sales manager to vice president of International Division, November 1977.
7. Mexico had no foreign exchange restrictions at the time research for this article was undertaken.
8. Interview with executive of Wadsworth Group International, November 1979.
9. Interview with executive of the International Division, Harcourt Brace Jovanovich, January 1980.
10. Confidential memo, November 1977.
11. Blucher, October 1979.
12. A sample of catalogues for Spanish titles distributed in Latin America by major U.S. publishers showed that there were far more post-secondary titles or about fourteen to every one secondary- and primary-level title in one of the catalogues and a similar ratio in the other. Catalogues sampled included the *Catalogo General, Libros en Espanol, 1979–80* of McGraw-Hill and the *Catalogo General, 1978–79* of the Fondo-Educativo Interamerican, S.A. (Addison-Wesley).
13. Interview with an executive of Addison-Wesley, International Division, December 1979.
14. Mexico has a policy of providing free textbooks to all students in the first six grades of public and primary schools.
15. Interview with Addison-Wesley, December 1979.
16. These include McGraw-Hill, Inc., Addison-Wesley; CBS, Inc.; Harper & Row; Houghton Mifflin; Macmillan, Inc.; Prentice-Hall; and John Wiley.
17. It is worth noting that Spanish publishers are very active in Latin America for obvious reasons of language and cultural ties. The degree to which these companies are part of the transnationalization process needs to be explored but is beyond the scope of this paper.
18. See brochure of Addison-Wesley International Publishing Group.
19. Interview with regional sales representative of Wadsworth, November 1979.

15. The Modernization of Publishing: The Japanese Experience

Shigeo Minowa

Publishing figures for the industrialized nations show the United States at the top with $5.4 billion in sales, followed by Japan with $3.8 billion. These two countries constitute huge markets for publications, far surpassing West Germany ($1.8 billion) and France ($1.4 billion), placed third and fourth, respectively.[1]

In terms of quantity, Japan's publishing industry has achieved tremendous development. This is obvious from the colorful books flooding the shelves of bookstores, fashionable magazines launched one after another, and the great diversity of paperbacks, each costing less than a cup of coffee.[2] Japan is one of the most blessed countries in the world as far as publishing is concerned. If the ultimate aim of modernization is to better satisfy the masses and if this is defined as making more books available, then Japan's present situation, where nine books per head are produced and consumed yearly, can be regarded as a significant achievement when compared with other nations.[3]

A study of the development of Japan's publishing industry would provide direct, valuable lessons to developing nations as well as contributing to modernization and development theories. Today's development theories emphasize soft technology (regarding social institutions, organizations, and so on) which ensure the effective functioning of the hardware more than the transplantation of hard technology, and education and communication, which have direct bearings on publication development, are focal aspects of this.

Cyril Black, an expert on the comparative study of modernization, defines "modernization" as the objective adaptation of human beings to increased knowledge and the improved capability to utilize environment. He cites four facets as characterizing his approach: (1) it attributes great importance to the modernization capacities developed by society during the modernization era; (2) it sees the advancement of knowledge that characterizes the scientific and technological revolutions as distinguishing the modern from earlier eras; (3) it examines the capacity of a society to take advantage of the possibilities offered by the advancement of knowledge in political, economic and social terms; and (4) it critically evaluates the utility of various political policies in converting traditional institutions to modern uses and borrowing selectively from more modern societies.[4]

With modernization studies stressing such soft aspects of society as intellectual capabilities, cultural traditions, communication, and social integration, publishing (book) development seems to be an important aspect to consider. If we restructure the history of publishing in the context of development theories, what would we find? What lessons would we learn? Unfortunately, few attempts have been made to theoretically elucidate the process of publishing development.[5]

This chapter examines the Japanese publishing experience in the following four aspects. First, how much endogenous publishing development did Japan achieve before the Meiji years (prior to 1868), when technology began to be imported from the West? How relevant is this question to the tremendous development of publishing in Japan since the Meiji era? Second, what effects, if any, did Western technologies (both hard and soft), imported in early Meiji years, have on publishing development in Japan? Third, if the imported Western technologies (both hard and soft) did affect publishing development in Japan, why were they readily accepted by the Japanese society and what social impacts did they have? Fourth, what role did government policies play in facilitating such acceptance?

Technology in Publishing

Before trying to answer these questions, we should confirm the meaning of "technology" in publishing. To do this we have to clarify the relationship between publishing, on the one hand, and printing, bookbinding, and paper-making technologies, on the other. Publishing is a composite art that requires paper-making, printing, and bookbinding technologies. For this reason, historically, it was often linked with and then confused with these technologies. It was only in relatively recent times that publishing was established independently from printing or bookbinding.[6] In addition to these peripheral technologies, a number of different technologies are incorporated into publishing itself, including editing, proofreading, book designing/making, and bookselling.

The technology of publishing in this article refers to an integrated system of techniques for operating a publishing enterprise. Publishing can be appropriately regarded as a technology if one recognizes that it mobilizes various technologies to produce and market materials for a large number of unspecified readers. It is in itself a system operated by a set of knowledge and, in this context, is a form of soft technology.

The soft technology of the publishing industry does not merely consist of these systematic techniques in individual publishing houses. Various systems built up by the publishing industry as a whole—above all the marketing system—play important roles.

The concept of publishing development is often obscurely used with reference to one of the following areas: (1) development within the publishing industry as such, excluding such peripheral industries as printing, bookbinding, and papermaking; (2) development of publishing and related industries, including printing, bookbinding, and papermaking; and (3) total social development, corresponding to UNESCO's concept of book development, which involves the spread of public libraries and the reading habit, together with the problem of illiteracy, in the context of the greater realm of publishing-related industries. In this article, therefore, "publishing-related industries" will be used in the sense of (2) while "publishing" or "the publishing industry" will be used in the sense of (1). The three different levels—publishing development, the development of publishing-related industries, and book development—have to be consciously and clearly distinguished from one another.

Historical Model of Publishing Development

The history of books is as old as that of humankind. This is true even if we limit the history of books, or publishing, to its business aspect alone. In ancient Greece and Rome, booksellers were already operating on a commercial basis. Of course, the copies they sold were handwritten, but as more or less sufficient copies were prepared to meet an anticipated demand, those booksellers could be regarded as pioneer publishers in the sense that they reproduced original works for the purpose of distribution.[6]

However, it was not until the sixteenth century in Europe, or the seventeenth century in Japan, that publishing entrepreneurs who produced and marketed a great many copies of books for a large number of unspecified readers emerged. The medieval, or premodern, publishing industries, organized into guilds, developed so slowly that for a time they seemed almost stagnant. Nevertheless, they began to expand rapidly at one point in the process of modernization. This sharp increase in the yearly number of newly published titles can be regarded as the "publishing takeoff." The development process, which began in the sixteenth and seventeenth centuries, has leaped forward in the past several decades with the information revolution.[7]

The publishing takeoff first occurred in Germany and seems to be attributable to the spread of education.[8] The publishing takeoff took place in Germany in 1780, in Britain in 1825, and in the United States in 1850. In Japan the takeoff took place in or around 1870, only a few years after the Meiji Restoration. Japan completed in only two decades what it took Germany, Britain, and the United States a half century to accomplish. The indicator of the takeoff completion—5,000 new titles published a year—was achieved in Japan by 1890.

The second phase of modernization is characterized by a general drop in book prices as the result of mass production and mass marketing. Books did not necessarily become less expensive as a result of the takeoff. The industry also had to experience a marketing revolution. This point can be illustrated by several examples, such as the publication of books priced at 1 yen in Japan around 1930 or the launching in 1935 of Penguin Books in England.[9]

The history of the publishing industry can be divided into epochs through this analysis: phase 1, the small-quantity production of a small variety epoch; phase 2, the small-quantity production of a wide variety epoch; and phase 3, the mass production of a wide variety epoch.[10]

The First Transformation: Publishing Takeoff

The publishing takeoff in Japan began around 1870, and the first stage of modernization was reached by around 1890. What led to this development? Was it the westernization or the modernization of publishing in Japan? Clarifying this would answer the question of how effectively transferred technologies facilitate publishing development.

The modernization of the publishing industry in Western Europe was not necessarily triggered by hard technology. In Germany, changes in social background resulting from the spread of education led to a publishing takeoff that preceded this phase in Britain.[11] Of course, in Britain the modernization of printing and paper-making technologies, as a part of the Industrial Revolution, was taking place simultaneously with a publishing takeoff. Thus endogenous publishing development was supported by the progress of hard technology.[12] Therefore, book development in Western European could well be classified into the soft technology-oriented German model, where hardware had virtually nothing to do with the takeoff, and the hard technology-oriented British model.

Certainly there was a gap between publishing-related hard technologies in Japan and in Western Europe when the Japanese publishing industry was about to take off in the 1870s. Although the publishing takeoff in Western Europe was not necessarily triggered by progress in hard technology, by the 1870s the European publishing industry already had access to advanced hardware (paper-making machines and high-speed presses).[13]

In examining Japan's publishing takeoff it is important to consider what kinds of publishing-related technologies were transferred from Western Europe to Japan during the 1870s: were they only hard technologies or did they also include soft technologies such as publishing management and publishing institutions? Also, was the Japanese industry affected by these transferred technologies or were the publishing takeoff and technology transfer parallel developments, with the latter supporting the former?

Publishing Technology and Institutions

Both paper-making and printing techniques and management techniques played a role in publishing's development. Printing and paper-making technologies were transferred from Western Europe during Japan's takeoff phase. Whether or not publishing technology and institutions were transferred with the hard technologies is not so easy to determine because unlike the visible and tangible printing presses and paper-making machines, the invisible know-how of management is difficult to pinpoint.

What management techniques and publishing institutions were found in Japan in the 1870s? Was publishing technology recognized as such? Even in today's highly technology-oriented publishing industry, advertising and marketing techniques and distribution know-how are not always consciously recognized as technology; soft technology is generally not recognized as such. However, a technology must be socially recognized as an objective being to be deliberately transferred. Was publishing management technology in Western Europe and Japan in and around 1870 socially recognized? A survey of Japanese publishing institutions, especially the system of book distribution which is an embodiment of publishing technology, and of how the Japanese, during the takeoff, accepted the publishing technology and institutions transferred from Western Europe will indicate whether publishing technology was socially recognized.

As new styles of publication developed successively with progress in mass production and distribution, corresponding changes in institutional aspects, including marketing mechanisms and methods of transaction have occurred.[14] In "Book Prices and Readers' Purchasing Power," I divided the history of publishing development in Japan into three epochs and pointed out that the takeoff was not immediately followed by a fall in book prices but that small-quantity production of a large variety of books ensued. The price decline, owing to mass production, took place during the ¥1 book age in Japan.[15] Before that, though publishers and the contents of publications had undergone a sweeping change following the Meiji Restoration, publishing technology and institutions seem to have changed little. In other words, Japan's publishing industry *underwent no institutional changes* in its takeoff phase, and, therefore, its takeoff was not a result of any change in publishing institutions.

However, even though the takeoff phase showed no institutional changes and was not the result of any institutional changes, this does not demonstrate the absence of Western European influences. Although many Western technologies were transplanted during modernization following the Meiji Restoration, some of them failed to take root locally and were eventually abandoned.

In the case of publishing, were Western technology and institutions transplanted but discarded because of their incompatibility with the local soil, or was their transplantation never conceived from the outset? In the tide of modernization whose main function and feature were to respond to massive needs, the transformation of the Japanese publishing industry and the revolution of book distribution, marked by phase 3, were not matched in Britain, for instance, until 1935, after the emergence of ¥1 books in Japan.[16] In both Japan and Britain the publishing takeoff occurred during the period of the traditional publishing industry. Thus, there were no marked differences between the two countries as far as publishing technology and institutions were concerned. Since it is inconceivable for any technology or institution having no major basic difference to be deliberately transferred, we may assume that no publishing technology or institutions were transferred to Meiji Japan in its phase of publishing takeoff.

This conclusion can be corroborated with the opinions of a contemporary Japanese about publishing in Western Europe. Fukuzawa Yukichi, an enthusiastic advocate of enlightenment in the Meiji era and the founder of Keio University, was also a publisher and a distinguished writer. He wrote dozens of books in his lifetime and contributed articles to the daily *Jiji Shimpo* for many years; the twenty-one-volume collection of Fukuzawa's works, published by Iwanami Shoten, consists of well over 10,000 pages. As he launched the Keio University Press to publish writings of his own and others and joined the Tokyo Association of Book Dealers as a publisher, he can well be counted as one of the best versed in publishing among the early Meiji intellectuals. The problem of protecting copyrights from piracy particularly attracted his interest, and he discussed this matter in considerable detail in the third supplement to his *Seivo Jijo* (Circumstances in the West).

Fukuzawa made it his life's work to introduce Western culture and institutions to Japan through the tremendous number of pages he wrote, and his opinion of publishing in Western Europe would be a valuable testimony for us in tackling the problem of publishing technology transfer in the early Meiji years. Unfortunately, however, few remarks on publishing, much less on Western publishing technology and institutions, are found in his thousands of pages. The few statements he made on publishing are summarized below, extracted from his writings, as they concern publishing development.

In *Tsuzoku Kokken Ron* (A treatise on state power, 1878), referring to an argument that Japan had relatively few literary works, Fukuzawa attributed that relative scarcity to the inconvenience of publishing in the earlier times, which obliged many writings to remain in handwritten copies. However, he added, publishing was greatly facilitated after the Restoration as block copy engraving techniques advanced and typography was imported, resulting in an unprecedented abundance of published literary works.

What is notable here is his testimony that, after the Restoration, not only was typography developed but also there was technical progress in woodblock printing, which contributed to the prosperity of publishing. More important is the fact that before the Restoration, according to Fukuzawa, there had been many unpublished writings or brisk literary activities whose outputs circulated in handwritten copies.

This latter statement endorses our presumption that the importation of mechanized paper making and typography, even if it did facilitate the publishing takeoff in Japan, was a secondary factor and that the takeoff resulted from the ripening of a social situation which needed those technologies.

Fukuzawa often emphatically discussed the problem of copyright in his writings. This does not mean, however, that the concept of copyright, in a rudimentary form, did not exist in Japan before the Meiji era or that Fukuzawa's advocacy immediately led to its establishment.[17] The Japanese legislation on copyright was only gradually modernized as it developed from the Publishing Ordinance of 1875 to the Copyright Ordinance of 1887 and further to the Copyright Law of 1899. As a necessary infrastructure for publishing development, it constituted an important socal institution supporting the nation's publishing industry after its takeoff, but the chronological order of events does not endorse an assumption that the concept of copyright gave significant momentum to the publishing takeoff in Japan.

Fukuzawa frequently touched on the freedom of the press, which he considered an indispensable condition for Japan's rebirth as a modern state. Prior Western experience underlay his argument, and the influence of Western culture on the institutional aspect of publishing is apparent, as in the case of copyright.

However, as in the case of copyright, freedom of the press was not legally established until long afterwards. Until the revision of the Publishing Ordinance in 1887, the controlling authority had required a manuscript to be submitted for censorship before its publication was authorized. Far from the freedom of the press, there was a system of prior censorship. Publishing takeoff nevertheless did take place. In this respect, too, Japanese publishing took off before the adequate development of the publishing system as an infrastructure.

Although Fukuzawa was keenly conscious of copyright and the freedom of the press as social institutions and was interested in new techniques in printing and paper-making, he never touched on the institutional aspect of publishing or publishing technology as such. In contrast to his emphasis on newspapers, for which he specifically provided a column in one of his writings, he made no mention of the institutional or technical aspect of book publishing. This suggests that he noticed nothing different from traditional Japanese practices.

Had Fukuzawa, who was a publisher himself, noticed any meaningful difference between the Western way of book publishing and the traditional Japanese, the outspoken advocate of enlightenment could not have resisted the temptation to write about it. His silence supports the hypothesis that there was no major difference between Western Europe and Japan as far as the institutions and technology of the publishing industry were concerned; by the time Japan's publishing industry took off, it had developed institutions and technology to a level comparable to what Western nations had reached by the time their endogenous development led to their own publishing takeoff. Nothing can more persuasively endorse this presumption than his comment, quoted below, on the transpacific voyage of the Kanrin Maru, a feat in which Fukuzawa took part.

It is as yet no more than two decades since the Japanese learned the art of ocean navigation. They have nevertheless built a ship for themselves, had a national crew operate her on a voyage to an area which they had never known and shown her to the eyes of those who had never known any Japanese before. It is not without reason that the local populace was astounded. . . . Certainly it is only twenty years ago that they learned the art of navigation, but it is not just for two decades, or not even for two centuries, that they had been cultivating human wisdom which enabled them to learn it, but this wisdom is a legacy of the eleven-century-old civilization of Japan's own, which the present-day Japanese owe to their ancestors.[18]

Transfer of Hard Technology

Having demonstrated that before its nonpublishing takeoff Japan, as far as publishing technology and institutions were concerned, had reached a level comparable to Western nations at the time of their own publishing takeoff,[19] the remaining point is how did the transferred technologies of typography and mechanized paper-making influence, or fail to influence, publishing takeoff in this country? The mechanized paper-making technology, developed by Louis Robert in 1815 in the midst of the Industrial Revolution in Britain, had a significant impact on the cost reduction of books and the modernization of publishing in Western Europe. Between 1874 and 1880, as many as seven paper manufacturing companies were set up in Japan, all utilizing the technology of mechanized paper-making imported from Western Europe. However, those manufacturers of Western paper did not necessarily support Japan's publishing takeoff in the early Meiji years, because Japan had an established tradition of making Japanese paper by hand and because locally produced Western paper was exposed to competition from imported products.

In 1897, after Japan had completed its publishing takeoff, the output of handmade Japanese paper was four times as large as that of Western paper, and it was not until 1913 that the latter surpassed the former. According to foreign trade statistics for 1892, the total value of book and paper exports was one and a half times as great as that of Western paper imports in the same year. Although the exports were mainly destined for China, the fact that books and Japanese paper were among Japan's major export items makes the paper situation much less simple than it might seem to have been.[20] Competition with imported Western paper was a major constraint on the growth of the local production of similar paper. Early Japanese-made Western paper was not competitive with Japanese handmade paper or imported products both in quality and in cost.

The completion of Japan's publishing takeoff long before paper was being mass produced is understandable given the situation of publishing in Meiji Japan. During the first phase of publishing modernization immediately following the takeoff, the quantity of publications, though already diverse, was still small. It was not until the second phase, after the publishing industry had gone through its marketing revolution, that mass publishing began. This would have been impossible without the supply of machine-made Western paper.

Therefore the demand for uniform quality paper in large quantities was still absent. It is inconceivable that Japanese-made Western paper, which was uncompetitive with handmade Japanese paper even in price, had a revolutionary impact on publishing development in this country. The replacement of traditional Japanese paper production with Western mechanized paper-making was a gradual process.

In the seventeenth century, Japan had come into contact with two different systems of typography, imported from Korea and Western Europe. One was the art of printing using Korean copper type, brought back by the Japanese troops who had invaded Korea, and the other was that of printing Christian literature with a Western-type printing press carried back from Europe by a mission of young boys who had visited Rome in the Tensho period (1573–92). The failure of these imported printing methods to establish themselves in Japan and the return to woodblock printing are attributable to the then-prevailing market mechanism which made the latter more advantageous for the repeated printing and sale of relatively few copies at a time.

The revival of typography in Japan, this time as *modern* typography, required the adaption of the modern Western way of type printing to the Japanese language. A system of Japanese types capable of meeting the requirements of diverse expressions was needed. Motoki Shozo, formerly an interpreter of Dutch in Nagasaki, somehow completed such a system, reportedly in 1869.

Thus, the development of modern typography in Japan was by no means a mere transfer of Western technology but required thorough adaptation by the Japanese, and modern typography, once established, did not play a decisive role in the modernization, above all in the takeoff, of publishing in Japan. Certainly typography became a favorite of the times, fairly quickly developed in part by the government's industry-promoting policy, and it eventually led to a reformed book marketing mechanism and played a decisive role in the development of the local publishing industry. This historical process, however, was realized long afterwards, and typography was not necessarily a key factor as far as the publishing takeoff was concerned.

The shift from woodblock printing to typography was a fairly long, gradual process. For instance, of 164 titles published by organizations connected to the Ministry of Education between 1870 and 1884, years corresponding to the phase of publishing takeoff in this country, some 60 percent were woodblock printed and the remaining 40 percent printed with type.[21]

The relatively slow spread of typography is generally attributed to the high prices of types, the scarcity of technicians to handle them, and the still limited use of papier-mâché molds, which was a disadvantage to repeated printing. Until around 1877, woodblock printing remained less expensive than type printing. It was many years before the full impact of typography was felt.

The Second Transformation: Marketing Revolution

If the publishing takeoff can be regarded as the first transformation for publishing modernization, the second is the marketing revolution, symbolized in Japan by the emergence of ¥1 books in the early Showa years and in Britain by the launching of Penguin Books in 1935.

During the first transformation, the phase of takeoff, publishing in Japan was not influenced by Western technology or institutions, and even in hard technologies such as printing and paper-making Western techniques played no more than a supplementary role. Publishing development in Japan was a modernization brought about by highly endogenous factors.

The Japanese publishing industry accomplished its second transformation some fifty years later. In this transformation from the first to the second phase of modern publishing, quantity was the distinguishing factor. Modernization manifests itself above all as a matter of mass; what emerged was a mass society.

The basic problem of the second phase of publishing modernization was how to respond to the masses' demand for a large quantity. In publishing, this manifests itself as mass production and mass sales. Of the two, mass sales is more important. The technology for mass production had been available since the nineteenth century when the transplantation of Western paper-making and high-speed printing techniques coincided with Japan's publishing takeoff. The second transformation did not result from these technologies, but rather from institutions for mass sales. Therefore, we can regard the second transformation as a marketing revolution in publishing marked by the endogenous development of institutions for mass sales.

The mass sales system is expressed in three aspects of Japan's publishing industry: (1) a nationwide network of book distributors and retailers, (2) distribution by consignment (permitting returning of unsold books), and (3) resale price maintenance. The fact that these three institutions reinforced one another has enabled the Japanese publishing industry to achieve tremendous expansion. Most other nations suffer from inefficient marketing of books because they lack some or all of these institutions. The first two of these have no parallels in other countries, and anything resembling them are inadequate and much newer than their Japanese counterparts.

The system of distribution by consignment is said to have begun with the Jitsugyo no Nippon Press's 1909 decision to unlimitedly accept returns of unsold copies of its *Fujin Sekei* (Ladies' World) magazine. This policy helped boost the periodical's circulation to 250,000 (310,000 at its peak), an amazing level by the then-prevailing standard, and marked the beginning of the age of mass sales. The policy to accept returned copies was in the meantime applied by Kodansha to books as well, leading to the "¥1 book war" in 1927.

The system of distribution by consignment, unlimitedly permitting returns, was a sales technique tailored to the needs of the mass marketing age. It enabled the quick distribution of a great many copies of magazines and books by relieving retailers from the fear of loss incurred by dead stocks. Book retailing, additionally helped by the resale price maintenance system, was thereby substantially stabilized and made profitable, and the national total of bookstores rapidly increased from around 3,000 in 1912 to 6,000 by 1919 and 10,000 by 1927. Thus, a network of book retailers reached even the remotest corner of the country. Distribution by consignment further developed after World War II as one of the most remarkable features of Japan's publishing industry.

The second typical institution, the resale price maintenance system, is not uniquely Japanese; many nations have similar institutions. In Britain, such a system was fully established in 1829. In instituting this system the Japanese publishing industry had a precedent. It is a subject of historical inquiry whether or not Japanese publishers in the Meiji, Taisho, and early Showa years consciously learned lessons from foreign resale price maintenance systems and incorporated any of their features into their Japanese version, but we may safely assume that they did not. This is a mere conjecture, but Japanese publishers in those days were little interested in learning about the institutional aspect of overseas publishing.

The resale price maintenance system in Japan, developing totally endogenously, became effective for magazines upon the organization of the Tokyo Magazine Sellers' Association in 1919 and for books by an agreement of the Tokyo Book Sellers' Association in the same year. Thereafter publications retailed at their respectively fixed prices.

Between 1919 and 1927, as the number of bookstores rapidly increased from some 6,000 to 10,000, distributors, in the modern sense of the term, became established in this country. In 1928 the new building of the wholesale department of Tokyodo (the origin of today's Tohan), mainly dealing in the distribution of magazines, was completed and paved the way for mass marketing of publications.

The presence of many publishers and many book retailers is a prerequisite to the establishment of distributors on a commercial basis. If a publishing house can sell its output to only 500 or 1,000 bookstores, it can directly handle the physical distribution and the collection of bills for itself and may find it more economical to do so. However, it is not possible, much less economical, to deal with more than 10,000 retailers. The advantage of distributors as junctions between many publishers and many retailers becomes apparent.

The book distribution system is a uniquely Japanese institution. All developing and many developed nations lack enough publishing houses and bookstores to foster a similar system. In those areas, the benefits of the distribution system are not so evident as in Japan, and accordingly it has no obvious necessity. Book retailers and publishers are more interested in large profits and slow returns than small profits and quick returns.

Conclusion

Japan's modern publishing industry evolved endogenously from the pre-Meiji publishing traditions. It would have been impossible to achieve the development of the Meiji and post-Meiji years without such a background. For 200 years before its publishing takeoff, Japan had experienced a prosperous publishing industry, though still in a premodern state.

The transfer of hard technology from Western Europe in and after the Meiji era played a secondary role in the development of Japan's publishing industry. These technologies can be effectively transferred only when preceded by necessary social factors; by themselves they cannot stimulate publishing development.[22] Because of its long traditions in publishing and printing Japan's technological gap, if any, was narrow and the publishing industry had no trouble in accepting and assimilating Western hard technology. Furthermore, government policies from the Meiji years on never negatively affected and usually enhanced publishing development in Japan.

Publishing in Japan has continued to develop endogenously, maintaining its unique features, almost independently of Western Europe. Its ability to remain autonomous is obviously due to its geographical position, which has enabled the nation to retain its independence for well over 1,000 years and to constitute a unique linguistic culture, totally isolated from the rest of the world. Japan's geographical position, far enough from neighbors to discourage invasion and yet near enough to encourage cultural interchanges with nearby countries, greatly contributed to the autonomous development of publishing. Thus, more than 1,000 years ago, the cultures of China, Korea, and the Southern Islands, and through them those of India and nations beyond the Silk Road, reached the Japanese archipelago, and from the days of the great navigators Japan was also exposed to Western cultures. These aspects all contributed to the development of the unique Japanese culture.

Japan's premodern experience should not be forgotten; modernization was not achieved overnight. Today, developing nations are desperately groping for a path to modernization. Many of them experienced a discontinuity in the form of colonization, which Japan did not experience. This discontinuity has seriously hampered the sound development of their political, social, cultural, and linguistic traditions, and as such affects publishing. Therefore, the course of publishing development for these developing nations, so different from Japan in historical background, cannot be the same as Japan's.

Modal differences in learning and publishing between different cultural areas is another important factor in Third World publishing development. Western Europe, developing nations in the dry zone, those in the tropical zone, nations of the Indian subcontinent, and East Asian nations, including Japan, irrespective of whether or not they ever experienced colonialization, differ from one another in the mode their learning or publishing (communication) manifests itself. For example, Western learning is done by polemics, while the East Asian scholastic tradition attaches more importance to transcription. In the West, verbally putting forth a winning argument was the way of learning. Therefore, books were not necessarily of primary importance, and whenever a book was produced, it had to be demonstrative and logical. In East Asia, in contrast, merely recording and classifying an extensive collection of facts was regarded as learning in itself. Doing so, it was thought, would lead to the Truth. Perhaps the relative scarcity of paper contributed to the Western emphasis on verbal polemics. On the other hand, without the abundant availability of inexpensive paper in Asia, learning by transcription could not have established itself. Even today, one of the major factors supporting Japan's publishing industry seems to be the people's respect for, love of, and faith in books. They buy books because they believe keeping a large library contributes to their self-improvement. When they buy a book, they seek not necessarily the utility of its contents but its very being as an embodiment of learning. To them, buying a book is completely different from borrowing the same book from a public library.

Thus a Japanese would buy and keep many more books than he is likely to be able to read. This is one of the pillars of the prosperous publishing industry in Japan. Meanwhile, a scholar wins respect by writing books. The originality of their contents is of secondary importance. Putting together a book deserves respect, even if the writer adds nothing to what his master taught him. Accordingly, an ever-increasing number of books are written and published. The Japanese way of learning has been to import, introduce, and interpret knowledge from abroad for 1,000 years. It has not necessarily been the originality of the Japanese that has produced so many published books. In Japan, translation, too, is considered a part of learning.

The prosperity of publishing in Japan may be a peculiarly East Asian phenomenon and perhaps cannot be repeated elsewhere. In areas other than East Asia, or in a different cultural climate from what prevails in East Asia, communication may have to be achieved in a different mode.

Notes

1. UNESCO, *An International Survey of Book Production during the Last Decades* (Paris: UNESCO, 1982), p. 9.
2. In my "Shuppan kaihatsu no keizaigaku" (Economics of publishing development) incorporated into Shigeo Minowa, *Rekishi to shite no Shuppan* (Publishing as an aspect of history) (Tokyo: Yudachisha, 1983), I compared general book price levels and per-capita incomes in twenty-seven developed and developing countries and found that of these countries Japan offered the easiest economic access to paperbacks; in other words, the proportion of the typical paperback price to the per-capita income was the smallest in this country. In many developing countries, the price of a book is a ten to fifty times greater burden on the average citizen than in Japan.
3. In S. Minowa, *Shohi to shite no Shuppan* (Publishing as a consumer industry) (Tokyo: Yudachisha, 1983), I compared the per-capita numbers of copies of books produced in sixty-two countries. Japan, with a record of about nine copies per capita, was ranked first among nonsocialist nations. The corresponding figures were about seven for the United States, about three for the United Kingdom, and 0.1 or even less for many developing countries.
4. Cyril Black, "An Introduction to Modernization Studies" in Michio Nagai, ed., *Modernization Studies* (Tokyo: United Nations University, 1983).
5. Philip G. Altbach and Eva Maria Rathgeber, *Publishing in the Third World: Trend Report and Bibliography* (New York: Praeger, 1980) is a convenient up-to-date guide to publishing problems in the Third World. However, many of the references listed are descriptive, reflecting the lack of theoretical studies in this area.
6. For an argument on this point, see Shigeo Minowa, "Shuppansha no shuen?" (An end to publishers?) in Minowa, *Shohi to shite no Shuppan*.
7. S. Minowa, "Shuppan to kaihatsu: Shuppan kaihatsu ni okeru ririku gensho no shakaigakuteki kosatsu" (Publishing and development: A sociological consideration of the takeoff phenomenon in publishing development), *Shuppan Kenkyu* (Publishing studies), no. 9, (1978).
8. *Ibid.*, pp. 31–33.
9. S. Minowa, "Shoseki kakaku to dokusha kobairyoku: Shuppan kaihatsu ni okeru jidai kubun no kokoromi" (Book prices and readers' purchasing power: An attempt at demarcating epochs in publishing development), *Shuppan Kenkyu*, no. 11, (1980).

10. *Ibid.,* pp. 54–55.
11. "Shuppan kaihatsu," p. 31.
12. *Ibid.,* p. 33.
13. The publishing takeoff in the United States began in about 1850 and completed its first stage at about the same time as Japan's first stage, and so the time gap between the two countries was very small in this respect.
14. S. Minowa, *Shohi to shite no Shuppan* (Tokyo: Yudachisha, 1982), p. 77.
15. Minowa, "Shoseki kakaku to dokusha kobairyoku."
16. S. Minowa, "Unwin, Shuppan Gairon no Shuhen" (Around Unwin's *Truth of Publishing*) and "Penguin kakumei no seiko" (Success of the Penguin Revolution), both incorporated into Minowa, *Shohi to shite no Shuppan.*
17. Evidently publishers in Tokugawa Japan were keenly aware at least of publishing right as part of, or a counterpart to, copyright. Evidence can be found in agreements within their guild against pirate editions. See, for instance, Haruo Uesato, *Edo Shosekisho Shi* (Tokyo: Meicho Kankokai, 1965), pp. 97–112.
18. Yukichi Fukuzawa, *"Fukuzawa bunshu, 2-hen, maki 2"* (An anthology of Fukuzawa's writings, part 2, vol. 2) (1879), in Complete Works, vol. 4, p. 532.
19. This statement is also endorsed by the fact that, in both Japan and any advanced Western nation, the number of new titles published annually before the takeoff was in the order of hundreds.
20. For further arguments, which have been dispensed with for the convenience of foreign readers, see "Meiji Ishin to shuppan no kindaika" (the Meiji Restoration and the modernization of publishing), the Japanese version of this article Minowa, *Rekishi to shite no Shuppan.*
21. Katsumi Yahagi, *Mincho Katsuji* (Mincho Type) (Tokyo: Heibonsha, 1976), p. 31.
22. Experience with training courses and seminars for publishers from developing countries demonstrates this point. These projects, to which UNESCO has devoted utmost energy, must be restructured, recognizing that merely transferring knowledge will not bear fruit.

A Select Bibliography

Philip G. Altbach
Amadio A. Arboleda
S. Gopinathan

This bibliography is intended to provide a selective and up-to-date guide to some of the key literature on publishing in the Third World. We have defined the topic fairly broadly and have included some general discussion of important publishing issues as well as materials dealing directly with Third World publishing. Limitations of space have forced us to leave out a significant number of important references. Readers should refer to Philip G. Altbach and Eva Maria Rathgeber, *Publishing in the Third World: Trend Report and Bibliography* for a comprehensive review of the literature published prior to 1979.[1] A more recent bibliography relating mainly to Africa is Hans Zell, *Publishing and Book Development in Africa: A Bibliography*.[2] Journals such as *African Book Publishing Record, Publishers Weekly* (USA), *The Bookseller* (Britain), *Asian Book Development* (Japan), and *Scholarly Publishing* (Canada) provide current analysis.[3]

This bibliography is arranged by area and by topic. We have included geographical listings first and topical listings next. Our stress is on books and journal articles. We have not included dissertations, government reports, and other materials that we felt are quite difficult to obtain. The bulk of the references are in English, reflecting in part the nature of the literature but also the items available to the compilers. It is hoped that this bibliography will provide a useful guide to those concerned with publishing in the Third World. It reflects a rapidly growing literature—and a literature which is unfortunately sometimes difficult to obtain.

Notes

1. Philip G. Altbach and Eva Maria Rathgeber, *Publishing in the Third World: Trend Report and Bibliography* (New York: Praeger, 1980).
2. Hans Zell, *Publishing and Book Development in Africa: A Bibliography* (Paris: UNESCO, 1984).
3. There are several additional publications that may be of interest to those concerned with Third World publishing. Among these are *Indian Book Industry* (New Delhi), *Singapore Book World* (Singapore), *Asia Pacific Book News* (UNESCO Regional Office for Book Development, Karachi, Pakistan), *Newsletter of the International Association of Scholarly Publishers* (Oslo), *Bulletin of Information* (UNESCO Regional Center for Book Promotion in Africa), *CERLAL News* (UNESCO Regional Center for Book Promotion in Latin America and the Caribbean), and *Book Promotion News* (UNESCO, Paris).

Africa
Books

Chakava, Henry. *Books and Reading in Kenya.* Paris: UNESCO, 1983.
Ethiope Publishing Corporation. *Publishing in Nigeria.* Benin City: Ethiope, 1972.
Financing Culture and the Book Industry in Zaire. Kinshasha, Zaire: SOCEDI, 1983.
Heissler, N. P. Lavy, and A. Candela. *La diffusion du livre et le developpement de la lecture en Afrique.* Paris: Culture et Development, 1965.
Oluwasammi, E., E. McLean, and Hans Zell, eds. *Publishing in Africa in the Seventies.* Ile-Ife, Nigeria: University of Ife Press, 1974.
Ricard, Alain. *Livres et communication au Nigeria.* Paris: Presence Africaine, 1975.
Taubert, Sigfried, ed. *African Book Trade Directory, 1971.* New York: Bowker, 1971.
UNESCO. *Book Development in Africa.* Paris: UNESCO, 1969.
Zell, Hans M. *The African Book World and Press: Directory.* Oxford, England: Hans Zell, 1983.

Journal Articles

Akiwowo, Akinsola A. "Textbooks and Materials for Africa," *International Social Science Journal* 31, no. 1 (1979): 10–20.
Armstrong, Robert Plant. "Developments in African Publishing. Book Publishers in Sub-Saharan Africa." In *The African Experience,* edited by John N. Paden and Edward W. Soja, pp. 17–31. Evanston, IL: Northwestern University Press, 1970.
Chakava, Henry. "Publishing in a Multilingual Situation: The Kenya Case." *African Book Publishing Record* 3 (April 1977): 83–90.
Dodson, Don. "The Role of the Publisher in Onitsha Market Literature." *Research in African Literatures* 4 (Fall 1973): 172–188.
Dodson, Don, and Barbara Dodson. "Publishing Progress in Nigeria." *Scholarly Publishing* 4 (October 1972): 61–72.
Hill, Alan. "Educational Publishing in Anglophone Africa." In *Education in Africa: Research and Action,* edited by R. Jolly, pp. 285–300. Nairobi: East African Publishing House, 1969.
Irele, Abiola. "The Ethiope Experience." *African Book Publishing Record* 1 (January 1975): 27–36.
Keim, Karen. "Popular Fiction Publishing in Cameroun." *African Book Publishing Record* 9, no. 1 (1983): 7–12.
Lindfors, Bernth. "Interviews: John Nottingham, David Maillu, Terry Hirst." *African Book Publishing Record* 5 (April 1979): 81–93.
Lottman, Herbert R. "Ghana Enters the Publishing Age: 2 Parts." *Publishers Weekly* 202 (March 6, 1972 and March 13, 1972): 34–36 and 43–44.
Lottman, Herbert R. "Publishing for 60 Million Nigerians: 2 Parts." *Publishers Weekly* 201 (March 20, 1972 and March 27, 1972): 38–39 and 59–60.

Mwiyeriwa, S. S. "Printing Presses and Publishing Houses in Malawi." *African Book Publishing Record* 4 (April 1978): 87–98.

Nottingham, John. "Establishing an African Publishing Industry: A Study in Decolonization." *African Affairs* 68 (April 1969): 139–144.

Olanlokun, S. O. "Nigerian Book Trade." *International Library Review* 2 (January 1979): 69–75.

Randall, Peter. "Minority Publishing in South Africa." *African Book Publishing Record* 1 (July 1975): 219–222.

Randall, Peter. "Publishing in South Africa: Challenges and Constraints." *African Book Publishing Record* 9, no. 2–3 (1983): 105–108.

Rathgeber, Eva Maria. "Africana Acquisitions Problems: The View from Both Sides." *Library Acquisitions: Practice and Theory* 6 (1982): 137–148.

Rathgeber, Eva Maria McLean. "Nigeria's University Presses: Problems and Prospects." *African Book Publishing Record* 5 (January 1979): 13–18.

Rea, Julian. "Aspects of African Publishing, 1945–74." *African Book Publishing Record* 1 (April 1975): 145–151.

Smith, Keith. "Books and Development in Africa: Access and Role." *Library Trends* 26 (Spring 1978): 469–478.

Smith, Keith. "Who Controls Book Publishing in Anglophone Middle Africa?" *Annals of the American Academy of Political and Social Science* 421 (September 1975): 140–150.

Udoeyop, N. J. "Scholarly Publishing in Nigeria." *Scholarly Publishing* 4 (October 1972): 51–60.

Williams, G. "The Zambian Publishing Scene: A Commentary." *African Book Publishing Record* 3 (January 1977): 15–22.

Yesufu, A. R. "Mbari Publications: A Pioneer Anglophone African Publishing House." *African Book Publishing Record* 8, no. 2 (1982): 53–57.

Zell, Hans. "Publishing in Africa in the Seventies." In *Acquisitions from the Third World*, edited by D. A. Clark, pp. 105–124. London: Mansell, 1975.

Asia

Books

Ahmed, Ziauddin. *Problems of Book Publishing in Pakistan*. Karachi: National Book Council of Pakistan, 1981.

Altbach, Philip G. *Publishing in India: An Analysis*. Delhi and New York: Oxford University Press, 1975.

Aprieto, Pacifico N. *Book Publishing and Philippine Scholarship*. Manila: Daily Star Publishing Co., 1981.

Asian Cultural Center for UNESCO. *Report on Typography in Asia*. Tokyo: Asian Cultural Center for UNESCO, 1976.

Byrd, Cecil. *Books in Singapore: A Survey of Publishing, Printing, Bookselling, and Library Activity in the Republic of Singapore*. Singapore: Chopmen Enterprises, 1970.

Ghai, O. P., and Narendra Kumar, eds. *International Publishing Today*. New Delhi: Bookman's Club, 1983.

Israel, Samuel. *A Career in Book Publishing*. New Delhi: National Book Trust, 1983.

Kaser, David. *Book Pirating in Taiwan*. Philadelphia: University of Pennsylvania Press, 1969.

Kimman, E. J. J. M. *Indonesian Publishing: Economic Organization in a Lagganan Society*. Baarn, Netherlands: Hollandia, 1981.

Kumar, Vinod, ed. *Book Industry in India: Problems and Prospects*. New Delhi: Federation of Publishers and Booksellers Associations, 1980.

Malhotra, D. N., and Narendra Kumar, eds. *Indian Publishing Since Independence*. New Delhi: Bookman's Club, 1980.

Minowa, S., and A. A. Arboleda, eds. *Scholarly Publishing in Asia: Proceedings of the Conference of University Presses in Asia and the Pacific.* Tokyo: University of Tokyo Press, 1973.

National Council of Applied Economic Research: *Survey of Indian Book Industry.* 2 vols. New Delhi: National Council of Applied Economic Research, 1976.

Nickerson, Thomas, ed. *Trans-Pacific Scholarly Publishing.* Honolulu: East-West Center Press, 1963.

Nunn, G. R. *Publishing in Mainland China.* Cambridge, MA: M.I.T. Press, 1966.

Problems of Book Distribution in Pakistan: A Survey. Karachi: National Book Council of Pakistan, 1981.

Richter, Harold. *Publishing in the People's Republic of China: Personal Observations by a Foreign Student.* Hamburg: Verband Stiftung Deutsches Ubersee-Institut, 1978.

Siddique, K. M. *Economics of Book Publishing in Pakistan.* Karachi: National Book Council of Pakistan, 1981.

Taubert, Sigfred, and Peter Weidhaas, eds. *Book Trade of the World, Vol. 3—Asia.* New York: K. G. Saur, 1981.

UNESCO. *Book Development in Asia: A Report on the Production and Distribution of Books in the Region.* Paris: UNESCO, 1967.

Journal Articles

Allworth, E. "Central Asian Publishing and the Rise of Nationalism." *New York Public Library Bulletin* 69 (October 1965): 493–522.

Altbach, Philip G. "Book Publishing in a Developing Regional Culture: The Case of Maharashtra, India." *International Social Science Journal* 31, no. 2 (1979): 328–340.

Altbach, Philip G. "Publishing in a Transitional Society: The Case of India." In *Perspectives on Publishing,* edited by P. Altbach and S. McVey, pp. 141–156. Lexington, MA: Lexington, 1976.

Arboleda, A. A. "English Language Scholarly Publishing in Japan." *Scholarly Publishing* 6 (April 1975): 257–266.

Baraheni, Reza. "The Perils of Publishing: Iran." *Index on Censorship,* no. 5 (1978), pp. 12–17.

Benjamin, C. G. "Book Publishing in Korea." *Publishers Weekly* 194 (August 19, 1968): 35–37.

"Books and China." *Publishers Weekly,* April 15, 1976, pp. 44–46.

Carnese, Paul J. "China Diary." *Publishers Weekly* 215 (June 4, 1979): 27–34.

Clark, Alden. "Some Notes on Prospects for Trans-Pacific Co-operation." *Scholarly Publishing* 3 (October 1971): 11–16.

Gopinathan, S. "Publishing in a Plural Society: The Case of Singapore." In *Perspectives on Publishing,* edited by P. Altbach and S. McVey, pp. 157–173. Lexington, MA: Lexington, 1976.

"Hongkong: Time to Branch Out." *Asiaweek,* August 5, 1983, pp. 52–54.

Israel, Samuel. "The Colonial Heritage in Indian Publishing." *Library Trends* 26 (Spring 1978): 539–552.

Kan, L. "Present-day Publishing in Hong Kong." *Library Resources and Technical Services* 22 (Winter 1978): 47–60.

Koch, H. W. "People and Publishing in China." *Physics Today* 32 (August 1979): 32–39.

Lim, Beda. "Scholarly Publishing in Malaysia." *Scholarly Publishing* 4 (April 1973): 271–278.

Lottman, Herbert R. "China: The Inside Story." *Publishers Weekly* 218 (September 19, 1980): 102–127.

"Malaysia: Reaching a Wider Audience." *Asiaweek,* September 30, 1983, pp. 52–55.

Minowa, S. "Scholarly Publishing in Japan." *Scholarly Publishing* 3 (October 1971): 17–27.

Noyes, Henry H. "How Chinese Publishing and Bookselling Works." *Publishers Weekly,* March 15, 1976, pp. 44–45.

Nunn, G. Raymond. "Modern Japanese Book Publishing." Occasional Papers of the Center for Japanese Studies, no. 8. Ann Arbor: University of Michigan, 1964, pp. 59–94.

"Printing and Publishing in Indonesia." *Printing and Publishing* 18 (Summer-Fall 1977): 20–28.

"Printing and Publishing in Iran." *Printing and Publishing* 19 (Winter 1978).

"Printing and Publishing in Japan." *Printing and Publishing* 19 (Summer 1978).

"Publishing in Japan: A PW Special Report." *Publishers Weekly* 214 (October 16, 1978): 50–95.

Shimizu, Hideo. "In Pursuance of an Asian Publishing Culture." *Asian Book Development* 10 (October 1978): 4–9.

Siwek, M. "Publishing in Korea." In *Bowker Annual of Library and Book Trade Information, 1973*, pp. 262–272. New York: Bowker, 1973.

Smith, Datus. "Books and the 'Asian Century.'" *Asian Book Development* 13 (Autumn 1981): 4–7.

Smith, Datus. "The New World of Books in Asia." *Asia* 5 (Spring 1966): 1–15.

Skedgell, Marian. "Book Publishing in India." *Publishers Weekly*, March 30, 1984, pp. 24–27.

Valdehuesa, M. E., Jr. "Scholarly Publishing in the Philippines." *Scholarly Publishing* 4 (April 1973): 257–264.

Latin America

Books

Andrade, O. de Souza. *O Livro Brasileiro*. Rio de Janeiro: Editora Paralebo, 1974.

Augsburger, Alberto E. *The Latin American Book Market: Problems and Prospects*. Paris: UNESCO, 1981.

Hallewell, L. *Books in Brazil: A History of the Publishing Trade*. Metuchen, N.J.: Scarecrow, 1982.

Penalosa, Bernando. *The Mexican Book Industry*. New York: Scarecrow, 1957.

Puigvert, Alfredo. *Mercados del Libro: Argentina*. Madrid: Puigvert, 1967.

Turner, Mary C., ed. *La Empresa del Libro en America Latina*. Buenos Aires: Bowker Editores, 1974.

Journal Articles

Alleyne, Alvona, and Pam Mordecai. "Educational Publishing and Book Production in the English-Speaking Caribbean." *Library Trends* 26 (Spring 1978): 575–590.

de Nohra, Flor Romero. "The Writer, The Public and Publishing in Latin America." *Cultures* 4, no. 2 (1977): 36–50.

Hallewell, Laurence. "Erratic Growth in the Argentine Publishing Industry," *Bulletin of the Society for Latin American Studies*, no. 16, January 1973, pp. 23–27.

Hallewell, Laurence. "From Managua to Peru: A Brief Look at Some of the Secondary Book Producing Centres of Latin America." *Bulletin of the Society for Latin American Studies*, no. 20, May 1974, pp. 5–12.

Holt, Patricia. "Publishing in Mexico: Its Time has Come." *Publishers Weekly*, April 25, 1980, pp. 33–46.

Lottman, Herbert R. "Argentina: A Book World, a World Away." *Publishers Weekly*, September 18, 1981, pp. 100–119.

Lottman, Herbert R. "Brazil: A Long Way to Go." *Publishers Weekly*, November 21, 1980, pp. 20–33.

"Printing and Publishing in Mexico." *Printing and Publishing* 20 (Fall 1979): 17–25.

Middle East

Books

Ben Cheikh, A. *Book Production and Reading in the Arab World.* Paris: UNESCO, 1982.

Journal Articles

Botros, Salib. "Problems of Book Development in the Arab World with Special Reference to Egypt." *Library Trends* 26 (Spring 1978): 567–574.
Lottman, H. R. "Publishing in Israel." *Publishers Weekly* 215 (March 19, 1979): 33–36.
Rizk, Nadia A. "The Book Publishing Industry in Egypt." *Library Trends* 26 (Spring 1978): 553–566.
Thoumy, A. S. "University Publishing in Lebanon." *Scholarly Publishing* 13 (July 1982): 355–362.

Bibliographies

Books

Altbach, Philip G., and Eva Maria Rathgeber. *Publishing in the Third World: Trend Report and Bibliography.* New York: Praeger, 1980.
A Select Bibliography on Book Publishing and Related Subjects. Karachi: UNESCO Regional Office for Culture and Book Development in Asia, 1982.
Zell, Hans, comp. *Publishing and Book Development in Africa: A Bibliography.* Paris: UNESCO, 1984.

Journal Articles

Altbach, Philip G. "Publishing in Developing Countries: A Select Bibliography." *Scholarly Publishing* 6 (April 1975): 267–279.
Zell, Hans. "Publishing and Book Development in Africa: A Bibliography." *African Book Publishing Record* 2 (April 1976): 95–103.

Books—General

Books

Books for All At Low Cost. New Delhi: National Book Trust, 1983.
The Bowker Annual of Library and Book Trade Information. New York: Bowker, annually since 1955.
Delaven, Emile. *For Books: UNESCO and Its Programs.* Paris: UNESCO, 1974.
Escarpit, Robert. *Trends in Worldwide Book Development, 1970–1978.* Paris: UNESCO, 1982.
Gault, Michel. *The Future of the Book: Part II—The Changing Role of Reading.* Paris: UNESCO, 1982.
Hasan, Abul. *Promoting National Book Strategies in Asia and the Pacific: Problems and Perspectives.* Paris: UNESCO, 1982.

Journal Articles

"Book Publishing in Foreign Countries: A Comparative Analysis." *Printing and Publishing* 2 (October 1970): 20–25.
Shimizu, Hideo. "The Role of the Book." In *An Introduction to Book Publishing World,* pp. 6–18. Tokyo: Asian Cultural Centre for UNESCO, 1974.

Children's Publishing

Kotei, S.I.A., and Colin, Ray. "The Legon Seminar on Writing and Production of Literature for Children, April 5–10, 1976." *African Book Publishing Record* 1 (October 1976): 227–229.

Soriano, Marc. "Children's Books and Human Rights." *Prospects* 7, no. 2 (1977): 204–225.

Copyright

Books

Bogsch, A. *The Law of Copyright Under the Universal Copyright Convention.* New York: Bowker, 1968.

Boguslasky, Mark. *The USSR and International Copyright Protection.* Moscow: Progress Publishers, 1979.

Carter-Ruck, P. F., and E. P. Skone James. *Copyright: Modern Law and Practice.* London: Faber and Faber, 1965.

Copyright in Developing Countries. London: Commonwealth Secretariat, 1974.

Copyright International Conventions Handbook, Vol. 1. New Delhi: Copyright Office, Ministry of Education, 1967.

Copyright Laws and Treaties of the World, 1956–1977. 3 vols. Paris: UNESCO, 1977.

de Freitas, Denis. *The Copyright System: Practice and Problems in Developing Countries.* London: Commonwealth Secretariat, 1983.

Gidwani, N. N., ed. *Copyright: Legalized Piracy?* Bombay: Indian Committee for Cultural Freedom, 1968.

Harvey, Edwin R. *Derechos de autor, de la cultura y de la informacion.* Buenos Aires: Ediciones Depalma, 1975.

International Copyright: Needs of Developing Countries. New Delhi: Ministry of Education, Government of India, 1966.

Kaplan, Benjamin. *An Unhurried View of Copyright.* New York: Columbia University Press, 1967.

Khosla, G. D. *Know Your Copyright.* New Delhi: Orient Longmans, 1977.

Mouchet, Carlos. *America latina y el drecho de Autor.* Buenos Aires: CSIAC Consejo Panamericano, 1973.

Newcity, Michael. *Copyright Law in the Soviet Union.* New York: Praeger, 1978.

Ploman, Edward W., and L. Clark Hamilton. *Copyright: Intellectual Property in the Information Age.* London: Routledge and Kegan Paul, 1980.

Whale, R. F. *Copyright: Evolution, Theory and Practice.* London: Longman, 1970.

Journal Articles

"African Study Meeting on Copyright." *Copyright Bulletin* 15, no. 2 (1963): 171–187.

Barker, R. E. "Copyright Concessions for the Developing Countries." *The Bookseller,* no. 3364, June 13, 1970, pp. 2598–2602.

Barker, R. E. "Copyright Concessions for the Developing Countries—II." *The Bookseller,* no. 3365, June 20, 1970, pp. 2678–2684.

Barker, Ronald. "International Copyright." *The Bookseller,* no. 3688, August 28, 1976, pp. 1522–1528.

Bhatkal, S., *et al.* "Copyright—National and International." In *Book Development: Some Problems, 1969,* edited by T. V. K. Krishnan, pp. 97–107. New Delhi: Federation of Publishers and Booksellers Association in India, 1969.

Bortnick, Jane. "International Information Flow: The Developing World Perspective." *Cornell International Law Journal* 14 (Summer 1981): 333–353.

Esezobor, J. E. "Implications of the Copyright Law for Authors, Artists, and Other Originators of Creative Work with Particular Reference to Nigeria." *Copyright Bulletin* 10, no. 4 (1976): 40–51.

Graham, W. Gordon. "The Piracy Picture Worldwide: Gains by Pirates Demand Action by Publishers." *Publishers Weekly* 216 (July 16, 1979): 33–34.

"The Great Copyright Debate." *Asiaweek* 10 (June 1, 1984): 54–57.

Hasan, Abul. "Copyright and Development." *Copyright Bulletin* 26, no. 1–2 (1982): 10–15.

Henry, Nicholas. "Copyright: Its Adequacy in Technological Societies." *Science* 186 (December 13, 1974): 993–1004.

Karp, Irwin. "Downgrading the Protection of International Copyright." *Publishers Weekly* 200 (September 27, 1971): 143–147.

Koutchoumow, J. A. "Copyright and Piracy." *Asian Book Development* 12 (March 1981): 13–14.

Leavens, T. R. "In Defense of the Unauthorized Use: Recent Developments in Defending Copyright Infringement." *Law and Contemporary Problems* 44 (Autumn 1981): 3–26.

Nelson, Dale. "China Moves Toward Copyright Law." *Wilson Library Bulletin* (May 1983).

Olian, Irwin A., Jr. "International Copyright and the Needs of Developing Countries." *Cornell International Law Journal* 7 (May 1974): 81–112.

Parsons, Ian. "Copyright and Society." In *Essays in the History of Publishing*, edited by A. Briggs, pp. 29–60. London: Longman, 1974.

Pitman, Michael I. "Why Copyright?" *Scholarly Publishing* 13 (January 1982): 118–126.

Ringer, Barbara. "The Demonology of Copyright." *Publishers Weekly* 206 (November 18, 1974): 26–29.

Said, Rafik. "The Role of Copyright in the Promotion of Development." *Copyright Bulletin* 11, no. 4 (1977): 49–52.

Schrader, Dorothy M. "Armageddon in International Copyright: Review of the Berne Convention, the Universal Convention, and the Present Crisis in International Copyright," *Advances in Librarianship* 2 (1971): 305–355.

Valdehuesa, Manuel E. "Need to Stop, Look and Listen: Copyright and Piracy at the 21st IPA Congress." *Asian Book Development* 12 (October 1980): 9–12.

Weinberg, Louise. "The Photocopying Revolution and the Copyright Crisis." *Public Interest*, no. 38, Winter 1975, pp. 99–118.

Development and Publishing

Books

Books and National Development: Seminar Report. Seoul: Korean Publishers Association, 1968.

Los Rios, F. G. *El libro y el desarrollo economico.* Bogotá: Centro Regional para el Fomento del Libro en America Latina, 1971.

The Reading Habit: Report of the Regional Seminar on the Promotion of the Reading Habit. Singapore: National Book Development Council, 1983.

Journal Article

Jennison, Peter S. "Book Publishing and National Development." *ALA Bulletin* 57 (June 1963): 512–517.

Distribution and Bookselling

Books

Bailey, H. E. *The Economics of Bookselling.* London: Hutchinson, 1965.

Kurian, George. *The Worldwide Markets for English-Language Books.* White Plains, NY: Knowledge Industry Publications, 1978.

Mumby, Frank, and Ian Norrie. *Publishing and Bookselling*. London: Jonathan Cape, 1974.

Journal Articles

Graham, Gordon. "The Shrinking World Market." *Publishers Weekly* 225 (May 4, 1984): 20–21.

Grannis, Chandler B. "Book Distribution in Developing Countries." *Publishers Weekly* 204 (September 24, 1973): 131–135.

Isenberg, Artur. "Toward Better Book Distribution in Asian Countries." *Indian Book Industry* (August-September 1970): 35–55.

Lightfoot, Martin. "The Distribution of Books: Weak Link in the Publishing Chain." In *Perspectives on Publishing*, edited by P. Altbach and S. McVey, pp. 71–82. Lexington, MA: Lexington, 1976.

Mann, Peter. "Books, Book Readers, and Bookshops." In *Media Sociology*, edited by J. Tunstall, pp. 351–362. Urbana, IL: University of Illinois Press, 1970.

Mohamed, N. I. "The Bookseller and the Academic Community." In *Scholarly Publishing in Southeast Asia*, edited by B. Lim, pp. 103–107. Kuala Lumpur: Association of Southeast Asian Institutions of Higher Learning, 1975.

Economics of Publishing

Books

The Business of Publishing: A PW Anthology. New York: Bowker, 1976.

Smith, Datus. *The Economics of Book Publishing in Developing Countries*. Paris: UNESCO, 1977.

Taraporevala, Russi J. *Economics of Book Publishing and Need for Capital in Book Development*. Bombay: Federation of Publishers and Booksellers Associations in India, 1969.

Vanier, Dinoo J. *Market Structure and the Business of Book Publishing*. New York: Pitman, 1974.

Wegman, Edward. *International Circulation of Books*. Paris: UNESCO, 1982.

Journal Article

Aoki, Haruo. "Business Management in Publishing." In *An Introduction to Book Publishing World*, pp. 19–47. Tokyo: Asian Cultural Centre for UNESCO, 1974.

Educational Systems and Publishing

Kyle, John H. "Books, Education, and the Developing World." *Scholarly Publishing* 6 (January 1975): 107–112.

Lottman, Herbert R. "Educational Materials in the Third World." *Publishers Weekly* 200 (November 22, 1971): 16–18.

International Aspects and Neocolonialism

Books

Amadi, A. O. *African Libraries: Western Tradition and Colonial Brainwashing*. Metuchen, NJ: Scarecrow, 1981.

Mattelart, Armand. *Multinational Corporations and the Control of Culture: The Ideological Apparatuses of Imperialism*. Sussex, England: Harvester, 1979.

Nordenstreng, Kaarle, and Herbert I. Schiller, eds. *National Sovereignty and International Communication*. Norwood, NJ: Ablex, 1979.

Price, Paxton P., ed. *International Book and Library Activities: The History of a U.S. Foreign Policy*. Metuchen, NJ: Scarecrow, 1982.

Schiller, Herbert I. *Communication and Cultural Domination.* White Plains, NY: International Arts and Sciences Press, 1976.

Journal Articles

Altbach, Philip G. "Center-Periphery: Publishing in the International Knowledge System." *Asian Book Development* 13 (Winter 1981-82): 6–9.

Altbach, Philip G. "The Distribution of Knowledge in the Third World: A Case Study in Neocolonialism." In *Education and the Colonial Experience,* edited by P. G. Altbach and G. P. Kelly, pp. 229–252. New Brunswick, NJ: Transaction, 1983.

Altbach, Philip G. "Literary Colonialism: Books in the Third World." *Harvard Educational Review* 45 (May 1975).

Golding, Peter. "The International Media and the Political Economy of Publishing." *Library Trends* 26 (Spring 1978): 453–468.

Lorimer, Rowland. "Multinationals in Book Publishing: Culture Homogenized." *Media Information Australia,* no. 39, August 1983, pp. 35–41.

Schiller, Herbert I. "Decolonization of Information: Efforts Toward a New International Order." *Latin American Perspectives* 5 (Winter 1978): 35–48.

Smith, Keith. "The Impact of Transnational Book Publishing on Knowledge in Less Developed Countries." *Prospects* 7, no. 2 (1977): 299–308.

Varis, Tapio. "Aspects of the Impact of Transnational Corporations on Communication." *International Social Science Journal* 28, no. 4 (1976): 808–830.

Language Issues and Translations

Book

Hasan, Abul. *The Book in Multilingual Countries.* Paris: UNESCO, 1978.

Journal Articles

Milburn, Stanley. "The Provision of Vernacular Literature." *Library Trends* 8 (October 1959): 307–321.

Miner, Earl. "On the Desirability of Publishing Translations." *Scholarly Publishing* 11 (July 1980): 291–299.

Mukerjee, Sujit. "Role of Translations in Publishing of the Developing World." In *World Publishing in the Eighties,* pp. 65–73. New Delhi: National Book Trust, India, n.d.

Smith, Datus C. "Translating Books for Newly Developing Countries." *Publishers Weekly* 190 (August 1, 1966): 22–26.

Libraries

Books

Clarke, D. A., ed. *Acquisitions from the Third World.* London: Mansell, 1975.

Fry, Bernard, and Herbert White. *Publishers and Libraries: A Study of Scholarly and Research Journals.* Lexington, MA: Lexington Books, 1976.

Kaser, David, C. W. Stone, and C. K. Byrd. *Library Development in Eight Asian Countries.* Metuchen, NJ: Scarecrow Press, 1969.

Journal Article

Oyeoku, Kaul K. "The Library and the Third World Publisher: An Inquiry into Lopsided Development." *Library Trends* 26 (Spring 1978): 505–514.

Publishing as a Profession

Books

Balaban, Meriam. *Scientific Information Transfer: The Editor's Role.* Dordrecht, Netherlands: Reidel, 1978.

Butcher, Judith. *Copy-editing: The Cambridge Handbook.* Cambridge, England: Cambridge University Press, 1975.

Kachroo, P. *Handbook of Editing and Production.* Calcutta: Kothari Publications, 1968.

Journal Articles

Chek, Chia Hearn. "Asian Conference of Editors." *Asian Book Development* 14 (Summer 1982): 9–12.

Lane, Michael. "Shapers of Culture: The Editor in Book Publishing." *Annals of the American Academy of Political and Social Science* 421 (September 1975): 34–42.

Junokawa, K. "An Introduction to Editing." In *An Introduction to Book Publishing World,* pp. 48–57. Tokyo: Asian Cultural Centre for UNESCO, 1974.

Philipson, Morris. "Publishing as a Profession." *Scholarly Publishing* 6 (Spring 1975): 221–228.

Publishing—General

Books

Altbach, Philip G., and Sheila McVey, eds. *Perspectives on Publishing.* Lexington, MA: Heath-Lexington, 1976.

Asian Cultural Centre for UNESCO. *An Introduction to Book Publishing World.* Tokyo: Asian Cultural Centre for UNESCO, 1974.

Bailey, Herbert S., Jr. *The Art and Science of Book Publishing.* New York: Harper & Row, 1970.

Coser, Lewis A., Charles Kadushin, and Walter W. Powell. *Books: The Culture and Commerce of Publishing.* New York: Basic Books, 1982.

Dessauer, John P. *Book Publishing: What It Is, What It Does.* New York: Bowker, 1974.

Dorsch, Petra, and Konrad Teckentrup, eds. *Buch und Lesen International: Berichte und Analysen zur Buchmarkt Forschung.* Gutersloh, West Germany: Verlag für Buchmarkt und Medien Forschung, 1981.

Report of the Regional Seminar on Commercial Factors Involved in Mass Market Publishing. Karachi: UNESCO Regional Office for Culture and Book Development in Asia, 1979.

Taubert, Siegfried, ed. *The Book Trade of the World.* New York: Bowker, 1972.

Taubert, Siegfried. *The Book Trade of the World, Vol. 2 USA, Canada, Central and South America, Australia, and New Zealand.* New York: Bowker, 1976.

Unwin, Sir Stanley. *The Truth About Publishing.* London: Allen and Unwin, 1960.

Journal Articles

Lacy, Dan. "Reading in an Audiovisual and Electronic Era." *Daedalus* 112 (Winter 1983): 117–128.

Marshall, Hilary S., and Ian Montagnes. "International Publishing." In *Royal Commission on Book Publishing: Background Papers,* pp. 154–172. Toronto: Queen's Printer and Publisher, 1972.

Taubert, S. "International Section." In *The Book Trade of the World,* vol. 1, edited by S. Taubert, pp. 10–54. New York: Bowker, 1972.

Vaughan, Samuel S. "The Community of the Book." *Daedalus* 112 (Winter 1983): 85–116.

Scholarly Publishing
Books

Harmon, Eleanor, ed. *The University as Publisher*. Toronto: University of Toronto Press, 1961.

Lim, Beda, ed. *Scholarly Publishing in Southeast Asia*. Kuala Lumpur: Association of Southeast Asian Institutions of Higher Learning, 1975.

Minowa, S., A. Arboleda, and N. Raj, eds. *International Scholarly Publishing: An Overview, 1976*. Tokyo: University of Tokyo Press, 1976.

National Enquiry Into Scholarly Communication. *Scholarly Communication: The Report of the National Enquiry*. Baltimore, MD: Johns Hopkins University Press, 1979.

Journal Articles

Alemna, A. A. "Scholarly Publishing in Ghana." *Scholarly Publishing* 12 (January 1982): 174–178.

Altbach, Philip G. "Scholarly Publishing in the Third World." *Library Trends* 26 (Spring 1978): 489–505.

Armstrong, Robert P. "The University Press in a Developing Country." *Scholarly Publishing* 5 (October 1973): 35–40.

Bohne, Harald. "The Crisis of Scholarly Publishing." *Journal of Canadian Studies* 10 (May 1975): 7–14.

Colwell, Ernest Cadman. "The Publishing Needs of Scholarship." *Scholarly Publishing* 6 (January 1975): 99–106.

Massil, S. W., and H. W. Lee. "Scholarly Publications: Considerations on Bibliographical Control and Dissemination." In *Scholarly Publishing in Southeast Asia*, edited by B. Lim, pp. 212–214. Kuala Lumpur: Association of Southeast Asian Institutions of Higher Learning, 1975.

Meyer, Sheldon, and Leslie Phillabaum. "What Is a University Press?" *Scholarly Publishing* 11 (April 1980): 213–220.

Munro, John, and Zahi Khuri. "The University Press as a Special Dimension of Extension Education." In *The Role of the University in Extension Education*, edited by M. Bashshur, pp. 108–119. Beirut: American University of Beirut, 1982.

Orlov, Ann. "Demythologizing Scholarly Publishing." *Annals of the American Academy of Political and Social Science* 421 (September 1975): 43–55.

Philipson, Morris. "What Is a University Press Worth?" *Encounter* 40 (May 1973): 41–49.

Smith, Datus. "Scholarly Publishing in the Third World." *Scholarly Publishing* 12 (April 1981): 195–218.

Sociology of Publishing
Books

Lindsey, Duncan. *The Scientific Publication System in Social Science*. San Francisco: Jossey-Bass, 1978.

Machlup, Fritz, and Kenneth Leeson. *Information Through the Printed Word: The Dissemination of Scholarly, Scientific and Intellectual Knowledge: Vol. 1: Book Publishing*. New York: Praeger, 1978.

Mann, Peter. *From Author to Reader: A Social Study of Books*. London: Routledge and Kegan Paul, 1982.

Journal Articles

Altbach, Philip G. "Publishing and the Intellectual System." *Annals of the American Academy of Political and Social Science* 421 (September 1975): 1–13.

Bell, Daniel. "Teletext and Technology: New Networks of Knowledge and Information in Post-Industrial Society." *Encounter* 48 (June 1977): 10–29.

Coser, Lewis. "Publishers as Gatekeepers of Ideas." *Annals of the American Academy of Political and Social Science* 421 (September 1975): 14–22.

Lacy, Dan. "Culture and the Media of Communications." *Scholarly Publishing* 13 (April 1982): 195–210.

Lane, Michael. "Books and Their Publishers." In *Media Sociology,* edited by J. Tunsall, pp. 239–251. Urbana, IL: University of Illinois Press, 1970.

Lane, Michael. "Publishing Managers, Publishing House Organization and Role Conflict." *Sociology* 4, no. 3 (1970): 367–383.

Neavill, Gordon. "Role of the Publisher in the Dissemination of Knowledge." *Annals of the American Academy of Political and Social Science* 421 (September 1975): 23–33.

O'Brien, Rita Cruise, and G. K. Helleiner. "The Political Economy of Information in a Changing International Economic Order." *International Organization* 34 (Autumn 1980): 445–470.

Technological Developments and Implications
Books

Book House Training Center. *Training in Book Publishing: A Guide and Course Handbook.* London: Book House Training Center, 1981.

Eisenstein, Elizabeth. *The Printing Press as an Agent of Change.* 2 vols. Cambridge, England: Cambridge University Press, 1978.

Hill, Mary, and Wendell Cochran. *Into Print: A Practical Guide to Writing, Illustrating and Publishing.* Los Altos, CA: Wm. Kauffman, 1977.

Oakeshott, Priscilla. *New Technology and the Publication Chain.* London: British National Bibliography Research Fund, 1983.

Zeitlyn, Jonathan. *Low Cost Printing for Development.* 4 vols. New Delhi: Center for Development of Instructional Technology, 1982.

Journal Articles

Bailey, Herbert, Jr. "The Traditional Book in the Electronic Age." *Publishers Weekly* 212 (December 5, 1977): 24–29.

Bergendahl, Carl A. "The Supply of Cultural Paper in Asia." *Asian Book Development* 10 (March 1979): 4–9.

Graham, Gordon. "Managing Change in Professional Publishing." *Scholarly Publishing* 14 (October 1982): 3–8.

Textbooks
Books

Heyneman, Stephen P. *Textbooks and Achievement: What We Know.* Washington, DC: World Bank, 1978.

National Book Trust, India. *Educational Publishing in Developing Countries.* New Delhi: National Book Trust, 1980.

Neumann, Peter H. *Publishing for Schools: Textbooks and the Less Developed Countries.* Washington, DC: World Bank, 1980.

Pearce, Douglas. *Textbook Production in Developing Countries: Some Problems of Preparation, Production and Distribution.* Paris: UNESCO, 1982.

Journal Articles

Altbach, Philip G. "Key Issues of Textbook Provision in the Third World." *Prospects* 13, no. 3 (1983): 315–325.

Aprieto, Pacifico N. "The Philippine Textbook Project." *Prospects* 13, no. 3 (1983): 351–360.

Gopinathan, S. "The Role of Textbooks in Asian Education." *Prospects* 13, no. 3 (1983): 343–350.

Kumar, Krishna. "The Textbook as Curriculum." *Bulletin of the Indian Institute of Education,* no. 2, 1981, pp. 75–84.

Pearce, Douglas. "Textbook Production in Developing Countries." *Prospects* 13, no. 3 (1983): 327–342.

Wagner, Susan. "Textbooks in Third World Education: The World Bank's Changing Role." *Publishers Weekly* 215 (March 26, 1979): 41–43.

Yadunandan, K. C. "Nepal: For Better Planning of Textbook Production." *Prospects* 13, no. 3 (1983): 361–372.

Third World Countries–General

Books

Barker, R. E. *Books for All*. Paris: UNESCO, 1956.

Barker, R. E., and R. Escarpit. *The Book Hunger*. London: Harrap, 1973.

An Introduction to Book Publishing World. Tokyo: Asian Cultural Centre for UNESCO, 1974.

National Book Trust, India. *Publishing for Rural Areas—in Developing Countries*. New Delhi: National Book Trust, 1981.

Prakash, Om, and Clifford Fyle. *Books for the Developing Countries: South Asia and Africa*. Papers in Mass Communications, no. 47. Paris: UNESCO, 1965.

Report of the UNESCO Regional Seminar on Book Publishing in National Languages. Karachi: UNESCO Regional Office for Culture and Book Development in Asia, 1980.

Smith, Datus. *A Guide to Book Publishing*. New York: Bowker, 1966.

Thapar, Romesh. *Book Development in National Communications and Planning*. Karachi: UNESCO Regional Centre for Book Development in Asia, 1975.

Journal Articles

Altbach, Philip G. "Publishing in Developing Countries." *International Social Science Journal* 26, no. 3 (1974): 458–473.

Malhotra, D. N. "Overcoming Obstacles to Book Publishing in Developing Countries: Reflections on the World Congress on Books." *Asian Book Development* 14 (Winter 1982-83): 6–10.

Contributors

Philip G. Altbach is Director of the Comparative Education Center and Professor in the Faculty of Educational Studies, State University of New York at Buffalo. He is coauthor of *Publishing in the Third World: Trend Report and Bibliography* (1980) and author of *Publishing in India* (1975) among other books.

Amadio A. Arboleda is on the staff of the Office of the Secretary, United Nations University, Tokyo, Japan. He has been an editor at the Pennsylvania State University Press and at the University of Tokyo Press.

Alberto A. Augsberger is a consultant to CERLAL (The Regional Center for Book Development in Latin America and the Caribbean), Bogotá, Colombia.

Amu Djoleto is executive director of the Ghana Book Development Council, Accra, Ghana.

Fang Houchu is Chief, Research Office, The Publishers Association of China, Beijing, People's Republic of China.

S. Gopinathan is Head of the Department of Comparative Studies and Lecturer at the Institute of Education, Singapore. He has been an editor at Oxford University Press and has served as secretary of the National Book Development Council of Singapore.

Laurence Hallewell is a member of the staff of the University Libraries at Ohio State University, Columbus, Ohio.

215

Sherry Keith is on the staff of the World Bank, Washington, D.C.

Shigeo Minowa is Chief, Academic Services, United Nations University, Tokyo, Japan.

Fred Ojienda Okwanya is director of Foundation Books Limited, Nairobi, Kenya.

Edward Ploman is Vice Rector, Global Learning Division, United Nations University, Tokyo, Japan. He is coauthor of *Copyright: Intellectual Property in the Information Age* (1980).

Eva Maria Rathgeber is on the staff of the International Development Research Centre, Ottawa, Canada. She is coauthor of *Publishing in the Third World: Trend Report and Bibliography* (1980) and a contributor to *African Book Publishing Record* and other publications.

Nadia Rizk is Librarian, Post Reference Library, American Embassy, Cairo, Egypt.

John Rodenbeck is Director, American University of Cairo Press, Cairo, Egypt.

Alfredo Navarro Salanga is professorial lecturer at the Institute of Mass Communications of the University of the Philippines. He is also National Fellow for Criticism at the Creative Writing Center at the University of the Philippines.

Tejeshwar Singh is Director, Sage Publications, Ltd., New Delhi, India.

Index